*Discourses delivered to Swamis and Ananda Samajis of the
Nithyananda Order all over the world*

The meditation techniques included in this book are to be practiced only after personal instructions by an ordained teacher of Life Bliss Foundation (LBF). If some one tries these techniques without prior participation in the meditation programs of LBF, they shall be doing so entirely at their own risk; neither the author nor LBF shall be responsible for the consequences of their actions.

Published by

Life Bliss Foundation

First Edition: June 2008, 1000 copies
Second Edition : October 2008, 2000 copies

ISBN 13: 978-1-60607-013-0   ISBN 10: 1-60607-013-4

All proceeds from the sale of this book go towards supporting charitable activities.

Printed in India by W Q Judge Press, Bangalore. Ph.: +91 80 22211168

The Door to Enlightenment

Nithyananda

 Published by LIFE BLISS FOUNDATION

Life Bliss Program Level 2 - NSP, Vancouver, Canada

Contents

Mental Body 138

TABLE OF FIGURES

PREFACE

Death is the only inescapable experience of everyone's life. Yet it remains the greatest mystery and the greatest fear, controlling the tone and actions of all that we think and do.

In this intimate setting with the modern enlightened mystic, Paramahamsa Nithyananda, we undertake a journey with ourselves. We learn who we really are and how to remove the blocks that prevent us from living fully. Guided by a Master who has faced and transcended death itself, we peel back the layers of our being and learn that we too are ageless, deathless.

As we sit at the feet of this living Master, death is demystified once and for all and we are able to live freely, blissfully in every moment.

Nithyananda Spurana Program (NSP) is the second level meditation program designed by Paramahamsa Nithyananda. In it he teaches us about the seven energy bodies of our being: physical, *pranic*, mental, etheric, causal, cosmic, and *nirvanic* bodies, and what happens at the time of death. Using a combination of cognitive instructions, profound personal experiences and guided meditation techniques, Paramahamsa takes us step-by-step through the process of inner transformation. When we do this program with sincerity and intensity, we are born anew!

The physical body is just one of the seven bodies that we have. The remaining six bodies are subtle but powerful energy bodies. They are responsible for the vital elements of life – desires, thoughts, sleep, deep-rooted emotions like guilt, pleasure and pain, and finally, our very core, which is bliss.

The knowledge about these energy bodies and how to control these vital elements of life is closely linked to the clear understanding of the ultimate mystery of death. Once we understand the death process, we get an in-depth understanding about life and about who we really are.

'What is really the meaning of life...and death?'

You may be thinking, 'Why worry about death? After all, it is going to happen at the end of life.' Either you are afraid of death or you feel it is not important to know about it.

But, did you know that your whole attitude to life can radically change with the understanding of death?

Life Bliss Program Level 2 - Nithyananda Spurana Program is designed to...

- Make your intelligence and being flower

- Enhance your memory, concentration, creativity and spontaneity

- Create balance in all areas of your life

- Release deep-seated fears, dissolve guilt, remove pain and eliminate deeply engraved negative memories

- Develop your leadership potential

- Overcome childhood traumas

- Recreate your destiny

- Celebrate your life and live with confidence

This book is based on the talks of Paramahamsa Nithyananda in various sessions of LBP Level 2 - Nithyananda Spurana Program.

CHAPTER 1

Introduction

WHAT THEY SAY AFTER THE NSP…

"The NSP is truly a unique experience. It is something that I would not have even imagined would be possible. I had only fantasized about such things while reading spiritual books. But to be in the presence of a living Guru and feel the sheer authority with which he liberated me from my emotional baggage was an exhilarating experience. One has to experience it to believe it."

- Christopher Paul, Los Angeles, USA

"The NSP is a too-good-to-be-true program. Profound insight into the fear complex and its impact on life itself and a lifetime opportunity to unburden the Being, this program makes one feel reborn with a wonderful lightness at the levels of body, mind and spirit. The intensity of this program cannot be adequately expressed through words."

- Sunitha, Chennai, India

WHAT IS ANANDA? THE ENERGY THAT NEVER REDUCES…

I welcome you all with my love and respect. Let me first introduce the word *Nithyananda Spurana* to all of you.

Nithyananda - nithya is eternal, *ananda* is bliss. *Spurana* is flowering. Continuously, eternal bliss is flowering within us, happening within us; but we keep stopping it!

Ananda means the feeling or the energy that never subsides. The opposite of it is *nanda,* which means *that which can leave you*, which can be taken away from you. *Ananda* means *that which never leaves you*, which can never be taken away from you, which will never reduce. It can never be affected by a certain time or a certain space. It happens irrespective of time and space. Anything that changes based on time and space is *nanda*. Anything that will not change based on time and space is *ananda*. Right now, whatever you think of as *ananda*, is only joy; it is not bliss. And joy changes based on time and space.

At a particular time, we are blissful. In a particular space we are blissful. If we try to reproduce that same time or space, we find that we are not as blissful as before! That is what I mean when I say that the joy that we know is subject to time and space, and also inconsistent at that.

In each and every one of us, there is an energy continuously flowing, which never changes. There is an energy that can never be taken away from us. Of course, again and again, all the Masters who appeared on planet Earth say that in every being, *ananda* is flowing. Apart from the Masters saying, even if we start searching inside, we will understand that if there is no *Ananda* sustaining us at the bottom line, we won't be able to move even an inch in our lives. Even the inhaling and exhaling is happening because of the underlying bliss. Our life continues because either we experience this bliss, or we hope to experience this bliss some day. The hope of bliss is what keeps us alive even if we are not aware of it.

Only because of this *ananda*, that even our inhaling and exhaling happens. Either we experience, or we have an idea that we *will* experience. It is the continuous flow of *ananda* that makes our life also flow. Otherwise, our life will not flow. That is why still we are alive. That is why still we are breathing. That is why our system is still functioning. This energy that we call *ananda*, is continuously working within our being.

ALL MASTERS AGREE ON ONE POINT – THAT WE ARE BLISS

There is a beautiful saying in the *Upanishad* (*Vedic* scriptures), 'If two *rishis* (sages) agree on some point, be very clear, one of them is a fake!' No two *rishis* will agree on any one concept. They will always have some conflict, because each one expresses things in a different way. All of their experiences are the same, but each of their paths and expressions is different. That is the problem.

If we ask about food, some of them will say to have only vegetarian food; some will say that we can have non-vegetarian food; some will say that we should fast unto enlightenment! Some will say that there are no food restrictions. Each one will have his own opinion about it.

If we ask about marriage, some will say, 'Don't marry, be a celibate.' Some will say, 'You can marry; being a householder is ok.' Some will say, 'You can marry even four or five times.' Marrying four or five times is the straight way to enlightenment! If we marry four or five times, we can't manage our life without enlightenment! It becomes a basic need then. If we marry once, enlightenment is an option. If we marry more than once, enlightenment is a basic need without which we can't live!

Anyhow, jokes aside, each of these Masters has got their own idea, their own opinion on every subject. No two Masters agree with each other on the same subject. But, when it comes to this one concept *'ananda'*, all of them agree to the statement, 'We *are* bliss. Our inherent nature is bliss.'

There is no being on planet Earth that is not filled with bliss. In every one of us, bliss is flowing. In every being, bliss is continuously happening. As far as this one concept is concerned, there is no Master who disagrees. If all the Masters are agreeing on this point, it must be a fundamental Truth.

IN THE MYSTERY OF DEATH LIES THE ANSWER TO LIFE

In USA, 115 years ago, a young lady asked the great sage Vivekananda, 'What is life?'

He said, 'Come with me to India. I will teach you.'

She asked, 'What will you teach me?'

He said, 'I shall teach you how to die.'

The question is about life but the answer is about death! It seems strange! What Swami Vivekananda is saying is, if you know the secret of death, the quality of your life will be different. Your very understanding and attitude towards everything will change.

Death is not a mere incident at the end of your life. It is a profound knowing. If you know how to die, you know how to live. Living and leaving are two sides of the same thing. Your life will be totally different once you understand death.

The NSP journeys you through your own life, simultaneously revealing the secrets of death. It makes your inner space pure and clean by unloading the baggage of emotions that you usually carry with you. It teaches you to live blissfully and leave peacefully. It puts death in the right perspective so that your life becomes more joyful and meaningful.

NEITHER DOUBT NOR BELIEVE. HAVE THE COURAGE TO EXPERIMENT!

People who don't believe will never allow these words to enter into them. That is one group. Those who believe never have the courage to experiment. That is a big problem also.

People who believe and people who don't believe - both are not going to be helped! Both are going to be in trouble. When we start believing, we don't experiment. I always tell people: the moment we declare that we believe something, we stop experimenting with it; we stop following it; we just hang it on the wall. The moment you hang my picture on the wall, you have made plans to escape experimenting with what I have to say. Worshipping me is a very convenient way of escaping from me.

We classify things continuously. The moment we classify, we start thinking that we have understood everything about it; that we know everything about it.

That is why I always tell people, only for a maximum of six months, you live with your husband or wife, that's all! After that, you create an image about him or her and your spouse in turn creates an image about you. After this is done, you live only with the images. You don't live with the real person! You don't live with the real being. It takes real intelligence to live with the person instead of living with images. The problem is there because continuously, we classify things. The moment we classify, we stop relating with the real person.

How To Get The Best From This Program

Come With an Open Mind

The best way to get the most out of the NSP is to come with an open mind.

When you come in with an empty mind, with no prejudice, you can completely absorb what I am saying in its totality. If you come in with your knowledge, you will be constantly comparing every word of mine with what you know, with what you have heard about from someone else earlier, and you will simply miss what I am trying to tell. You can absorb me only if there is some space in you to take me in. If you are already full, you cannot take me in.

If you want to experience me, if you really want to gain something for having taken the time out for these few days, just be like an empty cup here. I will then fill you up beautifully.

Be totally open and receptive. Be like a child - innocent and curious; like a sponge, ready to absorb; that is enough.

Why are we not able to relate directly? Why are we not able to listen with an open mind? For this, we need to understand the science behind the working of the mind.

HOW THE MIND WORKS

How does the mind work? The diagram shows how the information that enters through the eye is processed; actually, not just the information through the eye but information through all the five senses, that is through the nose, the ears, the tongue, touch and the eye. As an example, we are now taking the eye. Let me explain it to you.

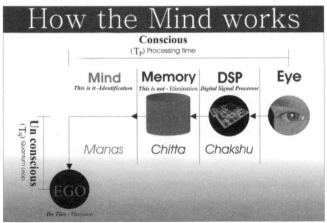

Figure 1: How the Mind Works

When you see something, first, the eye sees it. There is something called *chakshu* in Sanskrit, which digitizes the information seen by the eye. It is something like a digital signal processor – the DSP. The signal or the input is converted into a digital file by this *chakshu*. As I said earlier, this conversion happens to the information received through all five senses, not just the eye.

Then, the file goes to the memory - *chitta*. In the memory, a little more work is done on the file. It analyses the file received, through the process of elimination, as the first step to identify what has been received. For example, if you are seeing me now, the file is processed through the *chakshu*, and taken to the *chitta*, memory. The memory starts analyzing it. It starts saying, 'This is not an animal, this is not a plant, this is not a rock,...' It does the process of elimination.

Then, the file goes to the mind or *manas*. The mind does the job of identification. It concludes, 'This is a human being, a human being who is teaching a class.' The mind concludes, 'This is it.'

Next, the whole file takes a quantum leap to the ego and your ego decides to act based on your past experiences. If you have stored past experiences with similar classes, say yoga or meditation, and they have been alright for you, you will decide to sit here, or else you will think it is better to move on!

Let us go through the process again. The first step is you seeing me. The eye passes the information to the *chakshu*. The *chakshu* converts it to a digital signal. The memory then does the elimination work on the file – 'This is not...', 'This is not...' Then, the mind does the identification of the file – 'This is it.' Then the whole file takes a quantum jump to the ego. In this zone of stored memories, you decide whether to sit here or leave.

Introduction

I always give this example to understand the process of elimination versus that of identification:

Let us say that you want to find the word 'Home' in the dictionary. You start from the letter 'A' and you eliminate: not A, not B, not C, until you come to the letter 'H'. Until you come to the letter 'H', it is only an elimination process. Once you come to 'H', it is an identification process. You start identifying 'HO', then 'HOM', and then you come to 'HOME'. Even in the identification process, there is elimination, but that cannot be considered elimination, because your whole attitude is different during this time. Until you come to 'H', you don't even look at anything; you only eliminate. Once you come to 'H', 'H' becomes a standpoint. Then you start looking for HO, HOM, etc. There is a difference in your attitude in the identification process when compared to your attitude during the elimination process.

It is like this: you have thousands of files stored in your mind. Now let us say that you are seeing me. You will first start eliminating: this is not a stone, this is not a tree, this is not an animal. Then you come to man and say, 'This is a man.' Once you come to man, you start identifying me: six feet tall, saffron clothed, talking about meditation, my master, Nithyananda! So, you are eliminating until you find the right classification. That is the first step. Going in-depth into that classification to identify what is seen, is the next step. Elimination is breadth, identification is depth. The elimination process is like handling many files. The identification process is like going deeply into a specific file.

Now, let us call the time for the process between the eye and the mind, Tp. Tp is the time taken for the process between the eye and the mind to happen. This process is a logical and conscious one. You are completely aware of this process. It happens with your awareness and you will be ready to take complete responsibility for this process.

The quantum leap from the mind to the ego is mostly unconscious. That is the time when the actual decisions are made. So it means that the decision-making happens without your awareness. Let us call this time Tq. During this time, you decide hastily and illogically; you decide against your logical thought process. You make an illogical decision.

Why does this happen? Why do you decide unconsciously and regret it later?

The reason is that this unconscious zone is filled with restlessness and negative memories. All of your past memories, which we call *samskaras* in Sanskrit, are stored in this zone as different files. In the field of psychology *the word *engrams* is used to denote these stored memories. There are so many of these files stored in this zone. Without any logical connection between each other, these memories or incidents are stored together here.

What happens is that when the incoming information takes a quantum leap to this zone, the heavy data stored here causes so much restlessness in you that the incoming file does not even reach the ego properly for a decision. The stored engrams just start playing on the information received. They just impose themselves and cause havoc in the decision making process.

As a result, the ego makes a hasty decision purely from an instinct level, and passes the file back. It happens as an unconscious process.

For example, according to the data that you have collected, you know that smoking is injurious to your health; it is not good for your body or your mind. But once the mind takes the leap to the ego, the engrams just instruct you to smoke; you simply decide to smoke! The conscious process says, 'No, it is not good for my health'. But the unconscious process says...actually it doesn't even say, it *just* makes the decision and you execute it!

It is because of your engrams that you repent what you have done and regret your decisions most of the time. You wonder, 'Why did I behave in that fashion? This is not me! How did I allow this to happen? How did I make that decision?' This happens because the unconscious mind that is filled with all your *samskaras* has emotional attachments to your memories. If you only remember the past in a detached way, you learn from it and the resulting intelligence is used to make better decisions in the future. But if there are positive or negative emotional attachments associated with your memory, what happens? You are not able to see anything objectively. You look at the present through tinted glasses of the past, tinted by the memories of the emotions that you went through when so-called similar incidents happened in the past. You are not able to look at this incident as a fresh and new moment of your life.

The NSP is all about going deeply in and cleaning your deep-rooted *samskaras* that are controlling and playing havoc in your life. We will understand in depth about the various layers or energy bodies that we have and which emotion *or samskara* each of them is ruled by. This intellectual understanding along with the actual cleansing of the *samskaras* is the essence of the NSP.

THE HEALING EFFECT OF THIS PROGRAM

The NSP has a complete healing effect at the physical, mental and spiritual levels. People come and ask me how I heal through meditation. Please understand: I do not heal through my physical body. It is my *presence* that heals. When the sun rises, the lotus blooms by itself. The sun does not go and open the petals of the lotus. Similarly, in the presence of the Master, healing happens. Be very clear that healing is not *done*; it *happens*.

I can heal your body since it is in my presence. In the same way, if you open your mind too, it can be healed. In the NSP, that's what we do - opening of minds. You are asked to write down about yourself - about your pains, desires, guilt and pleasures. You will not be showing these to anyone else. It is for you to know clearly what your deeply embedded *samskaras* are.

During the NSP, people ask me why I have them write down all this since they are neither expected to show them to me nor to each other. Understand: by writing it all down, you are opening your mind in my presence. You are opening your mind and hence I can heal your mind. If you open your wounds, the sun can heal it. Similarly if you can open your mind, the energy will heal all the wounds.

NSP is opening up your energy layers one by one. Your pains, pleasures, guilt and desires are opened up. Once these open up and get healed, you experience a glimpse of God within you. At the end of the program, you don't even have to search for God, your mind will be so clear and relaxed that you will realize that God is already within you and is not something separate from you.

START RELATING WITH REALITY

There are seven energy layers or bodies in us.

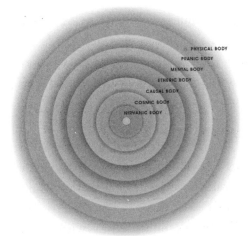

Figure 2: Seven Energy Bodies

You need to understand three things.

The first thing is that it is because of these layers that you are not relating with reality as it is. The mystics always say, 'The world is God. God is everything. Whatever you see is God. Everything is God.' But we don't experience everything as God. We always see everything as evil! We always think,

'Everyone is trying to exploit us. Everyone is trying to enter into our territory. Everyone is trying to disturb us.' So what the mystics say is one thing, and what we feel is a totally different thing. Why do we feel this way? It is because we are not able to relate with reality as it is.

So the first thing you need to understand is that because you are not experiencing these layers as you should be experiencing them, they just become a cancer. Whenever something is not becoming part of your being, it becomes a separate growth, a cancerous growth.

Unless you express, unless you start living these layers, you will never have the satisfaction that you lived. Because, if the major portion of your life is unlived, you will never have the satisfaction in your life - not only in spiritual life, but also in the material world.

THE POWER OF VISUALIZATION

One more thing: we will be working with so many techniques related to visualization; you will be asked to visualize so many things. Generally, we have a very deep disrespect for visualization. We always think, 'Oh... with my imagination, what can I achieve?' Understand: your whole life is nothing but your visualization. Your whole life is nothing but your imagination! So, it's like using one thorn to remove another thorn. If one thorn enters your foot, you take another thorn and remove it with the other thorn, is it not? In the same way, so much of imagination has entered without your knowledge, without your consciousness. To remove them, *conscious* imagination is going to be put into you and the process will be done. So, whenever meditation instructions are given, just put your total energy into making them happen. Don't bother about your opinion of them.

THE INSPIRATION FOR THE NSP

The person who creates a formula to re-create his experience of the outer world is a scientist. For example, Newton created the law of gravity. He had a certain experience. When he saw the apple falling from the tree, he had a certain experience. So he created a formula to reproduce the same understanding about gravity for others.

A person who creates a formula for others to understand the experiences of the outer world or the things of the outer world, is a scientist. A person who creates a formula to reproduce the experiences of the inner world is a Master! Understand, a person who creates a formula to reproduce the things of the outer world is a scientist. A person who creates a formula to reproduce the inner world experiences is a Master. This whole program is a formula created by me to reproduce certain experiences that happened in me a few years back. So we will see what those experiences were and how this formula appeared.

First, we will see how this experience happened in me, and second, how this formula will reproduce the same thing in you. Unless we understand these two things clearly, we will not be able to work with the formula.

DEATH IN MY PRESENCE - BEFORE ENLIGHTENMENT

The whole motivation for the NSP came out of two incidents in my life.

The first one happened before enlightenment.

Figure 3: Varanasi, India

It was probably in the year 1999. I was in Varanasi – Kasi. There was an elderly *sannyasi* – a very old *sannyasi* suffering from cancer. He was in the hospital, in the Intensive Care Unit.

I had the responsibility to take care of him. He was a great *sannyasi*, but not an enlightened person. He was a great *tapasvi* – spiritual seeker undertaking severe asuterities. Everyday I used to bring him food, take care of his needs and stay in the hospital.

One day, the person in the third bed from him was slowly passing away; he was dying. I was just sitting on the bed and watching the whole thing. The doctors were standing around him. They were trying their best to help, but they were not able to do anything.

Even though I was not enlightened at that time, I had had my conscious experience of death by that time - one of the most wonderful spiritual experiences I had ever had. Because of that, I was able to see what exactly was happening to him.

Slowly, he started suffering and struggling. First, he started suffering tremendous pain in the physical body. His face started showing the pain. Next, he became breathless. He started inhaling and exhaling erratically. I was able to see very clearly, the pain and the agony. The pain was what it would be like if one thousand scorpions were stinging him at the same time. His whole consciousness was being torn. Just imagine... if we cut our little finger with a blade, how much pain we would experience! Now imagine... his six-foot body was as if it was literally being cut into pieces along its length. Imagine the suffering!

I was able to experience the pain, the agony, the feeling which he was undergoing. Of course, slowly, very slowly, he started moving away from the physical body.

Even though it is a little difficult to receive this whole thing logically, even if it is a little difficult to understand this intellectually, this is what really happened. Understanding this whole thing is like working with a formula like $X \times 2 = 4$. To understand the formula, to understand how to solve it, first we assume some value for X. First we assume that $X = 2$. Then, we replace 2 in the place of X. Then, we understand: 2 x 2 is 4. Once the answer is right, we know X is 2. Until the calculation is done, we have to have a little patience. But when I say, let us assume X = 2, immediately if we start raising the question, 'No, why not 3? Why not 1? Why not 4?' we will not be able to proceed at all. Even if we understand it as a hypothesis, it is enough. At the end of the calculation, we will be able to understand how this whole thing happens. It is the same as what I am sharing with you. It may be difficult to understand logically, but just relax and take it as a hypothesis for now.

I was able to see and experience the tremendous pain and agony of that being. It was an excruciating pain and deep suffering. The being started moving from the physical body to the *pranic* layer, which is the second layer body. *Pranic* layer is our breathing energy.

All these seven bodies are seven energies, energy layers of our being. When the being started moving towards the *pranic* layer, again there was a deep suffering! Our *prana shareera* – breath body - is filled with all our desires. Our breathing and our desires are very closely related. If we change our breathing, our desires can be changed. Our desires and breathing are very closely related. So, when the energy was moving into the *pranic* layer, all the desires of the being started coming up. The being started suffering with all the unfulfilled desires.

Then, when the being started moving towards the next level body, all the guilt started rising - 'Oh! I should have lived in that way, I should have lived in this way, etc.' In this fashion, slowly, the being moved layer by layer and finally died. I saw the whole death happening right in front of my eyes. I was able to see the whole process of death very clearly. But

I was not able to help in any way. I was not enlightened at that time. I was not able to help. I just witnessed the suffering. But the pain created in me just by seeing the suffering itself was too much.

I started feeling the pain similar to what we might experience if we witness a nasty accident on the road. What will happen? Will we be able to eat for the next two days? If we see a terrible accident on the road, will we be able to eat soon after that? No! It was the same kind of feeling for me. In an accident, we see only one body. But I was able to see all the seven layers, all the seven bodies. Then imagine the pain I would have felt. The pain became so deeply engraved in me. It was recorded in my being so deeply. I was not able to eat or sleep for the next three to four days. Anyhow, after a few days, I left Varanasi and wandered further.

DEATH IN MY PRESENCE - AFTER ENLIGHTENMENT

I continued with the *tapas* and after about a year, became enlightened. Then, driven by the will of Existence, I came down to South India. I stayed there for one or two years. It was around that time that again, I had one more opportunity to see death happening in front of my eyes.

Again I saw the second death in a hospital, and in an Intensive Care Unit. This second person did not suffer at all. He simply passed away moving through one layer after another seamlessly. I was surprised. I asked his relatives if he was a highly spiritual person. They said that he was very far from it; he probably never went to a temple in all his life. Nor did he meditate or do anything remotely related to spirituality. I started analyzing, 'Why did the first person suffer and why did the second person not suffer?'

The death that I saw in Varanasi was so painful; there are no words to describe it fully. But the death that I saw the second time was so different! I saw that the person neither experienced pain nor did he have any suffering. He was moving beautifully from the first body to the second layer, to the third layer, to the fourth layer and so on! Like how a ball rolls in the snow, just like that his being was moving! I was surprised. As I was watching, his being slowly moved away and just disappeared. He became enlightened! He was liberated.

When I was pondering over these two incidents, suddenly the truth jumped up: the second man left his body in the presence of an enlightened being. That was the reason why he left the body painlessly. When the first person was dying, as I told you earlier, I was not enlightened; I had only had a conscious death experience myself. So, my presence did not in any way influence his death. Whereas, when the second man left his body, I was there in his presence and the very enlightened energy caused him to leave the body easily.

No sooner did this revelation happen than did the means to design a program for human beings to leave the body painlessly and consciously come up! That is the formula based on which the NSP is done today.

My Own Death Experience

Let me narrate to you my own conscious death experience in Varanasi. Let me describe exactly what happened within me when I had my experience with this technique. I always used to think that I should have an experience of death, that I should face death directly. But somehow, that thought never became a priority.

Introduction

Any thought has to become the topmost priority, only then the corresponding experience can happen; it should not just be in one corner of your mind.

Usually on our 'to do' lists, we have washing, cleaning, paying the rent and phone bill, and finally if time permits, enlightenment also! And if time permits, meditation also. No! Enlightenment will not happen if it is this way. Only when it becomes a top priority, only when the urge becomes urgent, everything around you will start aligning itself for the experience to happen in you. And this is the case not just with enlightenment. With anything, it is true. Understand, if at all you are complaining that what you wish to happen is not happening, it is because it has not become the topmost on your priority list, nothing else. Nothing else and no one else should be blamed for it. You will see that the moment it becomes the topmost priority, there will be an energy play that comes into being and it will simply happen. Until then, it will wait for you, that's all.

A small story:

One man goes to the doctor and says, 'Doctor I tried to commit suicide by taking 1000 aspirins.'

The doctor asks, 'But what happened?'

The man replies, 'No, after taking two, I felt better and I stopped.'

Understand: only when the desire is in the absolute top position in the priority list, the experience can be achieved. The death experience was not my top priority and so somehow, it was getting postponed.

In my wandering days, I had been to Varanasi, the holy city for Hindus. It has the largest floating population in the world. Per day nearly 300,000 people enter the city and leave. Further, per day, 300 dead bodies are burnt in a place called Manikarnika Ghat on the banks of the sacred river Ganga. It is traditionally believed that if somebody dies or somebody's body is burnt in that area, they will be liberated; they will have direct enlightenment. It is not just a traditional belief. Ramakrishna confirms it with his own experience. He says, 'I saw very clearly, Mahadeva (Shiva) himself going near every burning body, taking the soul, un-clutching it from the body-mind and liberating it!' So, you can't say that it is a mythological belief; it is a solid experience.

I had the fortune of going to Manikarnika Ghat. Traditionally, it is not only believed, but it is true, that for the last 2000 years, the fire that is used to light pyres has never been put off.

Figure 4: Manikarnika Burning Ghat, Varanasi, India

Whether it rains or shines or floods, people never bring fire when they come with the dead body to Manikarnika Ghat. The fire will already be burning and they will just take it from there and light the dead body, that's all. The fire has never gone off. It just continuously burns the bodies as they arrive. Sometimes I would see that two to three bodies are burnt at the same time, so many bodies keep coming!

Especially in the evenings, the bodies will be more in number. From near the place where the person dies, they will start walking, carrying the dead body, chanting *mantras* such as, '*Ram naam satya hai, Ram naam satya hai*' (It means Rama's name is the ultimate and eternal truth). By evening, they will reach Manikarnika Ghat.

The scene there, the very experience of just being there, I cannot describe to you verbally; only *you* have to be there to experience it. To tell you honestly, the fear of death just disappeared from my system. You see so many bodies continuously being burned every day. You feel, 'I am also going to go like this one day, alright', that's all! You feel there are so many people giving you company! It's like one more trip that you make, that's all; you don't feel lonely about death at all.

In your life, if you see may be one or two bodies being burnt, then you will still have the fear of death. But in that place, there will be no ritual done. They will bring the body and straightaway dip it in the river Ganga three times while chanting, '*Ram naam satya hai, Ram naam satya hai, Ram naam satya hai*'. By this time, the fire will be ready, and the wood will be arranged. They will bring the body straight from the water and burn it, that's all!

One strange thing you can see there, none of the relatives will stay there and do any further rituals. The moment they dip the body in the Ganga, they will place the body for burning there and go away, that's all! The people who maintain things there will take care of the rest. You will not know how long it will take for the body that you brought to be burnt completely. There will be a queue and bodies will be burning continuously.

I thought to myself, 'Let me try to sit here and see what goes on.' I sat. In just an hour's time, I felt that death is no more a strange incident which happens once in a while only for some relative or friend. I was watching bodies arriving one after another. It was like: ok, next, next, that's all. Different sizes, genders, ages, communities, of people arrived to be consumed by the same burning flame.

When you continuously see dead bodies being burnt, you actually lose respect for death! Now you have too much of respect, too many ideas about death. That is the problem. It is actually nothing but this: the breath that goes inside the body doesn't come out, that's all. Nothing much can be done about it. Neither you can rewind it nor fast forward it.

As I was watching this scene continuously, initially the little fear that I had for death also disappeared and slowly it became interesting to watch. I went near the people who maintain the fire and started helping them. As I was helping them, I was thinking to myself, 'After all, this body of mine is also going to become like this one day.'

When you remember that death is going to happen to you, the respect that you carry for your ego will come down. Because, whenever you think that something should not leave you, it is just the ego, nothing else. When you know for sure that everything is going to leave you, then the respect for the ego just drops drastically. The respect I had for my ego dropped at that moment.

Then I decided, 'After all I am going to die. Either I should have a conscious death experience now itself and live the rest of my life without the death-fear, or really die, that's all.' But I decided that I have to see the death happening to me one way or the other. There was a small Shiva temple around the corner and a small tower above the temple. I went and sat in that tower so that nobody would disturb me.

I sat in that tower and from there I started seeing the dead bodies being burnt.

Figure 5: Sitting in Manikarnika ghat, in the very tower where the death experience happened prior to enlightenment. (Picture taken during Varanasi tour, 2006)

I still remember the strong click that triggered the whole experience that was to follow an elderly lady's body being burnt. She had a big belly; the cloth was consumed by the fire and the fat that was in the belly started melting and flowing. Sorry for describing this so vividly! I could see clearly that because of the fat flowing, the fire was burning with full momentum. That gave a very strong click to me and I said, 'God! Yes, the same thing is going to happen to this body also. Let it happen!'

That click opened up a deep fear of death inside me. The fear spread all over the body, but I faced it consciously. I could see very clearly, the fear spreading all over the body, and when the fear met my awareness, when it hit my awareness, that became the death experience. I went through a conscious experience of my own death, and came out of it.

Whenever your fear is suppressed, it stays inside you as a suppressed fear. Whenever it comes out and you are not consciously facing it, it becomes a fear stroke, and shakes your whole nervous system and breaks it down. If it is faced consciously, it becomes the death experience, that's all!

If you just escape from the death-fear, when the fear happens, it becomes death. When you face it consciously, it becomes death experience.

Death-fear not expressed plus unconsciousness is suppression.

Death-fear expressed plus unconsciousness is a nervous breakdown.

Death-fear expressed plus conscious awareness is the death experience!

I have given a clear equation now. Understand again:

Death-fear plus unconscious-ness, is suppression or perversion.

Death-fear plus unconscious-ness means, you don't suppress but you don't face it either. You just get shaken, frightened, have a fear stroke, or a nervous breakdown.

Death-fear plus conscious awareness is a death experience.

I was able to see very clearly, the fear that arose. When I faced it consciously with awareness, it became my death experience. The body was dead; it was not moving.

For two and a half days I had no food, no water, no thought, no question, no doubt. The body was there. Only after the experience had passed, I realized that I had been like that for two and a half days! I could see with closed eyes that the body was dead, and there was no movement. Suddenly, after two and a half days, the click happened again, 'God! The body is dead but I still exist! I am there!' That clarity, when it clicked, became such intense ecstasy in me. The fear of death left me once and for all.

I was in such deep ecstasy, such joy, such bliss. I slowly opened my eyes and I was able to move the body. The first thing I felt was such a surge of ecstasy and gratitude. I went down to the Ganga, sprinkled a little Ganga water on myself, took the Ganga water in the *kamandalu* (small water pot that I used to carry, as wandering monks do), took a little ash from the fire, and went straight to the Kasi Vishwanath temple. I went up to the Shiva linga, offered the ash I had brought, did the *puja*. It was done with such inexpressible gratitude. I saw that Vishwanath was alive there.

Understand, because *I* died Vishwanatha became alive! Until the day before that, because *I* was still alive, Vishwanatha was always an ordinary stone. I had always felt that to touch this stone, 300,000 people are coming everyday from so far away... what foolishness!

You see, when you touch the deity yourself, you will tend to lose respect for it. In South India, you can't touch the deities in the temples. But in North India, you can touch it yourself and do the offering. Anyhow, I always felt that the Vishwanatha deity was an ordinary stone. I felt that way because I was still alive. When *I* died, I saw clearly, *He* is alive! Only one can be alive, either Him or you. When you see the Truth, He will become alive. *You* will not be alive anymore as you now think.

The fear of death left me once and for all. I can say that this is one of the very strong experiences that transformed me to search for the ultimate experience of enlightenment.

Life, Death and Inbetween States

What Exactly Happens During Death

– Passing through the Seven Layers...

There is a beautiful website on near-death experiences. An American doctor did this research. He started meeting people who had near-death experiences. 'Near-death' means those who are clinically declared dead and who come back to life after three to four hours. There are many such cases. In our Indian villages there will always be four to five cases.

The other day a doctor was telling me, 'There are so many cases of those who are medically declared dead, and who come back to life after four to five hours.' In some persons' lives, it happens three to four times even, and they come back to life. This doctor somehow got interested in this subject and he started going all over the world, meeting these types of persons. He met 10,000 people from all over the world and collected all their memories and their experiences of how they had their death experience. He did research for 30 years.

After analyzing all their experiences, he reached a conclusion. He made a statement, a beautiful statement that people on the planet Earth, only when they live, they are Christians or Muslims or Hindus or Jews or Buddhists. When they die, all of them die in the way that is described by Hinduism. We may be a Hindu, Muslim, Jew or Christian, but when we die we are a *Vedanti* (person who seeks the Truth).

In the *Kathopanishad* (ancient *Vedic* scripture), there is a clear description of death. This researcher says, in all these 10,000 people's experiences which he collected, everybody's experience exactly matches with what *Kathopanishad* describes!

Let us see how exactly death happens. First, we move away from the physical body. You may be thinking, 'I came to learn how to live, but he is teaching all about death!' Understand: unless we understand the mysteries of death, we will not have a clear idea about life. Our concept about death totally changes our concept about life. Our philosophy about life changes when our philosophy about death changes.

See, in the East, nobody cares for time. Things will happen at their own pace, taking their own sweet time. Why? Because all the eastern religions believe that humans have many births. They have eternity in their hands! If not today, tomorrow, that's

45

all. If it is not coming today, tomorrow, otherwise, next birth, so relax!

All western religions talk only about one birth. They say that after death we don't have any rebirth. That is why western people are so time conscious. Whatever has to be enjoyed has to be enjoyed in these 70 to 80 years. Nothing else can be done. We have to finish it. That is why their life style, everything is organized around time consciousness.

The idea of death changes the whole idea of life. So never think that learning about death is a waste of time. It is the basic lesson everyone has to learn.

First, a person moves from the physical layer, that is the body which we are having, to the *pranic* layer, which involves inhaling and exhaling, that is the energy or the air movement, the *prana* movement inside our system. *Prana* refers to the life force that is brought in by the air into our system when we breathe. It is the life sustaining energy needed for us. Air is just a medium to bring *prana* in. *Prana* is what is needed to sustain life.

When we move from the first layer to the second layer, all our desires, our unfulfilled desires, all the ways in which we wanted to live but did not live, all those things usually come up. When this happens, it is almost as if in a room, ten people are standing, kicking a football around. What will happen? Just like how the football is kicked from corner to corner, our consciousness will be kicked from all corners. In each corner, some desire will be standing and kicking it. At the time our consciousness is trying to leave the body, all our desires will be forcing us to enter back into the body so that we can fulfill and enjoy them further.

On one side, our desires will be forcing us to enter into the body again so that we can live and enjoy, while on the other side, the body will say, 'No! I am tired. I can't host you anymore, just leave!' On one side, the body will say, 'I am tired; I can't host you.' On the other side, the *pranic* layer that houses our desires forces us to live inside the body. That is what causes the pulling and pushing at the time of death. Pulling and pushing is nothing but the fight between our desires and the body.

Somehow, if we manage to move away from the *pranic* layer, we enter next into the mental body. When we enter into our mental body, all our guilt rises! All the guilt that we had about the way we felt we should have lived our lives but never lived, all the mistakes that we committed, all of our regrets, etc.

Please understand, desire is about the future and guilt is about the past. But actually, both are one and the same. The same thing, when it is about the past, it is guilt, and when it is about the future, it is desire! The way in which we *want to live* is desire, and the way in which we *wanted to live but didn't*, is guilt. I always tell people, guilt is nothing but reviewing our past decisions with updated intelligence.

Our intelligence is continuously being updated. The problem is that with this updated intelligence, we try to review our past decisions. For example, as a seven year old, your mother comes and calls you to eat your food. She says, 'You have played enough with your toys. Put them away, and come eat.' What do you say? 'No, I don't want to eat. I want to play.' If your mother comes and tries to snatch the toys, what do you do? You not only cry, you even curse her! But all these years later, now, you know that the toys are not so important as your mother is to you, is it not? Now, your intelligence is totally different. At that time, toys were so important to you that you cursed even your mother.

Now you know your mother is much more important. With this updated intelligence, is it good to create guilt? 'Oh! At that time, I cursed my mother. I feel so ashamed.' No! At that time, we had only that much intelligence. All our decisions are made with the available intelligence at that given point in time in our lives.

If we start reviewing our past decisions with updated intelligence we will always create guilt. All our guilt is nothing but trying to review past decisions with updated intelligence. All the guilt that we collect over our lives rises as we pass through the mental body. Then, if we move a little away, a little deeper , we come to the etheric layer that is related to all our sufferings. All the suffering that we went through during our life is stored here. Like this, each and every layer has got its own *samskara* or stored memories. Actually, traveling through these layers is what we can think of as hell. There is no other separate place called hell. Hell and heaven are not geographical locations; they are psychological spaces.

WAKING WORLD VS DREAM WORLD

One more thing: when we enter into the dream layer and start dreaming, we have seen that this whole world in which you live in now becomes black and white because we are in the dream world. We forget this whole world and the dream world becomes multicolour. If we come out of the dream, this whole world is again seen in 4 dimensions, like 4D.

Introduction

Now, when we are in this physical layer, this whole world is seen as 4D. We experience this world as 4D, in multi-colour. When we are in the dream world, we experience that world as 4D. So, when we are here, the dream world becomes black and white, and this world becomes 4D, and when we are there, the dream becomes 4D, and this world becomes black and white.

In the same way, when we move away from the physical layer to the *pranic* layer at the time of death, this whole world will become black and white. All of your achievements, your pride, your efforts, your sorrow, your happiness, everything will appear in black and white. You will wonder 'Why did I do all this work? Why did I think of all this as a base for my life?'

Let me explain why this happens. When we are alive we invest in our personality; we build up our personality based upon a few pillars. There are a few pillars or foundations on which we build our personality. Those pillars are money, name and fame, relationships, pride that we have a big community, support circle, etc.

If somebody asks you, 'Who are you?' what will you say? 'I am an engineer', 'I am a doctor', 'I am a lawyer'. Or you will say, 'I am the owner of four houses.' Or, 'I am such and such a person's husband or wife', or 'I am her husband', or somebody's son, or somebody's daughter, or somebody's wife. Our personality is built on these few foundations.

When we move from the physical body, all these foundations will be completely shaken. We can't sign our name on our cheques any more. Our signature is not accepted. Our bank balance is no more related to us. We can't handle our bank account. Our car will not be useful to us. At the most, only the ambulance will be useful! Our house will be filled with all our relatives. They will be weeping to see us dead. But neither our house nor our relatives will be useful to us. We can't even relate with our relatives. We can't talk to any of them. If we try to they will run away!

Your wife will come up to the last point in the procession and weep. Your son will come through to the end and do the last rites and rituals. But who will come after that? Nobody! Nobody can come. Only the conscious glimpse can come with you. In this way, whatever is the foundation for your being, that whole foundation will be shaken. When the foundation is shaken, naturally you don't have anything to hold on to.

Understand this one thing; if we suddenly hear of some loss in our business, we will feel that our whole body is suffering. The suffering will not be just in one portion. The whole body will be suffering. It will be almost like our being is crushed. We can see in our life, if we just sit in our office and worry about something, we don't have to do any work, if we just sit and worry alone, we will have shoulder pain! If we just sit and worry for ten minutes, what will happen? We will have shoulder pain.

So understand that when something moves away from us, our whole body suffers. When we move away from the physical body the same suffering starts happening in us. Whatever we thought was a foundation for our life is shaken.

As of now, this whole world will appear in 4D. All this talk about spirituality, meditation, growing the inner being, consciousness etc will appear as black and white. That is why, when I call people for meditation, they tell me, 'I don't have time to meditate. Let me finish all my work and then come. I have a few more years.' Never say, 'I don't have time to meditate.' Be very clear to yourself and say, 'I don't feel that it is that important in my life right now.' If we are ready to say, 'I don't think meditation is so important in my life,' then we are honest. But if we say, 'I don't have time,' then we are just fooling ourselves. Everyone has got the same 24 hours on hand to do what theye feel they should. It is not that the few who are meditating are jobless. It is just a question of priority, of *what* we want in our life. If spirituality and meditation appear as black and white to us now, we will not divert our energy in that area, that's all.

But what happens is that when we move away from the physical body at the time of death, whatever we thought of as 4D when we were living will totally disappear, everything will be totally shaken and appear as black and white! At that time, they will not have any basis at all. In them, we will not be able to find any space where we can rest. That is the reason why death is always a suffering. But at that moment, if we can have a conscious glimpse, or glimpse of consciousness from our past, then we can consciously enter into death!

Let me explain further. If we understand this concept completely, we will not develop attachment to whatever we think of as 4D. We may enjoy them but our personality will not be built on them. We will become intelligent, and when we are living, we will create at least one part of the foundation or one pillar in the other dimension that is spirituality!

You see, now we are in two dimensions, the material world and spirituality. Right now, what is happening is that however many pillars we build our personalities and life upon, all those pillars are based on the material world which appears to be 4D. Not a single pillar is based on consciousness or our inner space. Our whole personality is built only based on the outer space - our name, our fame, what society speaks about us, etc. Our complete personality is structured only on what society speaks about us. If everyone's opinion of us is that we are great, what do we think? We think we are great. If everybody says, 'You are useless', what happens? We start getting depressed.

This happens because not even a single pillar of our building is based on spirituality, our inner core, our being. The entire thing is based on the outer space. That is the reason that when those pillars are shaken by anybody, we start suffering terribly. If we have even one pillar from consciousness, we can depend on that to stand straight without suffering. One more thing: these outer world pillars are not in our control at all. Anyone passing by can easily shake them. Even if a small child comes up to us and says that we are a fool, we will get a little shaken, is it not? That child might have even said it only to try a few new words that he is learning! But you get shaken. So understand that these outer world pillars are that weak.

That is what the *Bhagavad Gita* says: what comes and stands in our mind at the time of leaving the body will alone decide about our next birth or enlightenment. If we have at least one pillar on consciousness, naturally we will not have suffering when we leave the body. All the other pillars will become black and white. But even if the other pillars become black and white, this one pillar will be there in multi colour − 4D. This one pillar will be there to take us through the process.

As of now we have no pillar to take us through, that is the problem. As of now, our whole personality is based on the outer space. All our pillars are made up of what we think is 4D *now*. And there is no inner space for us either. That is why, like a football, people can kick us from corner to corner in the outer space. Anybody can just throw one word towards us to make us depressed. If somebody says we are mad, we shout at them and prove that we are mad! A single word is enough to make us mad. Nothing much is necessary. We are almost like the street dogs - if we just throw one stone at it, it becomes mad.

If anybody throws one word at us, it is enough to make us mad or depressed. This happens only because we don't have strength in the inner space. Please understand that if we build at least one pillar based on our inner space, this pillar will shine in 4D at the time of death and help us leave the body beautifully.

FOUR STATES OF CONSCIOUSNESS

Vivekananda beautifully says, 'Even if we have one single thoughtless awareness experience in our life, that is, a single conscious experience in our life, that is enough. At the time of leaving the body, it will come up and we will leave our body peacefully. We will have just awareness without thoughts.'

The idea 'I' exists in all of us when we are awake. In deep sleep, is it there? No. In the same way, almost every one of us has thoughts when we are awake. In deep sleep, do we have thoughts? No. There are two states of mind and two states of being. These two criss-cross each other and create four states of being in which we exist and live our lives.

The first state is to be with 'I', and with thoughts. This is what we experience as our waking state. In Sanskrit, we call it the *jagrat* state; *jagratavastha* – the waking state.

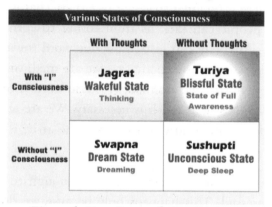

Figure 6: Four States of Consciousness

In the next state, there will be thoughts, but there will not be the sense of 'I' that we experience in the waking state. That is what we call the dream state. You may ask how is it that in the dream state we don't have the sense of 'I'.

Let me explain. Now, in the waking state, if you choose, you can control your thoughts, am I right? You can suppress them, alter them, and recreate them in a different way. You can do whatever you want with them because the frequency of 'I' is higher than the frequency of thoughts. 'I' is more powerful here.

But in the dream state the frequency of your thoughts is more than the frequency of the 'I' consciousness. That is why you are not able to control your dreams as you wish to. Are you able to control your dreams and dream the way you want to? No! Wherever the dreams take you, you have to go, that's all.

Introduction

In the dream state, the frequency of thoughts is greater. That is why they just flow. You can't do anything about it. If at all we have the opportunity to dream what we want to, we know what type of dreams we will be having! So understand, the dream state is when you don't have 'I' but you do have thoughts.

In the third state, neither have you the 'I' nor have you the thoughts. This is the deep sleep state, or sound sleep state.

There is a fourth state that we never experience. In that state one will have the 'I' consciousness but not have any thoughts. This is what we call *turiya* or meditation or *samadhi* or *atmagnana*, *nirvana*, the self-realization experience, whatever you want to call it. This is what we call *samadhi*. This is the state where you have the 'I' consciousness but no thoughts. This is what I mean when I say, 'thoughtless awareness' or 'consciousness'. Even one glimpse of this state is enough. Even one experience of this state is enough, that when you leave your body you will have your rest there!

As of now, this *turiya* state or *samadhi* state or consciousness... all these things will look like black and white to us. We will not give that much importance to all these things. We will think this is for philosophers or for people who are ready to die of old age. It will be very difficult to surrender to even the idea of this *turiya* state. It will be very difficult to work for this consciousness because it appears only as black and white to us, of little or no value to us.

You must be thinking, 'Who knows what the truth is? He must be telling something to do his business!' I always tell people that it is not so easy to understand all these things. It is not so easy to surrender to these ideas as of now.

The moment you hear the words 'consciousness' or 'surrender' or *'samadhi'* or 'meditation', immediately, what do you think? 'All this is very difficult for me.' And not only that, we will always have the fear, 'You may now tell me to surrender, but tomorrow you may take away my property or you may take away my husband or you may take my wife away from me. You may take away my kids also. Or, I myself may get inspired and go behind you!' There are so many troubles, so many problematic possibilities that you see when you hear all this.

It is very difficult to trust somebody. It is very difficult to enter into this fourth state or even come close to it. But it seems difficult only because all these things appear in two-colour now – black and white. But when you leave the body, then it will appear as four-colour and whatever you thought of as four-colour now will become completely two-colour, black and white.

DURING DEATH, EVERYTHING IN THIS WORLD BECOMES INSIGNIFICANT

Now, let us see how the second death happened so peacefully. Again the statement which I am going to make now is a little difficult to understand but I have no other way. The truth has to be explained as it is. The truth has to be expressed. Only then, you will be able to enter into the formula. This is the way the formula happened to the person who died peacefully in the second death that I saw in the ICU.

When the second death was happening, the moment the person left the first layer, because an enlightened being was there, because of my presence, somehow he was able to catch a glimpse of that consciousness! He was able to catch my presence. During the first death that I witnessed, I was not enlightened. I was only doing my *tapas* (spiritual practices). I was wandering all over India and doing *tapas*. But during the second death, I was enlightened. Somehow, because of that, he was able to catch a glimpse of consciousness. The moment he left the first layer, he was able to feel me or experience me. The moment he started experiencing me, his whole consciousness simply became centered on me.

Usually, what are the things that stop you from surrendering to the Master? The list is the same for everyone -your bank balance, your house, your car, your relationship, your wife, your own insecurity about your life etc. You may think, 'If I surrender to him, what will happen to my life? I may start becoming a servant to him. There are so many other things that I still have to do.' All these thoughts are stopping you from surrendering or entering into the consciousness. 'Surrendering' and 'entering into the consciousness', both are one and the same. But, for that person who was at the stage where death had started happening, all these things became valueless! They had no significance for him anymore! As I told you earlier, when you leave the first level, the body itself, all these things will become valueless to you. So whatever strings were pulling him down were already cut or disconnected. None of the usual attachments or fears was binding him.

As long as you think that the outer world is worthy, that it has got value and you fear that somebody may take it away, you are caught. You fear that somebody may snatch it from you and you can't surrender to the experience of consciousness. As long as you think that whatever you collected in your life is valuable, you will have tremendous fear of losing it. That is why I tell people, 'As long as you think these things are valuable, you will never be able to experience fearlessness.' There will be a continuous fear. The more you have the attachment to those things, the greater the fear. Continuously your being will be shaken. Every moment you will be waiting with fear as to what might happen next and what you may lose.

But for that dying man, at that moment, whatever can be taken away from him has already been taken away. Now there is nothing for him to lose. Trusting the Master is very easy at that moment. Somehow, fortunately for him, he had my presence there. He could simply see the whole thing! The moment the physical layer things were taken away from him, he understood that all the other things are valueless and of no significance, and that very moment his whole consciousness, without any doubt, without any difficulty, caught onto me. It became centered on me! Naturally, when he was centered on an enlightened being or conscious being, he simply dissolved into enlightenment without any suffering.

Whatever is stopping you now, will not stop you at that time. Understand: at that time you don't have to practice renunciation consciously. Everything will simply be taken away from you by force. That is the nature of death. Only as long as you have a choice, you have to practice commitment, renunciation, charity, righteousness and what not. At the time of death, you don't have to practice anything. Everything will simply be taken away from you without your permission or control. Then, what is there to practice? Renouce what? You won't have anything even to renounce!

Figure 7: A divine farewell to the departed soul of Sri Sri Nithya Arunachalananda Swami

In those moments there is nothing that can stop you from entering into the enlightenment experience. There is nothing that can stop you from entering into the conscious experience. But there is only one thing you need when you leave the body. You need a conscious being around you. Without that, it is not possible. Now, what am I supposed to do? I can't go and stand in all the ICUs in the world and ask people when they plan to die! How can I help so many people at the time of death without physically being there with them? So I thought about it seriously and the formula to achieve this revealed itself.

LEAVING THE BODY PEACEFULLY - THE GREATEST GIFT ANYONE CAN HAVE

From my own experience I tell you that leaving the body peacefully is the greatest gift anybody can have. If you have that gift, you have achieved whatever needs to be achieved. You have lived your life. Nothing else needs to be achieved. If you have not achieved that, nothing else is worth achieving.

After seeing this second death, I started seriously contemplating on how this could be reproduced. How can I help people leave their body consciously? As I was telling you, I cannot go and stand in all the ICUs. That's impossible.

Suddenly, like a lump, like a conscious ball, something landed in me. A formula happened in my consciousness. The formula revealed itself to me. This formula is what I call the Nithyananda Spurana Program.

The first thing you must know is that energy is not bound by space or time. Energy is beyond time and space. All we need is a tuning system, that's all. See, if you have a cable box in your house, you can just tune your television to any channel. If you tune to BBC, you will see BBC. If you tune to CNN, you will see CNN. Whatever channel you tune to, you can see the program on that channel.

In the same way, at the time of leaving the body, if you can tune yourself to consciousness, if you can tune yourself to 'thoughtless awareness', 'conscious experience', you will simply see that your life itself was a conscious experience. You will be able to beautifully and peacefully cross this ocean of *samsara* (worldly life of engraved memories that you lived in all along), or ocean of all these seven layers.

In this program we are going to work with this formula. Please understand, if you work seriously with the theory of gravity you can always understand fully what Newton experienced. In the same way, work with this formula. You can simply experience what that person experienced. What has happened in my consciousness can happen in your consciousness also. All you need to do is work with this formula intensely. Just go with this formula as intensely as possible. Nothing else needs to be done.

GOING BEYOND SAMSKARAS - ENGRAVED MEMORIES

Another important question arises here. 'Forget about dying... what about living?' Please be aware that as of now all the seven layers are not so clear as you think they are. It is like seven coats that you are having. If you are wearing the seven coats properly, you can remove them whenever you wish to and hang them on the wall. But as of now, you are not wearing these seven coats properly. The first coat button is locked with the seventh coat. The third coat button is locked with the first coat. The second coat button is locked with the fourth coat and so on! You see, if you can remove a coat whenever you want, it can be called a coat. If you can't remove it, then it is not a coat; it is a bondage.

If you have had a single conscious experience you will not be continuously tortured, pulled and pushed by your *samskaras* or engraved memories. If you look back at your whole life you will be able to understand what I am saying. If you look back at your whole life with a little intelligence, you will be able to understand that you never really lived. Only your engrams (engraved memories) lived through you. For example, suppose you have created a *samskara* that in the morning, at 7 o'clock, you need to drink coffee. At exactly 7 o'clock, you don't have to even see the watch, from inside you the alarm will sound, 'Coffee!'

Like this, you have many *samskaras*. For example, every morning at nine o'clock your mind will automatically start worrying about your office. In the evening at five o'clock you will start worrying about your house. In the night at eight o'clock you will start worrying about your kid's education. If this becomes a routine, even on Sunday, you will start worrying about your office at nine o'clock. Even if you don't have to go to office, you will start worrying about it. Suddenly, you will remind yourself, 'No, no. Today is Sunday so don't bother about it. We don't have to go to office.' Even then, you will continue to have that same low mood during that time. Even your worry, your mind, is nothing but recorded *samskaras*.

Never think you are really living. Your *samskaras* are living through you, that's all. These *samskaras* are recorded in all the seven layers. Only when you cleanse your *samskaras*, your mental habits, do you start really living.

When you can't sit with yourself, you miss a major dimension of your life. When I say, you can't sit with yourself, I mean when you can't sit enjoying your own reality, your own Self. And why can't you enjoy your own Self? It is because your *samskaras* are enjoying you. Your *samskaras* are living through you. You are not living. That is the reason why you can't sit with yourself. You are driven to continuously do something.

During these few days, all we are going to do is only one thing - work intensely and cleanse the *samskaras* and have the 'conscious experience' - at least one glimpse of 'thoughtless awareness'. Just one glimpse of thoughtless awareness is enough. I request all of you to please put your complete effort into this. Remember that as of now, whatever you think of as 4D, your precious life, will lose its value at the time of death. Internalise this truth completely. Your whole being, the very root, will be shaken the moment you move from the physical layer at the time of death. It is almost like you are building your own resort there, in the inner world.

The way in which you enjoy your whole life will decide how your last moment will be.

One more important thing, please understand. This might be shocking to you, but it is the truth. Only after seeing the first death was I able to realize this statement: even your *paapa* (sin) or *punya* (merit) doesn't come with you or count for anything, at the time of your death. Please understand: even your sin or merit doesn't come with you. Don't think that your sin or merit comes with you. Don't think that if you do some charity here, if you give some money to some temple here and get a receipt, you will be given a VIP pass there! No! There is no exchange offer between this world and the other world.

Then, the next question comes – 'If that is true then can I commit any sin?' Understand this truth: if somebody commits 100 murders, the attitude of committing murder goes with him upon his death. The exact number of murders does not go with him. The attitude goes with him. And one more thing: never think that because you commit sins you will therefore go to hell. You commit sins because you are in hell! A person who is happy will never be violent. If you are happy, will you torture others? If you are happy, will you be violent? When you are established in goodness, even if your staff or employee makes a mistake, what you will say? 'Alright, leave it!' So understand this important point: hell is not where you will go to. It is where you *are*. If you understand this, you will take back your question about committing sins!

In the same way, never think that you will do good things and therefore reach heaven. You do good things because you are in heaven. The mental setup that you have when doing an activity is what makes up your experience of hell or heaven. While doing something wrong, whatever mental set up you have that created your attitude and choice, that suffering itself is the only hell. While doing a noble thing, whatever mental setup you have that initiated such an action, *that setup and feeling is heaven*. So don't think your sins or merits come with you. Only one thing comes with you – the conscious experience that you had in your lifetime.

All of humanity can be categorized into just two categories: people who have had the conscious experience when they were living and people who have not had the conscious experience, that's all! All other concepts of hell and heaven are just beautiful stories. Please be very clear – there is no hell or heaven as you understand it to be. If at all you can carry something with you, there is only one thing that you can carry and that is this conscious experience. Either you can become enlightened, or you can come down for another birth according to your choice.

Please be clear, there are many people who are thinking, 'If I give this much money to that particular temple, that powerful deity will be standing there at the gates of heaven to take care of me.' Or, 'If I give this property to this church, God will be waiting with a special pass into heaven to let me in. Nothing like that will happen! People generally think, 'If I give this much of money to Venkateshwara Swamy, He will send a special flight from *Vaikunta* (His abode) for me.' No! This will never happen.

There is a beautiful story in the *Upanishad*, about a *rishi* by name Jadabharatha. One *rishi* called Jadabharatha somehow became attached to a deer. From morning till night, he used to spend his time taking care of that deer. When he was dying, he was not able to forget the animal. He started worrying about that animal, 'Oh! Who will take care of the animal? What will happen to it after my death?' He started worrying about all these things, because he was so attached to that deer. When he died, in the next birth, he was born as a deer. Beautifully the verse says that whatever you think in the *antima kaala* - in your last moment - you become *that*!

Some people think very cleverly, 'Let me live my whole life, the way I want to live. In the last few moments, I will chant *Hare-Rama, Hare-Krishna* or *Govinda-Shiva* and enter heaven somehow.' Or you may think, 'I don't have interest in spiritual things. I'll deal with it on my death bed.' It is not so. Only that which you thought of in your whole life, only that will come up when you leave the body. Don't think that at that moment you can play the game! No! Actually, when you leave the body your whole system will be in such agony, because 80 or 90 years of your life will run through in a fast-forward mode. All that will be seen are the scenes being fast-forwarded. Whatever experience you had intensely, or whatever you enjoyed intensely, only that will come up in multicolour. All the other things will run past in black and white.

If you have lived throughout your life only eating, then naturally, only that will come up in those last moments. When it comes up, what will you decide? 'After all, I am going to only eat in my next birth, so let me take birth as a pig!' You will think, 'Why take birth as a human body?' Suppose that you spent your whole life sleeping, you will decide, 'Why unnecessarily choose a human body and go to office? Let me take birth as a buffalo!'

I am not joking! It is only based on the way in which you enjoy your whole life that you decide in the last moment about your next birth. In the last moment, the whole thing will come up in fast-forward mode. What you enjoyed deeply, what was an intense experience in your life will appear like a pop-up; that will come up and appear in multicolour. All the other things will be in black and white as the background. If you had a single conscious experience, a single instance of thoughtless awareness in your life, naturally when you leave your body only that will come up in multicolour because that is the strongest experience anybody can have.

Please understand that 'thoughtless awareness' is the strongest experience you can have in your life. All the other three states are only shallow. Even for a single moment, if you had that experience, that is enough. Naturally, when you leave the body that will come up. That will come up and you will simply move into the light. That will act as a light and you will be able to move into the Consciousness.

One more thing is important to understand about the time of death. If you had met with an accident and died prematurely or committed suicide, if you did not have the conscious experience before your death you have to wait for the remaining years you might have lived before you can enter a new birth. For example, when you took this body, if you decided to live in this body for 90 years and then committed suicide at age 60, then for the next 30 years, you have to struggle, waiting for the next body. If it is a natural death, then there is no problem. Of course, disease is a natural death. But death due to murder or suicide will have to wait with a lot of suffering to get into the next body.

Never contemplate suicide. Why do we normally contemplate suicide? Because we think of this life as torture, as suffering. But if you commit suicide, only then you will understand that what you are going to go through will be a much worse torture. Never ever contemplate suicide.

If I have to describe the torture in a way, it will be like this: you will have sweets in front of you, but you will not have a tongue to taste or hand to take it and put it into your mouth. How much of suffering it will be! In the same way, the whole world will be in front of you, but you will not have the body to enjoy it when you float around waiting for your next body after having committed suicide. That is why I say never contemplate suicide.

A recent research report says that if a mother dies at a very young age, the child is prone to paralysis attacks. If the mother dies at a very young age, the child is prone to paralysis because that part of the energy given by the mother is not nourished by her presence, by her nearness. That is why in our ancient system until the age of 14, children were always kept in the nearness of their parents. They were allowed to sleep in their laps.

Till the age of 14, you should hug your children. Put them to sleep in your lap. Keep them always around you. Never put them in a boarding school. If you put your kids in a residential school before the age of 14, you need to get ready to go to old age home in your old age! They will put you in an old age home when it comes to that. If you put them in boarding school before the age of 14, they will put you in old age home later, that's all. There is no other way, because by putting them in boarding school, you would not have built a relationship with them. They will put you in the old age home at the time you need nearness. So please give them your nearness.

Within three *kshana* of death a person takes another body. It happens within three *kshana*. *Kshana* does not mean one 'second' of time. In *Vedic* mathematics or *Vedic* time calculations, the gap between one thought and the next thought for that particular person *is one kshana*. *Kshana* is determined by the individual and their thought flow. It is subjective to the person and not an objective calculation of time as we would think of one second on a clock.

If you lived a peaceful life, your *kshana* can be even two months. If you have lived a restless life, your *kshana* will be one microsecond. If you have lived a restless life hurrying and worrying, your *kshana* might even be one microsecond. If you have lived a peaceful life, a relaxed and especially conscious life, if your life was with a conscious experience, your *kshana* could be even three to four months. It can be extended to even one year.

CHRONOLOGICAL TIME VS PSYCHOLOGICAL TIME

There are two things - chronological time and psychological time. If you are sitting with somebody whom you really love, or who you really care for, you will not notice time pass. Even if you sit for three to four hours together, you will feel that the time flew by. Whereas, if you are sitting with somebody who doesn't interest you, whom you don't really care for, after every five minutes, what will you do? You will check your watch. You will wonder why time is not moving. You will feel so bored.

If the number of thoughts is too much, then the number of *kshanas* passed will be more and you will feel that too much time has passed whereas only a few minutes might have passed. This is what happens when you are with someone who doesn't interest you. Your mind becomes restless because of that. If the number of thoughts is fewer, the number of *kshanas* passed will be fewer and you will feel only a little time has passed, whereas a lot of time would have passed by. This is what happens when you are with someone whom you love. That is why we always say that if the number of thoughts is less, you are in heaven. See, for *devatas* (heavenly beings), our earthly one year is one day for them! Have you heard this before? Our entire year is one day for them! How is this so? It is because their number of thoughts is so few. So they don't even know how the chronological time moves past so quickly.

That is why in the Chidambaram temple in South India, which is considered to be the temple belonging to the heavenly beings, the presiding deity – Nataraja, will have only six *abhishekas* (ceremonial baths) in a year. He is worshipped by the *devatas*. In regular temples, usually we do six *pujas* per day. But in this particular temple, only six *pujas* are done in a year itself, because the calendar of the *devatas* is totally different. The number of thoughts for them is less; they are in heaven. So naturally their *kshana,* the time between two thoughts is more.

This concept of *kshana* should be understood clearly. From this we can understand how our one year is only one day for the *devatas*. The people who are residing in the sixth layer, the spiritual body, are called *devatas*. That space itself is called heaven.

You Choose Your Body, Your Birth

If you have lived a restless and continuously worrying life, the moment you leave the body, you will feel so restless that within three *kshanas,* you will take the next body. You cannot be without a body because you are so dependent on the body and mind to survive. You must quickly get another body so that you can continue to try to fulfill desires.

See, all along your life, your ten pillars, your foundation, were in the outer space of the world. Your attention was always directed outwards. So naturally you are dependent on the body to survive. You can't be without a body. What will you do? You will be in a great hurry to take another body. It is like this example. You wait in the railway station just to get into the first train that stops. You will not be bothered about which train is coming, which way it is going, which platform, etc. You will simply jump into it, that's all. If you have lived a simple life, a peaceful life, if you have had one glimpse of consciousness, a single glimpse of this *turiya* state, then when you leave the body, you will leave it beautifully, and you will have a VIP lounge there to wait in. There is no hurry and you take another body at your leisure. You will not be pushed and pulled by desires, guilt and painful experiences of your life. You will not be forced to take whatever next body is available. You can have a beautiful and relaxed way of living. You can wait and decide whether to take a certain available body or to wait further. It will all be your choice. All you need to do is work towards one conscious glimpse in this life and in this body.

If you have learnt to live without your body and mind for even a moment, that is what I mean when I say 'thoughtless awareness.' You will have the same thoughtless awareness at the time of leaving the body also. If you master the art of living with the body and mind, then, you will have the maturity and experience to know that whatever is taken away from you will not be you. You will have your inner space safe all the time. It is clear and there is no suffering. As of now you don't have that inner space. As of now, all we think as 'we' is based on the outer space only. Our inner space is simply corrupted with everything we encounter in the outer world. We never protect our inner space, our greatest treasure. That is the problem.

BE IN THE PRESENT

Ramakrishna says beautifully, 'If you put a little curd into milk and keep it in a corner for two to three hours, it will become curd. Then, you can churn or shake the curd. You will have only butter; nothing will go wrong with it. But immediately after putting the curd into the milk, if you keep on churning it, you will never have the whole thing as curd; the curd will never happen.' Now understand that for these few days, you need to keep your outside world connections away from your inner space so that the curd can form. Once the curd has happened, you can go back into the world. Then, anything may be done to you; nothing will shake you. But in these few days when the process is happening, please cooperate. We will be working intensely here.

Even if you try to get some information from your home or office, whether it is good or bad information, the problem is, your whole office mental setup or home mental setup will come back to you. And in just ten minutes, you will come down and become like how you were earlier. It is like this, even if you see a single encounter on the street, it is enough to create a chain of thoughts in you, is it not? So, please understand, in the next few days, even though it is a little difficult, try to avoid cell phone conversations. Avoid even the incessant mental chatter, the mental thoughts about your office, house, etc.

Whenever you remember this instruction, quickly bring your mind and consciousness back to the present moment. You can watch your breath or you can feel your whole body in order to bring yourself to the present moment. Continuously, come back to the present moment, just for these few days.

Introduction

Falling into Conscious State with Anesthesia

Around the world, thousands of people have worked with this NSP formula and have been successful. If you are successful in the NSP, that is, if you have had even one conscious glimpse during the program, not only at the time of leaving the body do you become conscious, but even if you are given anesthesia for any surgery you will enter into the conscious state at that time.

After the NSP, some people undergo minor surgeries in hospitals. They write to us that when they were given anesthesia, automatically they fell into the conscious state. Even under a full dosage of anesthesia, they fell into the conscious state! They say, 'We didn't feel pain, but were clearly witnessing what was happening. We were aware of the whole thing, and we were able to experience the whole operation very clearly.' This has happened not just with one or two persons, but with hundreds of people.

Even while doing some activity, if you feel giddy and fall, you will not enter into the darkness that you usually enter; you will not become unconscious. You will enter only into light.

Diseases Rooted in Mental Setup

All your major diseases are rooted in your mental set up. If you don't change your mental set up, when healing is given, what will happen? You will get the same disease in ten days' time and come back for healing again. As long as you have a knee, you will have knee pain. If you drop your idea about your knee, the pain will disappear.

When you have a conscious glimpse in your lifetime, no *karma* (unfulfilled actions) can touch you. Your frequency becomes much more than the frequency of *karma*. See, *karma* can work on you as long as you have thoughts. In conscious awareness, you go beyond thoughts. So naturally, you will start ruling *karma*!

MEDITATION - THE WAY TO EXPOSE YOUR CONSCIOUSNESS

It is said that meditation is like exposing your film directly to the sun. If the camera shutter opens for just one moment, whatever is in front of the camera will be recorded in the film, is it not? If the shutter is left completely open, what will happen? If the sun's rays directly fall on the film, what will happen? Whatever is recorded will be erased.

Now, when you took birth, for one moment the camera shutter opened, and life entered your body. So whatever was there in the scene got recorded. It means that whatever planetary positions existed at that moment got recorded. That is why the time of birth is very important. It is only based on that, your consciousness functions.

Now, consciously, I am keeping the shutter open for quite a bit of time during this program. So naturally, whatever is recorded... what will happen to that? It will be erased, meaning all your past *karma* is erased. That is why it is said that when you take birth it is like opening the camera shutter for one moment. When you are initiated, the shutter is completely opened. Naturally, the sun's rays enter and all your *karmas* are wiped out. That is why, when you are initiated, you are called *dvija* – twice born. You take a second life, a new life. And the one who operates your camera to hold the shutter open for that extra time is called the Guru.

How You Choose Your Next Birth

Based on all the intelligence that you have when you leave the body, you decide what type of a body you want to take next. It is based upon the lifetime you just completed. With the 'file' created by the experiences and impressions of the past life, you review the entire file. You ask yourself, 'What is the best experience that I wanted to have in my life?' Then you refer to the past life to see all the experiences you had in your life. Whatever you think was the best, even if it was just a glimpse, you choose. In order to repeat the same peak experience, you decide on the sort of place that would be good to be born in. Then you decide what type of father and mother are needed. After considering all this, you take birth. That's all.

Even Poverty is a Conscious Choice

Even poverty is a conscious choice! Please understand: poverty is a conscious choice. It is very difficult to understand this, but it is the truth. When you don't want to take responsibility of having and guarding money, you choose to be in poverty. Having money means a lot of responsibility. You are always in danger; anytime you can be harassed. You can be kidnapped and your money can be taken away from you. These are all the risks money will bring in life. Therefore, you may choose to be born in poverty! That is why we say even poverty is a conscious choice.

CHAPTER 2

Physical Body

The physical body is this body that we can touch and feel. The physical body is what makes us feel physical pain and suffering on the physical plane.

First, we will work on the physical body. There are three things that we are going to do: one is balancing the body, the second is erasing the body consciousness or the outer line of your body from your mind, and the third is just merging the physical body back to energy. The physical body is more like matter right now. It will be merged; it will be put inside energy.

BALANCING THE BODY

Why are we supposed to balance the body? Unless you balance your body, your mind will be continuously in the body. There is a beautiful saying by Patanjali: *sthiram sukham asanam*. Patanjali is a great, enlightened Master from India, known for his yoga science. The meaning of these words can be interpreted to mean 'When the shoe fits, the feet are forgotten!' Or, when the belt fits, the belly is forgotten, or when the chain fits, the neck is forgotten, or when the ring fits, the finger is forgotten. If the ring doesn't fit, you will be continuously remembering the finger, is it not? If the chain does not fit, you will continuously be remembering the neck; if the shoe does not fit, if it is either too tight or too loose, you will be continuously remembering the feet, is it not?

What is the scale to see whether it fits or not? If you have forgotten the feet, you can be sure, the shoes fit. If you have forgotten the belly, you can be sure, the belt fits. If you have forgotten the neck, you can be sure, the chain fits. If you have forgotten the finger, you can be sure, the ring fits. So... when you can forget the body, only then can you be sure, the body is comfortable! Whenever your body is not comfortable, you can never forget about it. If you are not remembering your body in any way, it means that you are comfortable in it.

If you can forget about your body, you can understand that you are healthy. If you don't remember your head, it means that your head is without any discomfort. If you have a headache, can you forget your head? No! That is why spouses always give headache to each other, so that you will not forget them! If some part of the body troubles you, you will never be able forget that part, is it not? If you forget that part, what does that mean? It means that you are not having any trouble with that part, that's all!

If the body is healthy, you forget about it. We can also say, when you forget the body, it becomes comfortable automatically!

So get ready for the first session - forgetting the body! If you are a little bit balanced, you will be able to forget the body and you will be able to enter into the second session. First thing, you need to balance your body in order to forget it. If the body is balanced, you will forget it.

Now we learn a small technique to balance the body.

Just think of your *mala* (red sandalwood chain that you are wearing) as the centre of gravity line of your body. If this line is straight, then it means the *mala* is in the rest position. If the *mala* is held to the side, then it is not resting. If I leave it, it will come back to the restful position. This down position, this *mala* is totally resting and comfortable. In the same way, your centre of gravity line should fall in a straight line. If it falls so, you will be totally comfortable in your body; you will be able to forget the body. Let me teach you how.

Just sit cross-legged on the mat, with the right leg on your left thigh. If you can't sit on the ground, then sit on the chair, but try your best to sit on the ground. Sit with the right leg on your left thigh; your legs should be seen. See, if your legs are really under your control, you should be able to do the *ardhapadmasana* – the posture I am telling you to sit in now. Only then, your legs are under your control. Otherwise, your legs are under someone else's control! You don't have to sit like this the whole day. Just once if you sit, it is enough. Then the whole day, you will be balanced; you will be comfortable.

It is good to sit often in the balanced posture at home or in office or car or wherever. Your whole body will be balanced. Until the age of seven, your body has its own builtin mechanism to balance itself. Once you have grown into society, you forget the original balancing technique. Now I am just giving the original balancing technique back to your body.

Once you learn it, you don't have to sit the whole day like this. You don't even have to sit straight. Whatever way you sit in it, the body will balance itself. It is like when you start training to ride a bicycle, you need to sit straight on the seat and hold the handles properly, but once you have mastered the technique, you can even put your legs on the handlebars and you will balance, is it not? So just the knack of balancing needs to be learned.

Actually, it is going to take only five minutes. Sit with the right leg on the left thigh. First thing: for one moment lean forward slightly and put your whole body's weight in front of you and feel the weight of the body. Naturally, you will feel that the whole body is being pulled by gravity. Now, slowly, inch-by-inch, if you raise yourself and make your body straight, at one point, you will feel weightless. You see, when your body is leaning forward, you will feel the weight, the heaviness of your body being pulled by the ground. Step by step, very slowly, in leaning backward to mid point, you will see the gravity becoming less. At one point, you will feel totally weightless. That is the line in which your centre of gravity falls in a straight line. Now, very slowly, lean backward and feel your weight again. Then slowly, bring yourself back to the straight position again. At one point, you feel totally weightless, relaxed. This is your center of gravity line. Now you will be able to feel this balance position well.

Only one thing should be understood. Your centre of gravity should be in a straight line, and you should feel weightless at that point. At that point which you feel you don't have any weight, at that point when you feel your body is the lightest, *that is the point* when your body is balanced. At this point the hip should be in complete rest; it should not be moved. It should be totally fixed. Now, start balancing your body. Do it very slowly. You need to observe your body well. Only the backbone should bend forward or backward, never the hip or thighs or legs.

If you are balanced, then close your eyes. You may also sit on a chair to do this balancing technique. Relax in this balanced posture for a few minutes.

We are going to do the next meditation sitting in this posture. Once your body learns the language of comfort, whenever you sit, automatically you will sit only in this posture. If you have observed me, you would have noticed that whenever I sit, and wherever I sit, my body will always be very straight. Only with specific instruction to it, I bend my back! With you, normally you will be bent; only by instruction you will sit up straight! So now, taste the comfort of sitting straight and balanced. If the body learns this you will see a total attitude change. The body's whole attitude will change and it will make itself completely comfortable. Now, we will do the meditation. This is a meditation that is actually working on the physical body, making your physical layer into energy.

MEDITATION TECHNIQUE 1

Stand with one and half foot space between your feet. Close your eyes and tie the eye band.

1. Inhale and exhale slowly and deeply.

2. Concentrate on your feet; forget all other body parts. Tense your feet. Visualize your body as a bean bag. Tense your feet as intensely as possible.

3. Now relax the feet completely *(2 minutes)*.

4. Next, tense your calf muscles as intensely as possible... Relax.

5. Now, tense your knees as much as possible to the point of pain... Relax.

6. Tense your thighs intensely. Do not allow even a single nerve to rest.... Relax.

7. Tense your hips... Relax.

8. Tense your navel region intensely... Relax.

9. Tense your arms intensely... Relax.

10. Tense your face intensely... Relax.

11. Tense the crown of your head intensely... Relax.

12. Finally, tense the whole body... Relax. Sit wherever you are.

13. Now, visualise and start inhaling and exhaling through the head. Visualize that the whole head is porous. Next, inhale and exhale through every pore of the face, ear, nose, eyes, mouth, neck, shoulders, hands and entire body.

MEDITATION TECHNIQUE 2

Actually, as of now, you are solid matter. But we will be making you totally porous to the energy of Nature. Mostly, all of us resist the energy of Nature. Understand: in the part of your body where you feel cold, where the cold air is touching you, if you don't resist and just allow the cold air to pass though you, you will never have a problem with Nature's energy around you. I walked in this very same dress when I lived in the Himalayas during my pre-enlightenment period. I walked in the Himalayan snow. Of course I never even wore sandals at that time. All the wandering ascetics live this way in the Himalayas, in the snow.

If you have this basic understanding, if you have this basic relationship with Nature, you will not fall sick due to cold and such things to do with Nature. At least that much you can manage. So this balancing will help you. And moreover, becoming energy will make you porous to Nature.

Meditation Technique:

Start humming as deeply as possible, and as loudly as possible. Think of yourself as a hollow vessel and start humming. Think of yourself as a hollow vessel; forget your body, forget your mind, just become the humming. Put your whole effort in the humming. Even if you have a slight tremble in the body, or cough, or burps, there is nothing wrong. Continue as deeply and intensely as possible; forget everything else; just become the humming.

Just put your whole effort into the humming; forget that you are an individual person. Drown yourself in the energy that is being created from the humming. Forget your body and mind in the humming sound. *(21 minutes pass)*

Stop!

Now, sit calmly and just witness all your thoughts; don't suppress any thought. Don't condemn any thought. Just see what is happening inside and outside your body. Whatever happens let it happen. Just be a witness to everything that is happening throughout your body. *(A few minutes pass)*.

Relax. Slowly, you can open your eyes.

This powerful humming meditation is called The *Mahamantra*. It helps you create a great current of energy. This energy circle will create 1000 volts of energy. Understand: if ten people put ten volts together, it becomes 100 volts. And if the same ten people touched that energy, just imagine what a shock they would have! In the case of energy, everybody in the circle gets the total energy. And when the Master's presence is there, the 100 volts becomes 1000 volts because his presence is like a step-up transformer! So if you can create one volt when you do *Maha mantra* alone, this *circle* will create 1000 volts for each of you.

MEDITATION TECHNIQUE 3 - DEATH MEDITATION

Sit down cross legged on the floor with your eyes closed.

Visualize that you have lost all your possessions, all your name and fame, all your wealth. See yourself as a nobody in society. Visualize that the people who respected you earlier no longer respect you. You have lost all money and have become a beggar begging on the streets. See clearly that you have become a nobody in society.
(10 minutes)

Visualize that you have lost your near and dear ones physically. Visualize that your most cherished relationships have broken to an extent they cannot be repaired.
(10 minutes)

Physical Body

Visualize that you have lost your body parts in an accident or through some disease. Your physical health has deteriorated to a great extent.
(10 minutes)

Bring in your fear of the unknown like the fear of ghosts, spirits and darkness. Live the fears to the maximum extent possible.
(10 minutes)

Get ready for your death. Lie down on your back keeping your eyes closed.
Your toes and feet are slowly dying...They are dead.
Your calf muscles and knees are dead.
Your thighs are now dead.
Your hip is dead.
Your upper body and your arms are dead.
Your neck and face are dead.

The soul leaves your body through the *sahasrara chakra* (on top of the head). You are dead.

Watch your dead body being surrounded by your relatives and friends. They are all grieving your death.

Watch your body being carried to the cremation ground by your family and relatives. Watch your body being prepared for the cremation.

Your body is now being burnt. It is burning and becoming one with Existence.

(A few minutes pass)

Now, enter back into your body and sit up. Open your eyes.

SHARING OF EXPERIENCE FROM NSP PARTICIPANTS...

I am a professional who had to quit my job because of a chronic heel pain. It was such a pulling pain that I had for over six years. It became so bad that I could not walk. I used to walk without my heel (left leg) touching the ground, literally hopping, and this was just when I was in my forties. I tried various systems of medicine and alternative healing but they were just temporary respites if at all any. As destiny would have it, I attended the NSP with Swamiji. On the very first day when Swamiji asked us to introduce ourselves to him, I told him my problem and he told me, 'Don't worry ma, I will take care.' At the end of the NSP, during *Ananda Darshan*, when I went up to Swamiji and again told him about my problem, thinking he might have forgotten, He smiled and said, 'I will take care.' Little did I realize then that these were not mere words, but a promise. He really took care. When I stepped out of the hall after darshan, I had no pain. In fact, from the very first day, my pain had subdued, but because of fear, I was afraid to walk with my feet touching the ground. I was still hopping. Over time, I relaxed and let my foot touch the ground, and the pain has never come back since then. It has been more than three years. I have got a job now. I do my meditation regularly. I have so much more energy and am able to walk long distances. Whenever I keep my feet down, I am filled with gratitude to Swamiji for the energy he has given me.

In eternal gratitude,
NC

CHAPTER 3

Pranic Body

The *pranic* layer is filled with all our desires.

WHAT IS *PRANA?*

Prana is the life energy that sustains us every moment of our life. Understand, it is not the same as the air you breathe in and out. *Prana* is the life energy that is carried by the air. For example, if you have to carry a truck of mud from one place to another, the truck is just the carrier. The mud is the real content you are interested in. Similarly, air is the carrier which carries the real content, *prana*. We don't need air to survive; *prana* is what is needed.

Prana is associated with five different types of movements or circulation in the body. They are: *prana* – inhaling of *prana*, *vyana* – *prana* staying inside the body, *udana* – *prana* spreading all over the body to every nook and corner, *samana* – *prana* leaving the body, and *apaana* – cleaning of the system.

Please understand that when your desires change, your *prana* flow or your air flow will change.

For example, if you are caught in lust or any intense desire, your inhaling and exhaling will become intense. The *prana* going in and coming out will increase.

With any desire, the *prana* flow will change appropriately. If you are in a silent and peaceful mood, the *prana* flow will be different. It will be so mild that you will not even know that the *prana* flow is taking place.

DESIRE IS ENERGY

Desire is nothing but energy. How should we handle this desire energy?

Mahavira, a great spiritual Master, says that when we are born on planet Earth, we bring with us all that we need to survive and achieve those desires for which we took birth. Yet, why do we feel we do not have enough? For instance, we take ten thousand dollars and set out to buy a car.

We meet someone on the way who talks of the latest television that one *should* buy if one can afford to. What happens? We are carried away by the friend's words and enthusiasm for the TV, and we end up buying the television. Then we find that we do not have enough money to buy the car that we actually needed! This is how we experience the inadequacies in our lives.

Those desires that you bring with you to fulfill in *this* life are called *prarabdha karma*. But after you are born, society imposes thousands of desires on you. You pick up desires from each and everyone whom you meet in life and from commercials and try to fulfill them. All the time, you are fulfilling someone else's desires and not your own, like the example of buying the latest television. You are caught in a trap. You do not have energy, money or time to fulfill all these desires. Therefore, forgetting that all those desires were really the ones that you picked up from others, you blame life and God for not being able to fulfill your desires. You do not feel a sense of abundance and the blessed showering of Existence in your life. Instead, you feel depleted and cheated.

How Do I Know Which Desire is Mine?

When you infuse energy into the *pranic* layer, only your real desires will stay. The borrowed desires will leave you! As with a tree when you shake it, the old and dry leaves fall while young leaves of energy stay, when you do this meditation, other people's desires will all fall away and only your dreams, your desires, will stay. Understand that your own desires that you came with, into this life are already imbued with the energy to fulfill them. Borrowed desires are not so deep and energy filled. But what happens is that you use the energy you came with to fulfill these borrowed dreams and complain that life does not supply you the energy you need to fulfill your desires. When you work on energizing the *pranic* layer, all the desires imposed on you by others will drop.

You design your desires when you are born. When other desires are imposed on you, your breathing changes; it becomes shallow. If you have observed kids when they are asleep, you can see that they breathe with their whole body. When social conditioning happens, your breathing becomes shallow and confined to the nose.

Prarabdha karma is your own *samskaras* that you brought with you. Borrowed *samskaras* change the way your *prana* happens. When you readjust your *prana*, all the false desires fall off. The purpose of this meditation is to strengthen your own desires, not to drop all desires.

If you do not work out the desires that you brought with you, that is your *prarabdha*, you become suicidal; you develop cancer. Right from birth we bring with us the plan for major events such as what we want to be in terms of career, marriage, children, etc.

The idea that your desires are never to be fulfilled is wrong. Drop that idea. *Prarabdha karma* itself means desires that you bring along with its own energy for fulfillment. Understand this very clearly.

Our desires are like Pandora's box! We have accumulated so many and kept them. Now, open Pandora's box and see what is inside. Do not condemn your desires; do not suppress them; do not judge. Whatever is there, let it out. We can classify desires into four types: desires to do with sensual pleasures, name and fame, material possessions and spiritual experiences.

Write down all your desires. Do not edit them as you write. Write in the language you think is the most effective way to express your desires. It is for you and only you. Write on a separate paper. When you have finished writing, go through your desires. Wherever you find a self contradicting thought or desire, change it to a positive thought. For example, instead of saying, 'I should not be poor', you can say, 'I should be wealthy.' Drop the word poor. Every time you use the word poor, you are empowering it along with the words 'I should not be'. So change the sentence to the corresponding positive statement: I should be wealthy.

Let go of the negative thoughts. You can follow this small technique to get rid of the negative words in your system: Talk to yourself especially in the mornings and before going to bed. Express all your thoughts only through positive words. Use that time to go deep into your system and spread only positive words and thoughts. Then your whole mental setup will change to a highly positive one. This very change will cause things to happen for you.

A man with an advanced mental age is the one who learns through intelligence; he is the one who clearly understands from his very first desire, that no desire, when fulfilled, will give him true happiness! He realizes that the ultimate goal lies beyond all desires. He will be able to see through the whole thing and analyze it. He will know that the real fulfillment comes from within himself, and not from outer world things such as desires.

Own Desires Vs Borrowed Desires

As we said earlier, your *prarabdha* is the desires that you bring with you when you come. Let us now analyse how exactly these borrowed desires take shape. It is not necessary that you yourself pick them up. Society also imposes them on you. Society is the one that first teaches you how to pick up desires from others. At a very young age, parents sow the seed of comparison in you for small things like academic performance, following cleanliness, keeping your things neatly and so on. They know to teach only by comparing you with others in all these contexts. They never just tell you the importance of it and leave it at that. This is how you learn how to borrow desires from others.

For example, when you are on your own at home, you will feel grateful for all things that you own and are blessed with. You will feel a pleasant feeling engulfing you, and a beautiful sense of gratitude overflowing from you. But the moment you open your eyes to the outer world, if you happen to pick up some desire that belongs to others, it becomes ugly again. The earlier beauty in you and your home disappears and the whole thing becomes ugly again. Again, you start pulling and pushing yourself with the freshly borrowed desires. Anything borrowed is ugly because it is not natural; it is forced or artificial, and anything that is artificial is not beautiful.

If you wish to be an artist but land up being an engineer because your father wanted you to be so, then, that again is ugly. You being an engineer is a borrowed desire. Had you been an artist, you might have been so beautiful. Who knows, maybe you were a born artist. Whatever is your nature, that is your own desire. The rest are borrowed. This is a great truth that I am telling you.

Understand this very clearly. **Whatever is your nature constitutes the desires that you brought with you when you came. If allowed to, these desires will express through you in a natural way and fulfill every moment of your life.** All other actions and miseries that happen in you are due to borrowed desires. Your own desires if allowed to be fulfilled, will by nature purify and expand your inner space. Borrowed desires on the other hand, will take you again and again to the outer world and put you only in depression. You will be true not to yourself or your own being, but to others and you will lose your way in life. You will waste your energy and land in depression and low energy again and again.

I tell you that almost every desire of ours is borrowed because our own desires are our nature! So if you sit and think, you will be able to clearly see how each and every action of ours is driven by what we picked up from someone. It is a very subtle game sometimes. But with intelligence, we will be able to trace the root of every action of ours. If we live with this awareness, it is more than enough. Just the awareness will take us beyond desires and keep us in peace and bliss.

In Jainism, there is a belief that when you are born, the entire quantity of food and energy that you will need during your lifetime is sent along with you. This is a way of saying that whatever are your true requirements in this birth, Existence equips you with the energy to fulfill them before sending you to planet Earth.

So understand that if at all you are feeling that your desires are not getting fulfilled, it is because of your own doing, not because of God or your parents or anyone around you.

One more important thing about desires, I want to tell you. Desires are energy for our body. It is the fuel without which we will not even get up from our bed. The reason why you even stir from your bed is because of the desire to do something. Without desire you will not even get up from the bed. To move out of bed, you need energy. That energy is desire. Desire itself is no problem. There is nothing wrong in having desires and fulfilling them.

The whole problem is we start having self-contradicting desires. For example, we want all the comforts, but we don't want to take up any responsibility. This is one major area of self-contradiction. Next, we want to take a vacation for which we need money. For money we need to work. These two desires are contradictory. What happens because of this? You lie on the Hawaii beach thinking about work! Misery starts! There is no fulfillment. This is exactly what I mean by self-contradicting desires. You pick up something from someone, you go behind it, but when you are trying to fulfill it, you start thinking about something else because you have picked up something else from someone else! This is why we need to bring awareness into our borrowed desires. They start becoming self-contradictory because you are picking up different things from different people!

Another more subtle example of self-contradictory desire lies in the language we use. If you want to get rid of a headache, what do you say? 'Let me not have headache.' But, the word 'headache' gets impressed in your inner space as deeply as the words 'let me not have'. The vibration of the word 'headache' is filling your inner space. So this is again self-contradictory because while you don't want the headache, you are repeatedly empowering it! And if you say 'I am healthy' you create another conflict within yourself since immediately another voice inside you will answer, saying 'That's not true. I'm not well.' Now the fight has started! Just say, 'Let me be healthy.' That's all.

NEEDS VS WANTS

Similarly, there is a difference between your needs and wants. Your needs are already taken care of in some way. It is possible to satisfy your needs, but it becomes impossible to satisfy your wants because they are changing and unclear all the time. Every time one want or desire is fulfilled, a hundred more come up. It is our nature to want endlessly, because we are continuously getting input through our eyes, ears, nose, mouth and touch! The more input we get, the more we want.

What is the difference between a need and a want? Take, for example, a creeper that is growing in your garden. For the creeper to grow upwards, it needs a support like a tree or a bamboo stick or a pillar or something. Without this support it will only grow horizontally and get crushed by people walking over it. This is an example of a need for the plants' survival. If you analyse all your desires with the help of this example, just imagine what will happen! You will see that virtually everything that you desire is a want and not a need!

The wandering *sadhus* (spiritual seekers) in the Himalayas live with so little. Their entire list of possessions will be a stick to wards off wild animals and a small water pot. That's all! I lived like that for so many years during my pre-enlightenment period! You don't know the liberation it is to live like that. You might say 'Swamiji, for *sanyasis* it is alright, but what about householders like us who have so many things to be done with husband, wife, children, etc.' Understand, I am not telling you to have only a water pot and stick, no! I am more practical than you - understand that first! I am only saying, first become clear of the difference between needs and wants. That is the first step towards more peaceful living. As this becomes clear, slowly, the want-based attitude in you will start changing and automatically, life will move from discontent to fulfillment, that's all. **You will see that fulfillment happens not because you got what you wanted but because you understood that you have all that you need!**

When this understanding happens, you will also stop picking up desires from others. You will stop comparing yourself with others. You will remain focused within yourself instead of outside of you. Once this happens, your wants will in no way affect your inner space.

There is a beautiful *sutra* in the *Shiva Sutras* where Lord Shiva gives a technique to handle one's desires. It says,

A Technique to Drop Emotional Attachment to Desire

Do you see how simple this technique is? But anything simple is complex for the human mind. To begin with, all simple things need you to be simple yourself. This is the basic requirement, or the pre-requisite to understand or internalize the technique.

Here Shiva directly says, 'Whenever a desire arises in you, consider it.' He means, 'Just see, don't judge'. Simply be an unbiased witness, an observer, not a judge.

If you judge something as right or wrong, you will not be able to drop the idea or desire. The moment you say that something is wrong; you have unconsciously begun to enjoy it because right from a young age you have been trained to derive pleasure in enjoying what society labels as wrong. The moment you judge something as right also, you start enjoying it because it is right!

Shiva says, 'See it, and the moment you see it, un-clutch from it!' He is teaching renunciation - simple and pure. People may ask, 'How can this be possible? How can we renounce?' I tell them, 'Then follow the method that you know to overcome it, that's all, simple!' You either learn from an enlightened Master, or life will teach you. Life is going to teach you. If you learn from the Master, it will be a lot easier for you because he will talk to you in the language that you can understand directly. You may not directly understand the language that life speaks in. Because of this, the process for you will be delayed and you will receive strong punches also. By the time you start realizing the punches, start interpreting and understanding the messages conveyed by the incidents in your life, it might be too late.

Please understand that it is always better to learn from the Master who is talking to you in the same language that you understand, the language that you communicate in, relate with. If you learn from him, it will be a lot easier for you as you do not have to go through all the painful experiences.

So, Shiva says, 'Suddenly un-clutch! Even before the mind starts arguing with you, even before the mind starts asking, 'Should I un-clutch or not?' suddenly un-clutch, that's all. If you keep arguing with the mind, you will never un-clutch.

I always tell people, 'Don't think before you jump. If you think, you will never jump'. If you keep thinking, you will never jump. You will jump only the moment you stop thinking. So don't think before you jump. There is a saying, 'Think twice before you jump,' or 'Look before you leap'. I say 'No! If you think, you will never jump.' Even before your mind becomes aware, un-clutch; you are enlightened.

There is a beautiful story:

One lady goes to Ramakrishna, the great enlightened Master and says, 'Master, my husband threatens me that he will become a *swami*, that he will leave me and go away, that he will renounce life and go away.'

Ramakrishna says, 'Don't bother, it will never happen'. She is surprised to hear this and says, 'No, no Master. He is not joking. He is very serious about what he is saying.'

Ramakrishna then narrates an incident to her.

There was one man threatening his wife, 'I will go away and become a *swami*. I will renounce life and go away.' This is actually a technique used by frustrated men mostly in India. They threaten their women because in India women are not economically independent. If the wife nags the husband too much, this is the way he will respond.

This lady goes and complains to the man's elder brother, her brother-in-law, 'Your brother is threatening me that he will become a *swami*, please advise him.'

The elder brother says, 'Don't bother, it will never happen.'

The lady asks, 'How do you say it will never happen? My husband is very serious about what he is saying.'

He replies, 'I shall show you how a person becomes a *swami*, just watch.' So saying, he removes his clothes and throws them away. He picks up a towel and walks away. He left the house and became a *swami*!

The elder brother shows, 'This is the way to become a *swami*,' and really became one!

The person who talks will never do. The person who keeps thinking also will never do. The person who is thinking will never jump. Ramakrishna relates this story and consoles the lady, 'Don't bother, the person who threatens will never move.'

When you are filled with some desire and you suddenly disconnect from it, you will experience a new inner space, an empty space - that inner space which is ready to experience your own reality. However, the big problem is that whenever you are ready to un-clutch from some desire, it is for the sake of some other desire! You are not ready to un-clutch completely. You are ready to un-clutch from one if you have the promise that the other will come to you. If you are greedy for some other desire, you are ready to un-clutch from *this* desire.

THREE LEVELS OF DESIRES

We handle desires at three levels. In the first level, we have too many desires that are always self-contradicting. Even if there are only two desires, they will contradict each other. In the second level, there is only one object. You fulfill that but still feel emptiness. You do not feel completely fulfilled. In the third level, there is no object, there is just overflowing energy. Desire without any object is bliss. In kids energy overflows as desires.

Pure desire is desire without any object.It is overflowing energy for no reason. Pure desire is actually just an overflowing, that's all. It is a causeless overflowing. When you further purify this with awareness, you come to the stage of *satori*; you get a glimpse of *samadhi*; that is, you are in a state of pure awareness. You reach this not by suppressing, but by being aware, by purifying it.

What is the root cause of desire? We feel we have to achieve something, some goal in life all the time. We feel we need to fulfill the purpose of life. All desires are to reach towards what we think is the goal of life at that moment. That brings us to the important issue of renunciation...

Do Not Renounce for the Sake of Reward

I have seen people who renounce drinking because they hear that in heaven, they are served much better liquor. This is part of the promises that are made to them. It is believed that in heaven you will have dancing maidens and you get different kinds of liquor and music. These people are fantasizing about heaven and renouncing this world! Of course in a way, it is good that they don't do these things here! But I always tell them, renouncing purely for enlightenment is renunciation; renouncing for some other desire is not renunciation. It is a bargain, a business.

A small story:

One man thought to himself, 'If I undertake austerities here and renounce everything, I may get all the best things in heaven.' So he was practicing all kinds of austerities, and became a big guru with many disciples and followers. One day, he died and reached heaven.

One of his disciples who was always with him thought, 'How can I live without my guru?' So he also died and reached heaven.

While he searched for his guru in heaven, he was thinking, 'My guru led such an austere life that he must have got the best rewards. He must be enjoying all the beautiful heavenly women and all the liquor that is served here. He must be really singing and dancing and enjoying this eternal pleasure.'

Suddenly, he saw the guru sitting next to a beautiful woman, probably a famous actress! He was sitting with her, drinking and enjoying. He approached his guru and said, 'Master! I am so happy to see your austerity well rewarded. O! What a gift she is for you!'

At that point, the girl immediately intervened and said, 'Stop! I am not the gift for your guru; he is the punishment for me!'

So do not expect any heavenly pleasures while renouncing! See, even in day to day life, if you meditate with the thought that you will have more power to enjoy pleasures later, that you will have other benefits, you are again using meditation as a utility.

WHAT IS THE PURPOSE OF LIFE?

This is a million-dollar question!

The answer to this is:

The whole of Existence, the whole universe, is purposeless!

Of course, it would be very shocking to hear this. From a very young age, we are taught and socially conditioned to believe that life has got some purpose. We are made to run towards some goal, towards some purpose, all the time.

'What is life without purpose?' you may ask. Any activity, let alone one's entire life, has to have a purpose, a definition, and an end point, to make it meaningful. That purpose is what drives us, motivates us and provides energy to carry on with our day-to-day activities.

So to hear a statement such as 'Life has no purpose', might confuse you. You would say, 'All our lives, we have been brought up to believe that we are here for a purpose.' This is because at every stage of our lives, a different purpose is drilled into our heads and we are made to work towards that purpose. As children, we are expected to do well in school. Once grown up, we are supposed to be married happily, and bring up children. During each phase in our lives, we have specific templates, specific guidelines, that society and our families have set up for us. So you might now ask, 'How can we let them down? How can we believe that all these expectations are wrong, and that there is no purpose to life?' You might feel that I am trying to turn your whole life upside down!

The more you run towards a goal, the more you are considered to be a successful person. More the speed, more you are respected; more the speed, more the rewards. From your birth, again and again, society teaches you that life has got some purpose, that life has some goal. Life without purpose seems meaningless to us. We cannot even comprehend such a possibility.

Just understand that this is only what you have been *brought up to believe*, and nothing else. This is not the truth of Existence. Life does not need any defined goal to make living worthwhile, meaningful and happy. In fact, the absence of purpose makes our life meaningful. The absence of goals makes living worthwhile.

The universe or Nature has no purpose. It just is. It exists. A river runs downhill towards the ocean because it is its nature to run downhill. It is not because it has a purpose to meet the ocean. Our life too, has no purpose. We were not born for a purpose. We were born to live, to enjoy life and to be happy. Instead, we set ourselves up for unhappiness by setting goals for ourselves. And almost always, these goals are based on fantasies, not on realities. In the process, we stop enjoying real life.

The more you run towards goals, the more you miss life itself, because when you run, you miss the wonderful touch of the earth beneath your feet!

The man who is continuously bothered about the goal will never be able to enjoy his life. He continuously lives in the future and ignores the present. When we are in the present moment, the 'here and now', we do not need a goal to guide us.

Just awareness of the present moment will automatically lead us to do what needs to be done at that point in time. When the present moment is taken care of with awareness, the future gets resolved by itself. As long as the path is right, whatever destination we reach will be right. We do not need to define the destination; the right path defines its own destination.

When we don't live with awareness in the present moment, our mind starts straying towards either the past or the future. That is the problem. We constantly worry about the future. We constantly think of the past, relate it to our future and define our expectations based on what we have missed in the past, or what we believe will provide us happiness in the future.

For example, when you are studying, you always think, 'When I have a job, my life will be happy.' When you have your job you think, 'After marriage my life will be happy.' After marriage, you think, 'When I have kids and my own house, my life will be blissful.' After you have kids and your own house, you think, 'When my kids grow up and support themselves, all my responsibilities will be over, and I will be peaceful and happy.' By the time your kids are settled, by the time your responsibilities are over, when you want to relax, your being is conditioned so much, that you can't relax!

A small story:

The emperor of a city came out from his palace for his morning walk. While he was walking, he met a beggar and asked the beggar, 'What do you want?'

The beggar laughed at the emperor and said, 'You are asking me if you can fulfill my desire?'

The King was offended by the beggar and said, 'What is it? Just tell me and I can fulfill your desire.'

The beggar told the emperor, 'Think twice before you promise anything.' This was no ordinary beggar! He was the emperor's spiritual Master from the king's past life. In the previous birth, the emperor missed the goal of enlightenment so the Master promised to return to awaken the emperor in the next life.

But the king had forgotten all this completely. Nobody remembers past lives.

In his arrogance, the emperor insisted to the beggar, 'I will fulfill anything you ask for. What is your desire that I cannot fulfill it? I am a very powerful emperor.'

The beggar said, 'My desire is a very simple one. Do you see this begging bowl? Can you fill this bowl with something?'

The emperor called one of his ministers and told him, 'Fill this man's begging bowl with money.'

The minister went, got some money and put it in the bowl. Soon it disappeared! Again he put in some money and again it disappeared. No matter how much or how often money was put in, the begging bowl remained empty.

The news of this spread throughout the whole capital, and a huge crowd gathered near the palace. The emperor's prestige was now at stake. He told his ministers, 'Even if the whole kingdom is lost, I am ready for it, but I cannot be defeated by this beggar.' Pearls, diamonds, emeralds, and his treasuries were being offered, all lost into the begging bowl.

As evening arrived the people stood and watched in utter silence. The king fell at the feet of the beggar and admitted his defeat. He said, 'You are right. I cannot manage this simple thing! Before you leave please tell me one thing, what is the begging bowl made of?'

The beggar laughed at the emperor and said, 'There is no secret. It is made from the same stuff as everyone's mind. It is simply made up of human desire!'

When you understand deeply that the mind is like the begging bowl that can never be filled, it can have a great, healing effect. This understanding can transform your life completely.

Let us get into the mechanism of desire. First, there is a great excitement, a great thrill and a feeling of adventure. We feel a great kick about the deisre. It could be a new car, a new house, increased bank balance...anything. But suddenly, there are moments when everything becomes meaningless!

What happens after some time? Our mind has dematerialized the whole thing. The car is standing in the garage, but there is no excitement anymore. The excitement was only in getting it. The desire is fulfilled, the car is in the garage, the money is in the bank account, but the excitement has disappeared. Again the emptiness is there, ready to eat us up. Again we have to create another desire to escape this abyss.

This is how we move from one desire to another desire. This is how one remains a beggar. Our whole life proves it again and again. If we observe the subtleties of it we will see that every desire only frustrates. The day we understand that desire will fail to satisfy us, then comes the turning point in our life.

Most of us need to get stressed out before we can relax. We don't know what it is to relax. When I tell people to relax during the meditation workshops, they ask me, 'Master, please give us a few guidelines how to relax!'

The tension of running behind something has become part of our being. It has become part of our conditioning. After that, resting will not be rest anymore; it will not be relaxation anymore. Happiness is where we are. It is not where we think we should be. It is good to have an idea about where we should be, in terms of business strategies, but it is not a good idea to have our happiness invested in it. The two are clearly exclusive. What happens to your goals is a separate thread. What you ARE is a separate thread. If you are able to separate the two, relaxing will never be a problem. It is only because you have tied happiness and your goals together, that you need to run behind the goals at the cost of your real happiness.

And one more thing: when you are too caught up in your goals, you might be shutting yourself out to so many beautiful things that are going on around you simply because you don't have the time to stop and look at them!

Another small story:

A life-long city man, tired of the rat race, decided that he was going to give up and move to the country. He wanted to become a chicken farmer. He found a nice, used chicken farm, and bought it. It turned out that his next door neighbor was also a chicken farmer.

The neighbor visited him one day and said, 'Chicken farming isn't easy. I will help you get started; I will give you 100 chicks to start with.

The city man was thrilled. Two weeks later, the neighbor stopped by to see how things were going. The city man said. 'Not too good. All 100 chickens died.'

The neighbor said, 'Oh, I can't believe that. I've never had any trouble with my chickens. I will give you 100 more.

Another two weeks went by, and the neighbor stopped in again. The city man said, 'You are not going to believe this, but the second 100 chickens died too.'

Astounded, the neighbor asked, 'What went wrong? What did you do to them?'

'Well,' said the city man, 'I'm not sure whether I'm planting them too deep or not far enough apart.'

Just imagine! The city man was actually planting the chicks! This is what happens when you are stuck with ideas and goals. You miss the many more beautiful ways in which things are done.

Be very clear that life has meaning but no purpose. Enjoy the path and the goal is reached!

Your very nature is bliss. Experiencing *that* every moment is the path **and** the goal.

THE ALCHEMY: FROM DESIRE TO COMPASSION

We may wonder why we exist when there is no goal to work for or look forward to.

We have to understand an important thing. When desire disappears, the energy behind the desire still remains. Man as such is energy. That should not be forgotten. We have always been trained to think that man is matter.

The first line of the *Isa Vasya Upanishad* is '*Isa vasyam idam sarvam*' - *All that exists is energy*. Desire is also a form of energy. That is why you can turn one desire into another. The desire energy at one point may be a manifestation of greed; in another moment, the same energy may transform into anger. In another case, it may transform into depression.

Energy cannot be destroyed. It can only be transformed. This is what science also says. What happens when we transcend desire? It cannot now be manifested as greed or fear or anger, which are all due to external causes. The whole energy manifests itself as pure causeless compassion! You cannot create compassion. It happens because of transformation of energy. Then the whole energy starts overflowing causelessly! That is the beauty and definition for compassion. It is the causeless overflowing of energy. It is causeless because there is no cause like greed or fear or anger or anything. It just IS.

THE POWER OF AWARENESS

An important thing to understand is that desire can exist only in unconsciousness. Only when you are unaware can desire exist. Look inside yourself when you have a desire or when you are angry or depressed. Look clearly at what is rising in you, what is happening inside you. The moment you look at the desire objectively, with awareness, you will see that the desire simply loses power; it just dissolves!

YOU CREATE THE REALITY AROUND YOU

A fundamental law of Existence is that you and your desires together create the reality around you. Existence responds to what you desire. For example, if you are afraid, that very desire of having fear will invoke the desire to frighten you in the other person. If you are not afraid, the desire in the other simply disappears.

Existence simply responds to what you ask for. Constantly, It is giving you what you request. We only need to have the intelligence to know what to ask for.

BLISS ATTRACTS FORTUNE

Your thoughts and energy directly affect your body, your cell structure, your decisions, your capacity to fulfill your decisions, the outer world incidents, and even accidents. Currently you are always centered in either greed or fear. Every action that you do, is out of either desire or fear. It becomes very easy for others to exploit you because of this. You become very vulnerable. You create a mental setup that creates and attracts similar incidents to you. You also corrupt your energy flow with this.

If you can change your mental setup from this type to one of bliss, or *ananda*, then your energy flow will start brimming and your thoughts will be much clearer and more in the present. When you do this, you have every power to control the outer world incidents because you and Existence have a very deep connection at the energy level. This is the thread that you need to catch in order to understand that Bliss attracts fortune. When you are blissful, when your mental setup is not one of worry, fear and greed but one that is in the present and always joyful, you will automatically attract all good things to yourself.

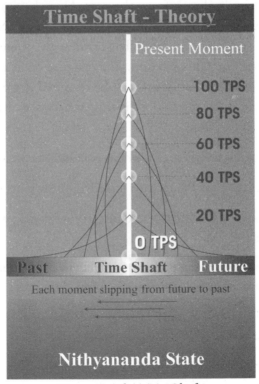

Figure 8: The Time Shaft

Desire is Never in the Present; Truth is Always in the Present

It is not that desire is right or wrong. It is also not the object of desire that is of concern. Desire itself will be dropped when we develop the maturity to realize that desire is never in the present; only Truth *is* the present moment.

Another thing we need to know is that desire is always from the past. We cannot desire something absolutely new. Can we desire something we do not have some idea about already? No! So desire is always from the past. Now, having said that, can you ask for anything from the past or future? No, because neither exist. The only thing that exists is the present. And in the present, you cannot desire. You can just be in it and enjoy it. So understand that desire can be dropped if we are just in the present moment and enjoying what is evolving every minute.

The *Bhagavata Purana* (an Indian epic) has a beautiful story:

Once a crow was flying with a piece of meat in its beak.

There were many crows pursuing it trying to grab a share of the meat.

The crow tried flying higher and higher to escape from them. It became tired and suddenly it dropped the meat.

Immediately the twenty crows simply followed the falling piece of meat.

Seeing this, the crow realized, 'How nice it is to carry nothing! The whole sky belongs to me now.'

The piece of meat he was carrying was creating all the trouble for the crow. The moment he dropped it, all the birds pursuing it simply disappeared!

Similarly, in our life also, once the meat of desire is dropped, the whole sky of enlightenment belongs to us!

Desiring means you have moved away from reality. You have moved away from that which IS.

Desire means you have fallen into the trap of a dream. Desire means you are not 'here' and 'now', you have gone somewhere in the future which doesn't exist. Desire means you are not satisfied with what you have. If you can be in the present moment and enjoy, you will drop from the vicious cycle of desires. This is the nature of surrender. Surrendering is non-desiring, which allows your nature to express itself.

FROM DESIRE TO CLARITY

When you light the candle of understanding, desire disappears. It is not a question of what you desire. The very act of desiring itself is misery. When you are desireless, the 'I' or the ego disappears, so the misery disappears.

All desires must disappear. Only in a desireless moment, will what you are asking for happen.

When we hear this, the next thing that occurs is your wanting to be desireless! But this is one more desire! You cannot desire desirelessness. You must simply understand the futility of desire. Through the understanding itself, the greed for desirelessness drops.

Watch every act that you do. Watch every thought, every desire that possesses you. As you watch, your chattering mind chatters less, because the energy that was earlier chattering and fuelling the desire is now being transformed into watchfulness. When this happens, clarity arises and the desire dissolves. Actually, the attachment to the desire drops.

When you watch your desire, you will be able to see two things: desire by its very nature cannot bring you fulfillment. When you realize this, the desire disappears. Second, you will see that only when you transcend desire do you reach fulfillment.

When you realize the very nature of desire, you accept that desiring is the nature of the mind. Please be very clear: acceptance is not the same as resignation. Resignation is defeat. One becomes resigned when one feels nothing more can be done about something. Acceptance is a totally different thing. Acceptance does not mean that you have accepted defeat. It simply means that there you have clearly seen and understood the real nature of something, that's all! Acceptance has nothing to do with defeat or victory. It is just clearly seeing what IS, that's all.

MEDITATION

Alright, now let us get into the meditation.

Sit down and tie your eye bands.

There are four steps to repeat here.

1. Inhale as deeply as possible.

2. Hold the breath, fill your lungs and remain that way for as long as possible.

3. Then, exhale through the mouth, emptying out your lungs.

4. Keeps your lungs empty for as long as possible. This is one cycle.

Start doing the meditation. Inhale very deeply; fill your lungs to the maximum extent possible, little by little. Hold on to it for as long as possible.

When you feel you can't hold anymore, try to extend it one second further. Then try for another one second. When you feel you have crossed your limit, breathe out through the mouth slowly and deeply. Exhale as deeply as possible, as slowly as possible.

Continue this cycle, but very slowly. Inhale as deeply as possible through the nose. Hold for as long as possible, then exhale gently through the mouth for as long as possible and keep the lungs empty for as long as possible. Repeat this cycle.

(After 10 minutes)

Stop the breathing and relax. Let your eyes be closed. Relax. Come to your normal breathing now.

Now slowly, very slowly, visualize all your dreams, all your desires. One by one, feel that all your desires are getting fulfilled, that all your desires have come true. Imagine as deeply as possible as if it has actually happened. Visualize consciously how your life will be after fulfillment of all your desires. If one of your desires is wealth, visualize how you will be when the desire is fulfilled and feel that way now. Visualise how you will live after getting all that wealth. Visualise realistically to the maximum possible extent, in a very detailed fashion. Don't think that any particular detail is silly to include. Include everything that you can think of.

Never condemn any desire. Never condemn the fulfillment that comes because of the visualization. Just ensure that you are completely fulfilled. Live the ecstasy, live the joy of having your desires fulfilled. It is completely alright to go through it.

Visualise all your desires having to do with name and fame. Visualise how your life and actions will be once the name and fame have been achieved. Visualise and enjoy your new social status. There is nothing wrong in doing so. Visualise how you will be attended upon by people because of your new status. Feel gratitude towards them and enjoy the whole scene.

Visualise all your sexual fantasies coming true. There is nothing wrong in doing so now. Go deep into them and visualize them coming true. Once your sexual desires get fulfilled, how complete you will feel, feel that way now. There is nothing wrong in this. Feel the relaxation and fulfillment upon satisfying all your sexual desires.

Once your spiritual desires are blessed, how fulfilled you will feel, feel that way now. Visualise all your spiritual aspirations coming true.

If there are any broken relationships that you desire be repaired, now is the time... Visualize that you have taken the steps needed to repair the relationship and that it has become alright. Feel the relief and joy because of the repaired relationship. Feel the joy of being able to talk to that person like the good old days again. Feel the joy of having the relationship healed.

Visualize and feel that all your desires.have come true. Visualize that your life now is in complete fulfillment, exactly how you would want it to be in all aspects. Consciously put your whole effort and visualize things in a detailed way.

Don't avoid this. Don't again push the desires to the unconscious. Bring them up to the conscious and live them. Live them totally with all the juice in them! Understand that there is nothing wrong in going fully ahead in your visualization. This is your best opportunity because you are in the Master's presence.

When you start visualizing all your desires, you will start automatically concentrating on the third eye, on the brow *chakra* located between the eyebrows. Allow that to happen. Encourage your mind to get concentrated on the third eye.

With all your power and consciousness, give life to all your desires. Live everything. Allow yourself to have life as you wish to. Let all your sexual fantasies come true. Let all your desires for wealth become reality. Let all your spiritual desires become reality.

Let your eyes be closed. Now, stand up with your eyes closed.

Give at least one feet gap between your feet and place them wide apart.

Stop all the movement of thoughts. Whatever thoughts may come up, just witness them. Just step away from your own body by one foot mentally and witness your thoughts, your breath, your mind and your body. Look at your whole body from a distance. Don't associate yourself with the body or the mind, just be a witness.

Witness the thoughts that are arising. Let your hands be loose and relaxed, just witness.

Now, relax. Slowly, you may open your eyes and relax.

When your mental body becomes empty, when your *pranic* body opens, your being becomes porous to the live energy.

When the desires become energy, you become porous to the energy. Many of your unconscious desires disappear. Many of your wants exist just because others also have the same wants. When you bring all those wants to consciousness, they will just melt and disappear. And the energy which was invested in those wants or desires will now aid in fulfilling your conscious desires. Those energies will become a support to fulfill your conscious desires.

Not only do the unconscious desires disappear, the energy that was locked in them now becomes a positive support for your conscious desires. You will start seeing that even when you don't ask, things start happening for you. The desires have started melting and becoming energy for you. Actually they *are* energy. They are not cancers as we think. We always think that desires are blood clots. No! They are not blood clots, they are *blood*. Because you have not brought consciousness into them, they have become blood clots. When you bring consciousness to them, they become blood again.

SHARING OF EXPERIENCE FROM NSP PARTICIPANTS...

I am usually a person who gets startled quickly. After my NSP, I noticed that the situations that would have jolted me earlier, caused no fear stroke or jumpiness in me! And I was able to disover this within that millisecond of reaction! I feel like a different person now. Things that used to affect me just do not touch me anymore. Anxiety, worry, just gone... desires too...

In Nithyananda
Anand Deoskar

I did my NSP at Yercaud in Tamil Nadu. During the course the most memorable experience for me was the *pranic* layer meditation. After writing down reams of desires for hours, when I went into the meditation, all I could recall were a handful of desires, and each one unconnected with anything material. I almost literally saw in my mind's eye a tree with a few golden leaves that Swami had predicted. Swami said that these few remaining desires were our *prarabdha*. I had no clue what He meant but was quite surprised that someone like me who had been an aggressive corporate warrior found nothing of material value to remember as my core desire.

But the course was magic. All that registered was the Master's guarantee: 'I promise you that none of you will take birth again if you do not wish to. You will be reborn if you wish in whatever form you wish to be.' I was so relieved that I was not going to be reborn.

Three months ago I would have dismissed this as the claim of a crazed soul. But sitting in front of the Master, (who was younger than my son!) I had no doubt that whatever He said would come true. The four days passed rapidly and the last night was a sleepless *Ananda Darshan* for nearly 300 people, all of whom received a spiritual name. I remember falling at the feet of everyone, young and old, with no thought as to who I was.

During the program we formed groups and performed skits. Swami sat on huge speakers and enjoyed the way we made fools of ourselves. During one skit that had an all female cast, a few of the participants made fun of the women in what I thought was an uncouth way. I could not help telling them to stop heckling the women. One of them I found especially distasteful and I was quite rude to him in front of Swami telling him to lay off. Surprised perhaps, this person did and the skits continued.

I forgot about the incident after that. But when I went back to the ashram for *acharya* training I started wondering why I was so critical of this person while Swami was laughing his head off at this man's antics. The thoughts wouldn't go away. 'If my Master didn't mind, why should I?' was the refrain that kept playing in my mind. 'How dare I? Who was I to judge?' I remember asking Ayya, Swami's secretary and senior disciple. He said that the very fact that I was thinking this way meant changes were happening in me. I had no idea about what these changes were.

A few days later this person was in the ashram for some work. I was near the kitchen beyond the Laughing Temple and I saw him approach from a distance of about 100 meters away. When he saw me I saw that he hesitated. Not surprising, since I had been quite rude to him during the NSP. Suddenly something broke within me. I can recall perfectly clearly the exact moment. I walked forward towards him with my arms open. As I hugged him half way down the pathway, I guess nobody would have been more surprised than this person. I had tears in my eyes. Neither had I anything to say, nor there seemed a need.

Today I know him very well. He has a heart of gold. We have nothing in common except the Master. Knowing what a wonderful person he is now, I realize what a judgmental person I was till my NSP days and what a poor judge of people I was. My judgments were based totally on social conditioning. Though I feel no guilt, thanks to my Master, I shiver involuntarily when I think of how silly I was.

From that moment it was as if all my negativities dropped. Anger, irritation, dislike ..emotions that made me operate previously in high gear seemed to drop in quick succession. Each time I felt a negative emotion about an event or a person, it was as if a hammer would knock my head saying, 'Wake up, you idiot, perish the thought.' True enough, they perished.

Attachments too dropped rapidly. Like the desires that dropped from the tree, there seemed no hold for attachments. For the first time in my life, I was free of conditioning, however much of a cliché it may sound. Looking back, NSP was when my transformation really began from a subhuman to a human.

Sri Nithya Advaithananda
CEO, Crucible Consulting

CHAPTER 4

Relation of Rituals with *Karma* – An Astounding Revelation

(Based on talks given by Paramahamsa Nithyananda in Himalayas 2007 Spiritual Tour)

INTRODUCTION

Most of us would have heard about the word '*karma*'. Each of us has some understanding of what *karma* is, based on what we have read from books or heard from others. The principle of *karma* needs to be understood by every individual because it is the basis of the cycle of our birth and death. We have to realize the understandings about life are very important; they are the bedrock upon which our ideals, principles and hence, actions are based.

For example, suppose you went for an adventure trip to a jungle with a group of friends. Let's say the group gets lost and you are all trying to find a way out. It is getting dark, everybody is scared and you need to find your way back before nightfall. In this situation of panic, suppose one person takes responsibility and says that he will lead everyone out. Now, this person does not have the required knowledge about the jungle but he is a little more courageous than the rest of the people. What are the chances that you will get out of the jungle?

Only a person who has seen the goal and knows the way can clearly and safely guide the group. A person in the group who climbs a tall tree, studies the landscape and then maps the way out is the true leader.

In the same way, the great Truths about life should only be learnt from reliable sources! An enlightened Master is one who has experienced and is living the Truth. He can simply transmit the experience to you if you are sincerely seeking and open to receiving it.

What follows is the unveiling of the deep mysteries about life and a logical understanding of the secrets about the inner workings of the cosmos, straight from an enlightened Master - a rare happening on planet Earth.

SEEING THE DIVINE IN THE DEITIES

An important difference you should understand between normal human beings and enlightened Masters. A normal person doesn't have the ability to make his body alive out of his will. Either a normal person's body is alive or it is dead, that's all. It is not under his control. But for an enlightened person, it is under his control. He can either make his body alive, or relax. Because of this ability, he can make another body also alive! When he chooses to make a stone or metal alive, it becomes a representation of his very self.

All the deities in our major traditional temples are those energized by enlightened Masters. Masters like Arunagiri Yogeeshwar from Tiruvannamalai, Patanjali from Chidambaram, Karurar from Thanjavur, Konganavar from Tirupati and Meenakshi from Madurai have energized the deities in these temples. So deities are considered to be the very bodies of the enlightened Masters, and disciples start serving the deities even after the Master leaves his physical body. The body of the deity is considered to be the body of the Master himself. That is the reason why the deities receive the same respect offered to an enlightened Master.

For example, all the disciples initiated by Arunagiri Yogeeshwar will worship the Arunachala temple for generations together. You will see that whatever is done to the Master, the same thing will be done to the deity also.

The deities possess independent intelligence. Energizing the deities is a big process. It is like giving birth. So understand, these energised deities directly will respond to your prayers. They will directly relate with you if you are open in relating to them.

If you see our *puja* (offering), and our ashram routine, you will see that in the morning they will play the appropriate song to wake the Lord up. Then they will give oil and tooth powder: a small cup of oil for His hair and a small cup of tooth powder for Him to brush His teeth! Then they will give Him a bath and offer fresh, ironed clothes, just like how they offer to the Master. Whether it is in Bidadi or Ohio or LA or Hyderabad, in all our temples, you will see the same routine. Then they also offer food and perform the evening *arati* (ceremoniously waving lit lamps and other items in front of the deities). Five times a day, they will offer *puja*. In the night, they will put the Lord to bed in a ceremonious way again.

Understand: all this does not add anything to the deity or to the Master; it adds to us! This is what is living with God! This is what is practicing the presence of God. Practicing the presence of the Master is *puja*. *Puja* is done everyday because it is a technique to remember everyday the presence of God.

If you decide to remind yourself of all the clicks that happened in you, all the Truths and ideas that you could feel connected to when they were uttered, that is what becomes your ritual then. It is a ritual because when you are dabbling in it, you raise yourself to the higher consciousness.

Whenever you are in a low mood or depression happens in you, if you remind yourself with the right click, you are doing a great service to yourself. The moment you remember the click, what will happen? You will come out of the low mood. You will simply come out of it.

SIGNIFICANCE OF RITUALS

I will now explain about how *karma* and rituals are directly connected, how our *prarabdha, agamya* and *sanchita karmas* and rituals are connected. I will tell you about these three *karmas*, and how performing rituals can directly eliminate the negative influence of these *karmas,* these *samskaras* or engraved memories. You can come out of them with this understanding.

Rituals are very powerful tools, powerful techniques. Many people ask me, 'You are enlightened; why you should perform rituals?' I tell them, 'Because I am enlightened, I am teaching people exactly how and why to perform rituals!' No ritual is needed for enlightened beings.

Let me tell you a small story:

One man went to a hotel and started eating *idlis* (Indian dish made of rice flour).

He ate eight *idlis*, and after the ninth *idli* his hunger settled.

The waiter came and gave the bill for nine *idlis*.

This man said, 'What is this? I will pay only for one *idli* - the ninth *idli* which put my hunger off! The first eight *idlis* did not do the job; only the ninth one did the job of satisfying my hunger. So, I will pay only for that *idli*!'

Doesn't it sound strange? In the same way, people who reject rituals are actually rejecting the first eight *idlis*. People who think that rituls are a waste and that they will go straightaway to meditation and spiritual experience are doing nothing but rejecting the first eight *idlis*. Understand that the ninth *idli* worked *because* of the first eight *idlis*. So, your meditation will work because of you having gone through ritual worship sincerely! If you reject all these preliminary things and think that you can directly eat the ninth *idli*, will it ever happen? Will your hunger ever get satisfied? Whoever thinks that they can directly eat the ninth *idli* will be just sitting and starving. Not only that, because they did not do things in a proper way, they will not experience what they should experience, and instead they will think, 'Maybe this is all that the experience is.' Such people are called *Vedantis* - the so called meditators. If you see them, there will be no sign of joy on their face. They will perpetually appear depressed and be missing something.

Ramakrishna beautifully says, 'As long as you think you have a body, you will be able to relate to the cosmic energy only through another body.' Only when you lose your body consciousness, you can see the Divine also as formless. Until that happens, you need some form, some reminding rituals, some deities to worship.

You see, in my first three years of the mission, from 2003 to 2006, I never gave any ritual along with meditation. Only in 2006, I added the *GuruPuja* to the everyday meditation - *Nithya Dhyaan*.

From 2003 to 2005, only 20% to 30% of the people who were initiated into meditation continued the meditation for at least three months. After three months, that also stopped.

But now, after I added the *Guru Puja* to *Nithya Dhyaan*, after it became more or less a ritual, more than 80% who take initiation follow it! I did a statistical study and discovered this. So I think it is good to have a ritual along with meditation, so that the regular habit of doing some *sadhana* – penance - will get cultivated.

Otherwise you won't do it regularly. The first day, you will think, 'Today my mother-in-law is here,' or 'I have too much work' and you will skip it. After two days, when your mother-in-law has gone, or the work is done, you will think, 'Let me enjoy my vacation after saying goodbye to my mother-in-law. I don't want to do it today.' Or, if you are happy, you will think, 'Today I am happy, then why meditate?' Or if you are depressed, you will think, 'Oh, today I am depressed. How can I focus on meditation?' Your mind tries to find some logic to skip it! But if it is made into a ritual, you will not find any logic to skip it. You will simply do it.

Now we will see how we go through the *janma marana chakra*, (cycle of life and death) and how these initiations and rituals can liberate us from it, how they can take us out of this cycle.

Sanchita, Prarabdha and Agamya Karma

Basically we have three layers of *karmas: sanchita, prarabdha and agamya. Sanchita karma* is like a bank, a reserve bank. See, this may not be the first time you have taken a body and come to planet Earth. You might have taken millions of bodies before! In those millions of bodies, whatever you learnt, whatever you did, all those engrams put together is called *sanchita*. In Sanskrit, there is one more word *samoochita*. That's one more Sanskrit word that they use for *sanchita*. When I say 'bank', it is not a collection or saving; it is a debt! You will have to finish all the credit out!

The next type of *karma* is *prarabdha karma. Prarabdha* means from this *sanchita* bank of the entire *karmas*, you take a little *karma*, create your body out of it, and decide to enjoy all those *karmas* through that body when you take birth. So *prarabdha* is just a small bit which you brought to enjoy or exhaust through this body.

The third type of *karma* is the worst thing. It is the *agamya karma* - the *karma* that you start collecting because of fresh thoughts, words and deeds after coming down to planet Earth.

Now, anybody who lands on the planet Earth has to exhaust his *prarabdha karma*. For example, let us say, you have 1000 *karmas* in your *sanchita*. I am just giving an example. Let us say, when you take up your body, when you assume your body, you take only ten *karmas*, saying, 'Let me exhaust these ten.' After coming down, you start collecting *karmas* based on the desires of others - borrowed desires and actions that you do because of others' influence over you. You end up collecting say 200 *karmas*.

129

By the time you go back, what will happen? Your bank balance has increased to 1200! You did not exhaust the ten *karmas* with which you came, but you collected 200 more.

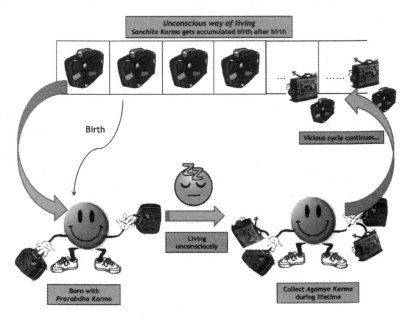

Figure 9: Collecting agamya karma

What will happen the next time you take the body? Your *sanchita* is now 1200 *karmas* - 200 karmas more than the last birth. Again you take ten out of it and come down; you collect some more and go back. This becomes a vicious circle. This is what we call *janma marana chakra* – life and death cycle: continuously taking a body and dying, again and again.

Instead, while you are living, if somebody gives you the knowledge that you are not the body, you are not the mind, it is just these *karmas* that are influencing you, then the influence of these *karmas* over you will start decreasing and you will start exhausting the ten *prarabdha karmas* you came down with.

Understand: for example, you brought ten *karmas* with you when you took this body and came down. Suppose in these ten *prarabdha karmas* you have three *karmas* which will put you in depression, which means three *samskaras* or three engrams whose tendencies will put you into depression. These three depression engrams have got power over you to put you into depression.

If you continue to obey those engrams and fall into depression, these three will not remain just three. They will probably become ten because, out of the depression, you will make decisions and take actions that will increase your karma and trouble . The additional seven *karmas* are the *agamya karmas*. Whenever you cooperate with *prarabdha*, you collect *agamya*.

On the other hand, whenever these three engrams put you in depression, if you have learnt how to come out of the depression, then these three will start losing their power over you! So, of the ten *karmas*, three have gone or been exhausted! Whenever you reduce the influence of *prarabdha* on yourself, the chances of accumulating new *karma, that is the *agamya karma,* will come down. Let us see how.

Whenever the *prarabdha* loses its influence over you, you stop collecting *agamya.* So when the influence of these ten engrams over you stops, the *agamya* collection will also stop.

Bringing yourself back to your inherent state of joy or your pure inner space - the unwavering, undisturbed inner space -

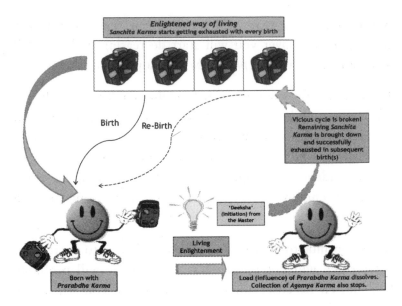

Figure 10: Dissolving prarabdha karma

not only reduces *prarabdha's* influence over you, it also stops the number of engrams getting collected as *agamya*.

Initiation by the Master is the ideas or knowledge given by him, which bring you out of these depressive thoughts, which brings you out of the clutches of your *prarabdha*. The knowledge which brings you out of the depressive thoughts, the influence of the *prarabdha*, is what we call the initiation or 'click'.

PUJA IS A REINFORCEMENT OF CLICKS... BURN YOUR SANCHITA WITH IT...

Puja is nothing but remembering, at least once, all the clicks that have happened to you everyday so that the necessary click will automatically come up whenever you have a problem.

Relation of Rituals with Karma

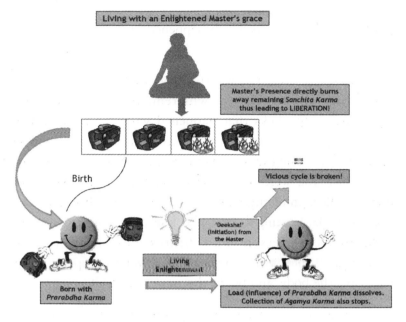

Figure 11: Deeksha by Master burns sanchita karma

See: when a Master teaches, it is not even a teaching, it is a powerful experience. When you don't use those *shaastra-shastras* (knowledge-weapons) repeatedlly, not only do they lose their power, you may not even be able to remember them again. That is the important thing to understand.

See, for example, let us say you have a cot. If you don't use this cot for two years, it is not that the cot will disappear. After two years, you can use it again. But the knowledge given to you, the initiations given to you, if you don't use them for two years, don't think they will be sitting in your bedroom; no! They will simply disappear, that's all.

So how do you remind yourself everyday of all the clicks that have happened in you? Everyday, sitting and reminding yourself of all the clicks which happened in you is what is *puja* or ritual.

Automatically, everyday, whether you want it or not, when you sit for the ritual, you will remember the initiation experiences, the clicks that happened with the Master. The ritual brings you back to pure consciousness everyday. The engrams start losing their power over you. When the engrams with which you were born start losing their power over you, further collection of engrams stops. When the collection stops and when the existing *karmas* also lose their power over you, naturally the person who brings you back to the superconsciousness again and again, the Master, appears when you leave the body, and burns the *sanchita* as well.

Understand: you can't do anything directly with *sanchita*. For *sanchita*, only *Guru kripa* – grace of the Master, will work. Only the Master's grace can do anything with the *sanchita*.

For example, if your child sits and tries very hard to build a small home, what will you do? You will say, 'Alright, don't bother. I myself will build and give you.' When a disciple sincerely works to remove his own *prarabdha* and *agamya*, the Guru's grace simply happens!

You see, the Guru's grace is not just dependent on me. Understand. Anybody who sincerely does *sadhana* (penance) or meditation, in spite of me, the grace has to land on him! It is not even dependent on me. It is an automatic mechanism!

Be very clear: it is just dependent on your receptivity, not on me. I am like an ocean - constantly available to whoever comes with whatever size vessel they carry. If you come with a coconut shell, you will carry back that much of me. If you come with a little bigger vessel, you will carry back the corresponding quantity of me in that. If you came with a still bigger container, you will carry back what that can hold. If you are intelligent... you will build a canal!

Initiation, or *puja* means, reminding yourself everyday of all the initiations, the great experiences that happened with the Master, and bringing yourself back to the same high consciousness repeatedly. When you are ready with the same high spirit, it means that now you are ready for the next 24 hours' drama! For the next 24 hours, you now have energy. That is the reason for doing *puja*.

MEANING OF *MAANASA POOJA MANTRA*

In the *Guru puja* – the offering to the Master, just the *maanasa puja mantra* (verse which pays obeisance to the Master through inner visualization) will remind you of all the clicks.

The first line of the *maanasa puja mantra* says, '*Hridpadmam aasanam dadhyaat*' - my heart is a seat for You. This very line implies that our heart has to be clean! It is an inbuilt reminder, a click!

'*Sahasraar achutaamrutaihi | Paadyam charanayor dadhyaat*' –

sahasraara amruta means when you overflow with gratitude, you will have a deep sweet taste in your tongue, and in your throat. During *Ananda darshan* you can feel this. How many of you have felt? In *Ananda darshans*, you can see suddenly that whole throat becoming so sweet; that is what is *sahasraara amruta* – the nectar that happens out of deep gratitude.

The nectar comes down from the *sahasrara* (your crown center) when you are feeling fulfilled and your whole throat will be filled with it. That very nectar is used as the *paadyam* or water, to wash the feet of the Divine! It means that when you sit at the *puja* everyday, in order to experience the nectar, remember the *Ananda darshan* experience, and you will bring yourself back to that same ecstatic state! If you don't experience that sweet taste in your throat, you can't offer *puja*. Because then you would be telling a lie! Only if you have that real feeling again are you authorized to use those words *sahasraar achutaamrutaihi | Paadyam charanayor dadhyaat* in the *puja*!

Manastu arghyam nivedayet – this means that you are offering your very mind as the food to the Lord. At the end of the NSP (Life Bliss Program Level 2 - Nithyananda Spurana Program), you offer all your *samskaras* or engraved memories into the fire. That is your *manas,* mind. So when you recite this line, you will automatically remember the action, 'Yes! How I offered everything there, now I am offering everything at Your feet.'

Tena amrutena aachamaneeyam – With that same ecstatic nectar, I do the *abhisheka* (holy bath) for You. This line will pull you back to that *Ananda darshan* experience, that joy, that ecstasy in order to experience that nectar again. So in this way, every step of this *mantra* reminds you and brings you back to the clicks, the initiation experiences that happened in you.

It is such a beautiful concept! If you understand this, it is enough. Automatically, all unwanted thoughts, words and deeds will leave you, and the Master's grace will descend upon you in no time. Once that happens, you are liberated.

CHAPTER 5

Mental Body

The mental layer is associated with the powerful emotion of guilt. Thoughts are much more powerful than we think they are. We think our thoughts can, at the most, affect only *us*. For example, we may think that if we have negative thoughts they can put only us into depression. Or when we are happy, we feel a positive outlook in our thinking for some time. But we don't understand an important thing: our thoughts do not affect just us, they affect everybody around us. In fact, our thoughts affect the whole world. We may not be able to believe this logically, but it is our collective thoughts that are responsible for every single incident happening in this universe.

Nothing is an accident. Nothing happens randomly. Because we don't understand the science behind what is happening, we call them incidents or accidents or coincidences.

COLLECTIVE CONSCIOUSNESS

For this, we need to clearly understand these deep yet fundamental Truths about life that will change the very way we look at life.

First thing, all our minds are not individual separate pieces of the universe. They are all one and the same. All our minds are interlinked. Not only interlinked, they directly affect each other. This is what I call 'collective consciousness'.

Your thoughts are as infectious as your cold. People may escape from your cold. It is not so infectious, but your thoughts are so infectious, much more than your cold is. If you catch a cold from someone, you might suffer physically for a few days and then get over it. But when you catch thoughts from people, not only do you suffer mentally, but the suffering is also forever. Similarly, anything that *you* think affects the people staying around you. It affects not only those who are staying closely around you, but everyone living on planet Earth.

Your intellect might resist, saying, 'How can this be true?' But the truth is, all of us are not different beings, or different minds. We are all totally interlinked, closely networked. Any of my thoughts can transform you; any of your thoughts can touch me. We are not separate individuals, we are not an island. There is only one whole thing - collective consciousness.

The second truth is that you are connected not only at the mental level, but even at the deeper conscious levels. The deeper you go, the deeper you are connected. We are all actually connected in the levels of all the seven energy bodies.

Now, in the physical layer, you, God and I can be represented as three different points quite far from each other, say 120 degrees away from one another. In the physical layer, the distance is so much.

If you come down a little to the *pranic* level, the distance is reduced. The three points come a little closer. If you come down deeper to the mental level, the distance between you and I is further reduced and so is the distance between you, God and I. When you travel deeper and deeper, and finally reach the *nirvanic* level, these three entities merge into one!

Please be very clear that at the deep end of all these layers - that is in the *nirvanic* layer - God, you and I are one. There is no distance between us.

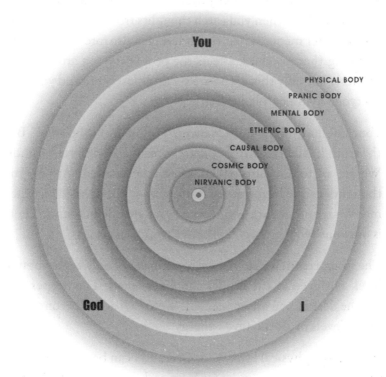

Figure 12: Relation between You, God and I in the Seven Energy Bodies

Let us go a little deeper into this truth. We all seem like different entities at the physical level. But what happens when you love someone intimately? His or her love and suffering affects you. It comes and goes out of your being. This is because, at a deeper level, there is no individual entity and each one of us is a part of the collective consciousness. Of course, you do not want the suffering. However, you cannot escape from the suffering. Have you noticed that whether it is physical pain, or mental suffering, or spiritual bondage, you get it again and again? This is because you are not aware that you are a part of the collective consciousness. Once you become aware and realize that you are a part of the collective consciousness, that you don't have an individual identity, you realize that you do not have a separate ego.

All of us think that we own our intellectual identity. However the simple truth is, in Existence, no such thing as a separate individual identity exists. Once we know this truth, we go beyond pain, suffering, depression and disease. Understand clearly that as long as we have this concept of individual identity, whether physically or mentally or at the being level, we will be continuously suffering. The moment we start thinking that we are an individual body that is separate from Existence, our whole body becomes our enemy.

You are a part, and everything is the Whole. If you fall in tune with the Whole, the Whole behaves as your friend. The moment you start thinking, discriminating or behaving with the Whole in opposition, it starts acting like an enemy. Remember, the Whole is not here to kill you or destroy you.

The Whole, the universe, is a hologram of which we are a part. Just as in a hologram, every single part of the hologram, even if split, reflects the totality of that hologram, we too reflect the totality of the Whole that is the universe.

The other day I read an interesting interview of this man who survived his jump into the Niagara Falls! This being an unusual event and a very daring one, there were many journalists questioning him. If you have been to the Niagara Falls, you would know… the depth of the fact that someone survived jumping down the Niagara Falls. I can't imagine someone surviving the Niagara Falls!

When asked how he managed this unimaginable feat, the man replied beautifully, 'When I jumped, I became a part of the Niagara Falls. I felt like I was a part of it. I never felt that I was different from those falls.'

When we are in tune with the collective consciousness, when we become a part of the collective consciousness, Nature is with us, Nature is our friend, and Nature protects us. Nature will not harm us.

When we start thinking that we are different from nature, that we are an individual consciousness, we will always experience Nature as our enemy. Let us be clear that as long as we are in tune with the collective consciousness, we experience Nature as that which protects us.

Wherever we want to achieve success, either in the social or economic world, when we tune in with the whole group, when we fall in tune with the collective consciousness, we will achieve what we want to achieve.

As long as we feel that we are separate individuals, as long as we want to keep our identity distinct, and wish to have an idea that we are 'somebody', be very clear: we will be resisted and we will be resisting. The moment we start resisting, we make a hell out of it.

Whether at home, office, workplace or industry, this is bound to happen. However, if we disappear into the collective consciousness, we will be protected and taken care of, again and again. We will attain complete success, not only socially and economically, but we will also experience it. It would be a feeling of fulfillment which is inexplicable.

A small story:

A man was suddenly informed that his wife has fallen into the river.

He immediately jumps into the river and starts swimming against the current.

Everybody is surprised and asks him, 'Hey, why are you swimming against the current?'

He replies, 'You guys don't know my wife. Even if she falls into the river, she would only swim against the current!'

As long as we resist the current, whether it is our workplace, our house, our company or any other place for that matter, as long as we do not disappear into the collective consciousness, we will be continuously creating hell for ourselves and for others.

Tao, the ancient Chinese philosophy, contains the same teaching. Tao is all about flow. It is about flowing with Nature. Water is the greatest illustration of such a natural flow. Water simply flows with the landline, around obstacles, smoothly and energetically. Tao talks about the reeds in the water that bend with the flow and straighten up once the flow reduces. This can only happen when we do not imagine ourselves to be different from our environment.

Even in the physical layer, if we think we are something separate, be very clear, we will be inviting diseases. Another point is that in the mental layer, if we think we are separate individuals, we will be sowing seeds of violence again and again in our system.

Seeds of violence are created whenever we feel we are an individual - unconnected and unrelated to others. We turn selfish, dogmatic, and violent. We turn into virtual terrorists. With individual consciousness, we dissect; we cut things into pieces. Understand that such logic always breaks things apart. However, with collective consciousness, we unify everything around us with us.

At the soul level, if we think we are separate individuals, spiritually, we cannot even take the first step. There is no possibility of any spiritual growth.

First of all, remember that at the physical level, we are not independent individuals. Our body and the body of the Sun and the Moon are pre-connected. Any small change in the body of the Sun can make changes in our body. Any small change in our body can change the body of the Moon, and vice versa. Some of us may have noticed that the phases of the Moon affect the state of our mind. We may not be able to logically relate these changes, but they are true.

In the mental layer also, we are not alone. At any given point in time, any thought rising from anyone's head comes and touches us, and any thought created in our mind goes and touches someone else. This is going on continuously. Be clear that any thought sown by someone else can touch us and affect us.

Thoughts are like ripples created on the water surface of a lake. If we are creating a strong wave, we will be creating an impression with our thought. We will be leading and inspiring others with our thoughts. However, if our thoughts are not solid enough, waves created by others will impress us!

Either we live as leaders or as followers. There is no in-between. The mind might think, 'I will not be a leader, as I cannot do that much. I will not be a follower either, so I shall maintain my own stand.' This is simply impractical. There is no such thing as 'my own stand'. Either we lead or we follow.

At the mental level also, if you continuously think that you are a separate individual, you will be resisted again and again. The moment you understand that you are a part of the collective consciousness, you will not be resisted; instead you will be welcomed and accepted.

The third truth:

Finally, at the spiritual level, the moment we understand that we are deeply, totally, and intensely connected to the whole group, to the whole universe, not only do we start experiencing the bliss, but we also start to actually live. This opening up leads to the opening up of the many different dimensions of our being.

We can't even begin to imagine the many different dimensions and possibilities that will open up to us when we disappear into this collective consciousness. As of now, with one body, it is such a feeling of joy sometimes, is it not? Then imagine what will happen when you have so many bodies!

Imagine that one body is an air conditioner and the other one is a heater; imagine three different bodies in different countries enjoying different cultures. Similarly if the multitudes of bodies increase, so will the joy, the bliss. Whatever we experience as individuals, we will be able to experience far more when we are a part of the collective consciousness.

NSP – A Gateway to Collective Consciousness

During the entire Nithyananda Spurana Program (NSP), you will realize that you are a part of the collective consciousness. It will not stop there… You will realize that not only are you a part of, but you *are* the collective consciousness.

Remember that you are not just an individual consciousness as you think. As you start traveling deeper and deeper, layer by layer, the realization will dawn that you are just one with everything. As a result, you start feeling a sense of well being in the mental layer, the *pranic* layer, the etheric layer, the physical layer, and all the other layers, and automatically all diseases disappear!

When you really experience that you are the boundary-less consciousness, it is an unbelievable experience that is difficult to describe.

I have seen people at the end of the program in such ecstasy, that they forget their name, their identity, their social status, their education, their qualifications, their wealth, their religion… everything that they are and that they have! They respect every other individual in the hall with such flowing love and gratitude. All of them fall at each other's feet!

I have seen the father-in-law falling at the feet of his daughter-in-law. In India, this never happens. It is too much to ask, as per the traditions followed in India! However, this has happened at the end of the program only because he is able to see the divinity in her at that moment. The mother-in-law sees the divinity in her son-in-law and falls at his feet. Grand parents touch the feet of grand children. Bosses or owners touch the feet of the people working under them.

This experience of oneness or collective consciousness makes us forget all differences in name, wealth, social status, and prestige. Whatever we think as ourselves, all of it just disappears, and what we truly *are* is revealed. I have seen that by touching the feet of their worst enemies, people simply forgive and forget the past. They experience such a deep level of consciousness, such bliss, that literally the ego disappears!

They just go around and see God in everyone, and they are in bliss, ecstasy, collective consciousness. Mind you, it is not that they are visualizing or hallucinating. When the experience happens, the whole group realizes that they are all one and the same; that they are not different entities.

A small story:

There was a farmer who grew superior quality and award-winning corn. Year after year, his corn won honor and prizes in the state fair.

One year a newspaper reporter interviewed him. The reporter wanted to find out something interesting about how the farmer grew the best corn. During the interview, the reporter discovered that the farmer shared his seed corn with his neighbors.

'How can you afford to share your best seed corn with your neighbors when they too are entering their corn in competition with yours each year?' the reporter asked.

'Why sir,' said the farmer, 'didn't you know? The wind picks up pollen from the ripening corn and swirls it from field to field. If my neighbors grow inferior, sub-standard and poor quality corn, cross-pollination will steadily degrade the quality of my corn. If I am to grow good corn, I must help my neighbors grow good corn too!'

The farmer gave a superb insight into the connectedness of life. His corn couldn't be better or improve unless his neighbor's corn also improved.

The farmer had learnt the secret to harmonious life.

If we choose to be at harmony, we must help our neighbors and colleagues to be at peace.

If we choose to live well, then we must help others live well too.

If we choose to be happy, we must help others find happiness.

We must work with others because we are all connected with each other, no matter how remote it may seem. The value of a life is measured by the lives it touches.

Only when we experience the collective consciousness can we realize and experience the meaning of the word bliss, eternal bliss, *nithya ananda*.

Mental Body

GURUKUL EDUCATION – FOUNDATION FOR NURTURING COLLECTIVE CONSCIOUSNESS

Figure 13: Nithyananda Gurukul

The problem is that from childhood, we are trained to be separate from others. In schools, we are taught to be 'somebody different', prove that we are 'somebody'. As adults, we are taught to compete with others.

We have to understand one thing: those who have created the present system of education, are not enlightened. The system of education designed and developed by the ancient sages in the East - the *Gurukul* structure is almost completely out of practice. It is almost dead today. It is an ancient Indian residential education system whereby the students study with and imbibe the energy and teachings of enlightened Masters.

149

Let me highlight a few points about the *Gurukul* education system that was initiated by enlightened Masters. In this system, any child who belongs to the country belongs to the Master. The Master takes care of all of them and parents have to hand them over to the Master and move out of the way.

Up to the age of seven, children in the *Gurukul* were not given the idea of wearing clothes. You might laugh at this, but it is a fact. This was done so that they do not get the idea that they are individual bodies. They were allowed to simply go around and relate with Existence, with the ether straightaway. They were allowed to relate with flowers, forests, trees, and the earth. This ensured that until the child's seventh year, the idea that they are an individual did not form in the mind.

This also taught them not to suppress the opposite gender that is alive in them. They were not given the idea that they are male or female. Understand that when we are born, all of us have the characteristics of both the genders within us. A man is only 51% male and 49% female. Similarly a woman is only 51% female and 49% male. It is our upbringing, dictated by societal rules that classify us into rigid gender differentiation right from birth. Therefore we end up suppressing the opposite gender within us.

In the *Gurukul* system, children were encouraged to keep their gender open. They were also not taught to separate their body from the environment.

Try to follow only these few things with your kids. First, do not separate their upper and lower body with clothes that grip at the waistline. Make them wear single piece clothes that cover the whole body as one. Next, do not encourage anything that will develop the idea in them that they are 'somebody'. We commonly believe that this is what builds their identity and self esteem, but this is where we are making serious mistakes.

In the ancient *Gurukul* system, at the age of seven, both boys and girls were given a meditation technique. Even if they formed such an idea that they are male or female, they used this meditation technique to dilute that imbibed feeling. This meditation technique helped them to flush out the feeling of gender uniqueness again and again, and helped them tune into the collective consciousness. This is what we now call the *Gayatri Mantra* (a sacred chant taught before adolescence). From seven to fourteen, they practiced the *Gayatri* through which they continuously connected to the collective consciousness.

By the age of fourteen, by the time they reached adolescence, they would have had a glimpse of the collective consciousness and its blue print. After they have had the glimpse of the blue print, depending on the intensity of that glimpse, they would be given deeper meditation techniques, so that they could go deeper and deeper into themselves. Thus by the age of 21, they had every opportunity to become enlightened.

I will tell you honestly that there was a time when 70% of all the people were enlightened. The remaining 30% were working towards it. The social structure created by the enlightened Masters consisted of people either already enlightened or those who were working towards it. There was no other category. Just two categories: achieved and working towards it: enlightened and seekers! Unfortunately, we have lost that system.

We have a *Gurukul* system in the Bidadi ashram in India. You should see the children... how joyful and alive they are! They wake up at 4:30 am every morning and start their day. They grow up doing various things from worship to studies to travel studies to what not. They are such lucky children, because their hero, their idol is an enlightened being! They unconsciously imbibe the enlightened body language.

Collective consciousness is what we call God. The Whole is what we call God. When you are Whole, you are holy!

You must have heard about the *raas purnima* described in the *Bhagavatam* - the full moon night when the *raas leela* was performed. It refers to the collective experience that Krishna gave his *gopikas* (his women cowherds). It is a beautiful example of collective consciousness. Most of us have no idea or a wrong idea about the *raas leela*. It has got nothing to do with the physical plane. It was actually a grand experiencing of collective consciousness. Krishna gave the ultimate experience of collective consciousness to the entire group.

OUR THOUGHTS CAN AFFECT A GLASS OF WATER

Our thoughts and energy flow have the capacity to create and attract incidents and people of the same nature. There is a beautiful research you should know about.

One Japanese doctor Masaru Emoto has done a beautiful research on water and published a book called, 'Hidden Messages from Water'. It is a beautiful book. He is a great scientist. He is not only a scientist, but a person who works on different possibilities untiringly, working on the power of the mind over matter.

He took many cups and filled them with water. All the cups were filled with water of the same chemical composition. Chemically, the water in all the cups was the same. He kept the cups in several rooms. All the environmental conditions like the room temperature, humidity etc. were the same. Everything was controlled perfectly.

Everyday he would enter each of the rooms and relate with the cups of water. In one room, he would create some positive thoughts like peace, bliss and joy for five minutes and come out. He would then go to the next room and create some violent thoughts like war, terrorism, violence and anger and come out. He would go to the third room and chant some words from the *Dhammapada*, Buddha's teachings. Finally he froze the water from each of the cups and took pictures through a microscope.

His results are published in his book 'Hidden Messages from Water'. The results are simply shocking. The water on which he used positive words was shining like a diamond. The water on which he used negative words looked like a ghost - dark, distorted and dense. The water on which he used Buddha's teachings looked divine and beautiful. Not once or twice, but he did this experiment several hundred times and found the same results. If you find time, go through that book, 'Messages from Water'.

Understand: if your thoughts can affect the water in the outer world - water in a small cup, can't it affect the blood which is flowing in your body? The first thing is to understand that your thoughts can affect the outer world. The second thing is that if you can affect the water in the outer world, why not the water flowing in your body? 80% of your body is filled with water — blood!

NATURAL CALAMITIES ARE A RESULT OF OUR COLLECTIVE NEGATIVITY

If five minutes of one person's negative thoughts can affect one tumbler of water, what happens when so many of us, harbouring so much irritation and negative thoughts, express our thoughts into nature? Won't nature be disturbed? Natural calamities are only because of our collective negativity. When we release so much negativity where do you think all this will be deposited? How else will it be expressed but only in the form of natural calamities.

Today science proves that one glass of water can become negative energy just by one man's five minutes of negative thoughts. Then imagine billions of people constantly radiating negativity, negative thoughts, negative words, and negative energy. Why will the ocean not be affected? Why will tsunamis not happen? Naturally, we are abusing nature by our negativity. We are imbalancing nature by our own negativity, and blaming nature for it.

GUILT – THE GREATEST SIN

A small story:

A great *rishi* (sage) was doing penance in a deep forest. Suddenly one night, he had an unexpected guest. There was a knock on his door. There was a man standing at the doorway. He requested the *rishi*, 'Can I stay here tonight? Tomorrow morning I will leave this place.' The *rishi* said, 'You are welcome. Please come and stay.'

The next morning, the *rishi* casually inquired, 'Who are you? Where are you from?' The man said, 'Please don't be frightened. I am a thief. Last night, I robbed the palace and escaped. I came to your hut straight away. I am very happy that you took care of me by giving food and shelter. I am leaving. Please bless me.' So saying, the man left.

The *rishi* felt very disturbed, 'What a big sin I have committed by giving shelter and food to a thief!' He started weeping, not knowing how to atone for the sin. He wanted to wash away his sin. He started praying, 'Oh God, please forgive me. I don't know what I should do to remove the sin. I gave shelter and food to a thief for one full night. Please forgive me.' He was weeping and wailing.

Suddenly he heard a voice from heaven. The voice was also weeping. He was surprised! He asked, 'Who is it weeping?' From above he heard a voice, 'I am God. I am weeping.' Surprised, the *rishi* asked, 'Why are you weeping?' God replied, 'You gave shelter to the thief for one day. You think that it is a big sin. I am giving him food and shelter everyday. Where will I go and wash my sins? That is why I am weeping.'

There is a beautiful thing to be understood from the story. The *rishi* had a strong idea that he is holier than the thief. He had more ego than compassion in him. His ego was shaken by God's message.

All our guilt, all our rules, all our morality and all our ideas of right and wrong are created only by these type of *rishis* and priests. Not all *rishis*, but these type who think they are holier than others, that they are purer than others, or that they are greater than others. They created the rules that created guilt in you.

According to me, guilt is the greatest sin. At least other sins will punish you after your death. Guilt will punish you when you are alive.

The guilt that retards your growth and puts you into a vicious cycle of misery and suffering is what society feeds on, what religion thrives on. It condemns all the basic emotions that humans have, instead of giving the techniques to transform the base emotions into higher ones.

Actually, if you go to see, all so-called activities of social service are to get rid of the guilt feeling that we might be having 'too much' money. But we don't realize that it is not money that is the problem, but the mind that is the problem. If the mind is not a problem, it will not matter how much money we have.

GO BEYOND RIGHT AND WRONG...

Let us look a little deep into guilt. What is the root cause of guilt? It is our idea about right and wrong, our understanding about what is right and wrong. Only from that, the guilt starts. What is right? What is wrong? Let us start analyzing.

After all, what is the scale to measure right or wrong? In Hinduism, vegetarianism is considered right. In Christianity, non-vegetarianism is thought to be right. In Hinduism, you can marry only once. In Islam you can marry several times. In Hinduism, you can't drink alcohol and liquor. In Christianity, Jesus himself consumed wine.

There are so many rules and so many regulations in different places, different situations, and different societies. In South India, fish is considered non-vegetarian food. In Bengal they call it *Gangaphal* - fruit from the sacred river Ganga!. Bengali *Brahmins*, a priestly class of people eat fish. Every Bengali house has a small fish pond in front of their house. They grow fish. They eat fresh fish. Ramakrishna Paramahamsa used to eat fish. For Bengalis, fish, sweet, and tobacco are the basic things in their life. Ramakrishna used to smoke. Vivekananda used to smoke. Of course, they smoked not as an addiction but for various practical reasons. Where is the scale for so all the so-called morality? It is just local customs! In the course of time, they become the morality.

If you read the ancient scriptures, the epics of India like the *Mahabharata*, Draupadi was married to five men! So many kinds of life systems, so many different customs are there. Mother Kunti had five sons from five different men! Draupadi lived with five men!

At different times, different rules were formed by different leaders. In a particular society, certain things that were considered morality were considered to be immoral in another society! Here in America, there are similar moral standards that I saw. In one state, casinos are allowed, whereas in the neighbouring state, casinos are illegal. A river separates the two states, and the border line between the two states passes through the river. So, inside the river itself, there is a big casino! On one side it is legal, and on the other side it is illegal! So, where is the scale of right or wrong? For one person, a particular food is *amruta* (nectar), whereas for another person, the same food is poison!

Where is the scale to measure what is right and what is wrong? There is no scale. Please understand that morality should happen out of integrity, not out of guilt. Guilt is a wedge inserted into your inner space. It makes you schizophrenic. It makes you take on double standards.

What do I mean by integrity? Being in the present moment and being only ONE and not many; seeing *reality* without the play of the mind. Once the mind steps in, duality also steps in. Just by being intensely aware of the present moment, you can achieve integrity where there is only ONE and not two or three or many, fighting in you. When you are aware, you will be ONE and moral. When you decide to stray from awareness, you will be many and immoral. Morality has to do with awareness, not with any other social rules. Awareness causes you to spontaneously take the right action in the right situation. Morality can very well cause you to do the wrong thing in the right situation because it doesn't have the right base. If you integrate yourself, you will be centered upon awareness. If you remain fragmented, you will depend on morality for guidance.

People who create rules and regulations in order to create guilt in you, are the ones who hide their personal lives under covers because their personal lives would be totally nonconforming to the rules set up by them. But they set up the rules so that they can rule you and exploit you. Once you have the idea of guilt sown in you, you can be cheated and exploited easily by society. That is why guilt is the first thing that society sows in you. With guilt, it is easier to control.

SANATANA DHARMA —THE ULTIMATE RULE BOOK

In *Santana Dharma* (another name for Hinduism), we have two main scriptures – the *shruti* and the *smriti*. *Sanatana Dharma* is the only courageous religion to have two kinds of scriptures. In all other religions on the planet Earth, they have only one scripture, only one book which is considered to be the ultimate! Almost all religions don't allow any scope for their holy book to be updated. But *Sanatana Dharma* is one of the courageous religions which says its book can be updated.

SHRUTI AND SMRITI

The main scriptures are divided into two portions: *shruti* (*Vedas*) and *smriti* (traditional sacred books). *Shruti* means the ultimate laws about enlightenment - the concept or realization about the universe. *Smriti* means the social laws, day-to-day rules and regulations which, when followed, will take one along the path to realize the goal of *shruti*. The courageous people declared that *smriti* can be changed. From time to time, enlightened Masters can create new *smriti*, because we know that no morality can be morality forever. No law can be law forever because morality and laws are based on the situation, on the type of people and culture at that time.

For example, if the deer population increases too much, you are allowed to hunt deer. In the same way, once upon a time in India, there were too many cows. That is why they started offering cows in the ritualistic sacrifices. Once the cow population became too low, they started to worship the cows.

The rules are created to maintain equilibrium in society and nature, to maintain harmony in the society. When we all live together we need some basic understanding and rules to happily co-exist. For example, you will not try to kill me so that I will not kill you. That is all. Then, both of us can live happily without fear. Like this, a few basic things are assumed and come into being. Slowly, by and by, they become rules. They become morality.

The problem is that as long as you understand the root of the moral rules, you will neither behave immorally nor will you get disturbed by them. When you don't understand the rules, once the rules are just spoon fed, when they become a set of forced rules, then not only will you try to escape from the rules, but you will also create a deep guilt in you with regard to them.

THE NATURAL INSTINCT TO BREAK RULES

When anything is a forced rule, you always try to get around it. For example, you always speed when you don't see the cop! Take children as an example. When you tell them not to do something, they will be most tempted to do it. As long as you don't mention anything about doing it or not doing it, they may not even be bothered about it. But the moment you tell them not to do it, they will be looking to do it.

Actually, there is a taste, a thrill in doing what you are not supposed to do.

A small story:

Once, a man became addicted to smoking. He came to me asking for help, 'Please help me to quit smoking. I don't know how I became addicted. Please help me.'

I asked him, 'How did you start?'

He replied, 'I never wanted to smoke. In fact, I hated the smell! One day my friend and I were talking in a street corner. My friend was smoking. My father saw from a distance and thought that I was also smoking.

When I went home he started yelling at me. I tried my best to explain to him that I was not smoking. But he was not ready to listen to me. Then I thought, anyhow, he is already thinking that I smoke. He is not willing to believe me. Then, why not smoke? That is why I started smoking.'

Most of the time, you develop an instant taste for something if you are asked not to do it. You feel a kind of a joy or satisfaction by doing it. That is the basic tendency in every human being. When you say 'no' to your parents, you think that you prove you are independent. As long as you say 'yes', you are only a child. When you start saying no, you feel you have matured.

You can see this in teenagers also. The moment they say no, they think they are grown up and mature. Only because of the joy in saying no to moral rules, there are so many rebellious groups, so many gangs. The habit of sowing guilt in people has backfired in this fashion. The general feeling is that when you say no, you prove that you are somebody special, you are somebody different.

DEAD RULES VS LIVE INTELLIGENCE

First, you try your best to escape from it. Next, you create a deep guilt inside your being for escaping from it.

The Door To Enlightenment

A small story about how we get caught up in superstitions:

An economic forecaster was known to have a horseshoe prominently displayed above the door frame of his office.

One of his colleagues saw it one day and asked him why it was there.

The forecaster replied, ' It is a good luck charm that helps in my forecasts.'

The colleague was surprised and asked, 'But do you really believe in this superstition?'

The forecaster replied, 'Of course not!'

The colleague was confused. He then asked, 'Then why do you keep it?'

'Well,' said the forecaster, 'it works whether you believe in it or not!'

Just see how strongly influential superstitions can get! It virtually destroys the intelligence in us. This is how we start making up rituals and following them with no clues about the truth behind them. We give in to a set of blind rules in our lives and fight with them as well.

Another small story:

One great *pundit* (learned man) wanted to take a bath in the sacred river Ganga. He had a *kamandalu* (small water pot) with him. He wanted to keep it in a safe place where no one would pick it up. He looked around but found nobody trustworthy to have hold the *kamandalu* while he went to take a bath. So he then made a small pit in the banks of the Ganga, put his *kamandalu* in the pit and covered it with sand. To mark the spot, he put a heap of sand on top of the pit. He then went to take his bath.

There was a farmer who watched the *pundit* from some distance. He thought to himself, 'Oh, before taking bath in the Ganga, one should make a small sand heap!' He proceeded straight to the banks of the river, made a sand heap next to the pundit's and went in for a bath.

Another man who was going to have a bath saw the farmer doing this and thought, 'Oh, it seems like a tradition to make a sand heap before taking a bath in the river Ganga.' So, he too made a small sand heap and went for his bath.

By and by, all the people started making heaps before taking bath in the Ganga.

The *pundit* finished his bath and came out of the river. When he came out, he saw hundreds of sand heaps all over the Ganga banks! He was shocked! Not only that. Now he had a big problem: where is *his kamandalu*? Which heap was it under? He started searching. He started to destroy the sand heaps to look under them.

Suddenly the farmer came by and shouted, 'Why are you destroying our *Shiva lingas* (symbol of Lord Shiva)? Why are you destroying them? You are a *pundit*. You should have some sense! Don't you know that you are supposed to make a *Shiva linga* before taking your bath? And not only that. You are disturbing our *Shiva lingas*! Don't you have sense?'

The *pundit* was shocked at the farmer's words and knew instantly what had happened. A heap of sand naturally looks like a *Shiva linga*! The *pundit* thought, 'What I did to save my *kamandalu* has become a Shiva ritual now! I seem to have started a ritual!

Of course, the *pundit* had to leave without his *kamandalu*.

If you look into your life, there are so many sand heaps that have entered in the same way! There are so many speed breakers and so many obstacles that have entered your life without your understanding. In the course of time, many regulations that had meaning earlier, became rules without any meaning now!

In India, during the times before electricity, clothes would not be sewn after sunset since sewing was done by hand with a needle and the tailors had only dim lanterns with which to do their work. Naturally, in the nighttime, in the dim light of the candle or lantern, it would be a strain to sew. Therefore, the work was always confined to daylight hours. But even now in India, the eldery people in the house will say, 'It is not a good thing to sew after dusk!' The very reason for not sewing at night doesn't even exist anymore. Electricity and bright lights are there! But it has become a ritual for them without any connection to its original purpose!

When you do not have or are not given the right understanding, things become dead rules in your life. When you have understanding, any rule can become a technique to live life happily. Rules and rituals are actually techniques for your own enlightenment. When I say enlightenment, I mean a blissful life full of clarity. Of course, when pursued deeply, it will lead to your ultimate enlightenment. When you are given the right understanding, you will understand that any rule was created just for you and others around you to live a happy and blissful life.

When the spirit of the rules are understood, there won't be any problem falling in line with it. And the juice will be there in your action or commitment to it. But if the spirit is missed, everything is missed. It becomes like setting out with the wrong foot. Take meditation, for example. Meditation itself is done to go inwards irrespective of the outer world scenes. I have seen some people, before starting their meditation routine, they will create so much noise in the house. They will go around telling everyone to keep quiet. They will practically take the whole house to task just for going about its normal routine when they are going to meditate! If they understood the spirit behind meditation, they would not be doing this. Only when the spirit is missed, things become dead rituals. They miss and mess!

ANY RULE INTERNALIZED WILL CREATE GUILT IN YOU

Generally, when you don't understand the root of morality, you start living in a dull and dead way, with guilt. According to me, any rule when internalized, will create guilt in you. That is because by your very nature you are a person who aspires for freedom. It is called *svabhava swatantrata* - free by the very nature. This means your nature itself is freedom. You arc a *nithya mukta* - eternally free person. You are by nature eternally free. You never want to be caged! You never want to be a slave of any rule!

Your entire struggle is nothing but the struggle for freedom. Even your search for money is the search for freedom. If you have more money, you have more choices or more freedom to choose a bigger house, a bigger car, more comforts etc. Your search for more choice is your search for freedom - the real search! Your search for money is nothing but the search for freedom.

RULES EXPLOIT YOUR FEAR AND GREED AND LEAD TO GUILT

So, by your very nature you are searching for freedom. When some morality is taught to you as a rule, either you try to get around it or if you can't, you take revenge on the people who imposed the rule on you. Imposed morality always causes you to be or feel revengeful. You may not be obviously revengeful, but it will be there in you as a subtle thread.

For example, people repeatedly tell me, 'My son is not taking care of me.' Be very clear that your son may be your foremost enemy because you have given him so many rules, so many regulations throughout his life. You must have given him so many laws. You would have been almost a master for him when he was young! Naturally, while one part of his mind will have respect for you, the other part will always harbour a revenge towards you. Don't think this is something new that I am telling you or this has to do with your son alone. No! This is a basic fact in society. It is not spoken about because it is too much truth for people to bear! Which son or which father will agree if I told them this fact? See, this fact is such a deep rooted one that most people are blissfully oblivious of it. But it is my duty to draw your attention to such base level things.

There are a few people who try to give you rules in a very subtle way or cunning way. They exploit your fear and greed by showing you ideas of hell and heaven and create the desire for heaven and fear of hell. They create so many concepts of hell and heaven and sell them to you. They say, 'If you practice these types of things, you will be rewarded with heaven; if you practice those things, you will be punished with hell.' This concept of heaven and hell is a subtle way of exploiting your being. When you are given rules based on greed and fear, you start creating a deep guilt in you.

There is a subtle relationship between fear and guilt. It is like this: when you accept fear, you go beyond it. But when you suppress the fear, when you reject it, it transforms into guilt. Anything suppressed, anything that is dealt with against nature, leads directly to guilt. The feeling of not being true to oneself is the root cause of guilt.

Many times you justify your guilt by labeling it as responsibility. No! How does one differentiate between guilt and responsibility? If you get into a low feeling when you think about it, it is guilt. If you feel intensity and integrity, it is responsibility! So you cannot confuse the two and try to escape. This is the clear scale. If you are pulled to low energy at the thought of what you did, then it is guilt. But if you feel good about it, then it is responsibility.

A guilty person can never be at ease with himself. He will always lack self-confidence. He starts looking for a leader for guidance. This is where religion steps in and exploits people. It exploits the deep guilt through a set of moral codes, through a set of do's and don'ts. The same religion can work in a positive way to get you out of guilt. How can it work? It can work through the power of prayer. You can exercise the power of prayer to intensify and integrate yourself. Prayer has immense power, especially when you are looking to integrate yourself. Instead of following religion as a set of rules, you could take it up as a technique to integrate yourself. As a sheer outcome of the power of prayer, the guilt in you will dissolve.

If you live from moment to moment, there is no question of repenting for what you have done; guilt will have no place. Guilt is not real. It does not have existential reality. You can choose to drop your guilt at any time because it is not natural. We carry the load of guilt most of the time because of our convoluted thinking.

NOBODY CAN LIVE LIFE BASED ON ANY LAW

An important thing... This is one of the ultimate laws that is very difficult to understand, but one of the ultimate laws. Nobody can live their life based upon any law. When I say nobody, I mean NOBODY. When I say any law, I mean ANY LAW. Life is much superior to laws. Any law, rule or regulation is based on a certain understanding of life. But life is beyond all our understanding and logic! That is why.

People ask me, 'Why is this life created at all?' I tell them, this WHY can never be answered because this WHY is based on your logic. But life is based on God's logic. Your logic and God's logic can never meet with each other. His logic is so big, so vast, and so infinite. You can never meet His logic.

Life is created by Him. Rules are created by you. Life is created by Him. Laws are created by you. Naturally, your laws can never match or fit with God's logic or God-created life.

Life is natural. Laws are societal. Life is physical. Laws are mental.

All your ideas, all of your do's and don'ts, all your morality, all your 'right or wrong' is given to you by society. You are called a saint or a sinner only by society. As long as society labels you a saint, you are a saint. The moment society labels you a sinner, you are a sinner.

If you kill someone in the society, you will be called murderer; you will be punished. But if you kill someone on the battlefield you will be called a hero. You will be given a big award!

When you start internalizing the laws of society, you create a deep wound in your being. You destroy your innate intelligence. According to me, children can be given a set of rules initially so that they don't move from the path of consciousness. But soon, they too have to be given the understanding of life and the need to operate from consciousness instead of conscience. If you live with consciousness, you will automatically live a moral life. To start understanding the need to live with consciousness, just look into your morality. You will realize that it is only skin deep. Society's morality is only skin deep, whereas consciousness comes from the very being.

Your consciousness is always trying to break through your conscience. Your consciousness continuously fights with conscience. Conscience is societal. Consciousness is natural. Conscience is a poor substitute for consciousness.

People ask me, 'What is this Swamiji? You are pulling down the whole social structure. Then how can we all live morally?' I tell them, 'Be very clear. It is only for kids that you need a forced morality. For them you need to say, 'Keep quiet, I will give you candy.' Of course, nowadays kids reply, 'I am happy. I don't need your candy. Who cares for your candy!' For a child you can say that you will give candy or you will restrict him. You can impose morality based on fear or greed. But for yourself, it is time to grow up. You are not kids anymore. Just stand up with consciousness.

GUILT IS THE ROOT OF THE 'FEAR OF DEATH'

A beautiful story:

Once there was a Zen Master. For some reason, the king declared that the next morning, the Master must be killed. The Zen Master was informed of this. The king had also said that until the next morning, the Master could do whatever he wanted to do. He could live as he liked. He was given full freedom.

Even after the death sentence, the Master was seen following his usual routine. He did his usual gardening, fetched water from the well, cooked, served the disciples and so on. He lived in exactly the same way as before, doing the same routine.

Some of his disciples were surprised and asked him, 'Master, tomorrow morning you are going to die. Don't you want to do something else, something special?'

The Master replied beautifully, 'My life flows from my understanding. This is the best way I can ever live. I am totally fulfilled. I have nothing else to do whether I am going to live for 24 hours or two hours. This is exactly what I want to do and what keeps me happy. I have nothing else as better enjoyment.'

For us it is different. If someone gives us this same deadline, that we will be alive only until the next morning, and that we could do whatever we wanted to do, just imagine what we will do! Be very clear: if you would do anything other than your daily routine, it means that you have lived your entire life based on morality that was just skin deep. This is the best scale to judge. What does it mean? It means that you are just controlling yourself, fighting with the morality imposed upon you every moment. You are not living your life with blissful consciousness.

As long as you don't live your life in its entirety, you will always feel that you are missing something. The feeling that you are missing something is the root cause for the fear of death also. Mostly, our fear of death is not the fear of dying itself. It is the fear of not having lived our life fully. Guilt is the root of the fear of death. When we harbour guilt, we don't live life fully. When we don't live life fully, we fear death.

GUILT IS THE ROOT OF GREED

Guilt is the reason for greed also. It works like this: when you are habituated to feel guilty for most of your expressions or actions, you stay away from freely expressing yourself and doing things. Although this may save you from falling into guilt, you unconsciously develop a greed for real life. Over many years, the suppression causes greed to build up in you.

If you have the intensity to break free from your guilt and express yourself, then you are liberated. But most often you won't even have the clarity that it is the guilt that is causing the struggle within you. You will simply fall into depression because you can't pursue the goals of your greed.

When greed arises in small doses and you are taught to deal with it with awareness, fulfilling the greed consciously can be a joyful experience. But what happens? When greed arises, society starts labeling it and condemning it. You start feeling guilty about all your desires. You start suppressing. Then the problem starts. The suppressed greed either becomes depression or any other aggressive expression.

The Stone of Guilt in the River of Your Mind - The Block in the Flow of Intelligence

You are designed to move like a freely flowing river. Guilt is like the rocks in the path of the water. They have been placed in you by society. A flowing river looks so happy, is it not? Society has branded happiness itself as a sin. That is the problem. That is why you will notice, when everything is going smoothly and happily, there will be a lurking feeling of guilt in you. We are taught by society that being happy and enjoying life is not our natural state. So we feel guilty. But when we feel sad and depressed, do we ever feel guilty? No! This is because you are taught very strongly that life is meant to be suffered and endured, with happiness only being allowed once in a while. This is also why people can't stand it when you are happy and smiling all the time. They try their best to bring you back to 'so-called' reality by instilling guilt in you.

When you are enjoying, dancing or relaxing at the beach for example, suddenly what happens? Guilt will start rising in you about all the work that you have kept pending, about the responsibilities you have put aside. This is wrong. Work while you work and play while you play, that's all!

Even when you are around me, if I give you a little too much attention, you start feeling guilty, is it not? There is no need to feel this way. Guilt has no basis and it simply destroys your whole life. If you can live without guilt, you will enjoy every moment and you will have no regrets in life.

The problem is that our being is a crowd of voices that don't belong to us. Understand, your being is no longer only *your* being. It is a totality of your mother's voice, your father's voice, your teacher's voice, your neighbor's voice and what not! All these voices are in there. If there is only one voice, you will never have any problem. Your mind will move like a river. But there are so many voices telling you so many things and pulling you back into guilt.

As long as you flow like a river, you will express extraordinary intelligence in your life. You will live with an energy that is overflowing every minute. The moment you allow guilt in you, the moment you are stopped in your free flow, you create energy clots inside your being. Especially, the older the culture, more guilt is there. We always feel proud of our ancient culture. If we are able to keep the idea behind the culture alive, it is alright. But most often, the older the roots of your culture, the more trouble for you because the more misconstrued and misinterpreted they will be.

Anger – A Way to Come Out of Guilt

You might have noticed that when you were harbouring guilt, if you got angry, the guilt reduced. The moment you express your anger, your guilt is released. This happens because anger and guilt are two sides of the same coin. The moment you become angry with the person who created the guilt in you, you come out of the guilt. If you created guilt based on somebody's opinion of something, the guilt is basically because of the respect that you have for that person. If you did not have respect for that person, it would not cause such a deep guilt in you. But the moment you become angry, naturally the respect is lost. So when the respect is lost, the guilt also disappears. You understand that you have been exploited and hence disturbed.

I am reminded of another incident that I share often at my discourses. One American woman brought her son to me with a complaint. She said, 'My son is not obeying my words, Swamiji. Please advise him.' I felt a little awkward. I myself never obeyed my mother when I was a boy! How can I advise him to obey? The boy looked very intelligent. But I had to do the job.

So I started talking to him, 'Why don't you obey your mom? She even made me obey her just now.' The boy asked, 'She herself is not happy. If I follow her words, where will I end up? I will also end up in the same way as her. Why are you asking me to obey her? Why are you asking me to listen to her?'

I was shocked. He made good sense. Somehow I managed to convince him. I think the next generation kids might even sue their mother or father if they fall into depression. They will say, 'These people didn't give me the correct mental setup. That is why now I am very depressed.' So watch out. If you try to sow the wrong seeds in your child, you might be in trouble later in your life.

We have to find out some method by which we do not create guilt in the kids' minds. According to me, intelligence is more solid than morality. Consciousness is more solid than conscience.

Of course you need a little patience to create consciousness in the child. You need to work with them, explaining every step to them. You can't give consciousness in teaspoons. You can give conscience in teaspoons - just do's and don'ts. But consciousness, you can't give in teaspoons. You need to work with them. Unless you have that much patience, think twice before bringing children to planet Earth. Some people tell me, 'But Swamiji, children are not in our hands. God gives us.' Just imagine! Only when you shed responsibility, you will talk these nonsensical things.

Some people tell me, 'It is very difficult Swamiji. If you have one kid, it is ok. You tell us all these things, but it is very difficult to manage them, very difficult to patiently give them intelligence. Naturally, we have to create guilt and give them rules.' Well, as I said, if you can't take responsibility to have patience and groom them, think twice before you decide to give birth, that's all.

Ask yourself, 'Have I solved my life's problems? Did I find solutions to all my problems?' If yes, then go ahead; bring the next generation to planet Earth. Otherwise, wait. There is every chance that the next generation will catch you and ask, 'What are you doing? Why did you bring me here?' Already, kids have come to the level of remarking, 'She herself is not happy. Why should I follow her?' So think before you decide.

PSYCHOLOGICAL ILLNESS DUE TO GUILT

Guilt is the sure killer of intelligence. According to me, guilt is the worst killer of intelligence. It will never let you move in your life.

Once one of our devotees had a tumor at the end of her spinal cord, near the root *chakra*. For twenty years she suffered. She came to me complaining, 'Please help me, heal me. I am suffering with this tumor for so many years. After undergoing surgery, it has reappeared.'

I started talking to her slowly to trace the origin of the problem. I asked her a few questions at the end of which she finally opened up and started weeping. I asked her, 'Do you have any guilt related to your sex energy?' She slowly opened up and started weeping. She said she was physically abused when she was very young. One of her close relatives abused her for many years. That guilt stayed with her. She said, 'I started hating that part of my body. I started feeling, 'that part of the body should not exist in me.' I felt, that part of my body was not my being. My hatred towards that person turned towards my own body.'

Her hatred was so deep. I continued speaking to her. Slowly, she opened up more and more to me. When she brought the guilt out, I started talking to her. She came out of the guilt. She was psychologically healed. I explained to her how this is a usual thing that happens.

Now researchers say one in four are getting sexually abused, especially in America. I read a report just the other day - one in four! Of course, kids don't open up. Kids don't tell you these things. Anyhow, she was psychologically healed when I explained to her what was happening. You will be surprised, in just ten days, the tumor simply disappeared!

I gave her a small meditation technique to meditate on that area. I told her, 'Express your anger towards that man. Weep, shout, cry, hit. Close the doors, take a pillow, imagine that it is him, and weep, cry, shout and hit. After that sit silently, and feel, that part of your body is also your own body. Feel love towards that part of the body.'

You will be surprised... in just ten days, the tumor disappeared! It never came back. It might be difficult to believe, but it is the truth.

Most of our ailments are due to psychological disturbances for which guilt is the main cause. Most of the time, your energy gets blocked because of your guilt. You have psychological illness because of your guilt. If you look deep, wherever you have fear, wherever you are not able to move, wherever you are not able to take decisions, there will be some guilt lurking.

THREE KINDS OF GUILT

There are three kinds of guilt that take root in you:

1. Guilt created by your immediate family

2. Guilt created by social laws

3. Guilt created by yourself

These are the three major kinds of guilt that kill your intelligence.

The mental layer which is related to thoughts is specifically associated with the feeling of guilt. Guilt is nothing but your past decisions and actions being reviewed with your updated intelligence. For example, when you were in school, you might have said a few mean things to one of your friends which caused a relationship to break. Now, this many years later, with the kind of intelligence that you have presently, is it right to review that incident and feel guilty? No! At that time you had only that much intelligence and so you behaved in that fashion. Now, you have updated intelligence. But, you can't review the past like that with your present intelligence.

Before the age of seven, guilt is created by your immediate family. Rules are imposed by family because they cannot logically answer and make you understand issues. This leads to guilt. The guilt about sex is created most definitely by the immediate family. That is the first guilt. The guilt based on greed is always the first guilt that is created by the immediate family.

From seven to fourteen, society creates guilt in you through its rules. The guilt based on fear is created by social laws.

The third guilt is the worst - that which you create for yourself. When you internalize the guilt based upon greed and fear, you create new types of guilt for yourself. If you analyze the situation, whenever you are stuck, these three kinds of guilt will be there in you.

The Useful Guilt

There is a certain guilt that is useful for you, a guilt if pursued intelligently, can cause you to move forward in life. It is like this: when you see that you have the potential to do something, when you feel that you have so much potential which you are not using at all, then, if you are intelligent, guilt will happen in you! This guilt can spur you to take steps to implement what needs to be done for you to reach your potential level.

Sometimes we see the state of things around us and we know in one corner of our mind that we can very well help turn the situation around. But, either due to laziness or due to the fear of confrontation, or due to the fear of taking responsibility, we will just keep quiet and watch. This type of situation can cause deep guilt in us. This guilt is significant. It can be called 'high level guilt'. If we take steps to correct the situation by helping, then the guilt will disappear and we will also move forward.

This type of guilt has the ability to immerse you in terrible misery. Because of that, it also has the property to drive you to do what needs to be done! Because of its very nature, you cannot harbour this guilt for long. You *have* to get over it. And the way to get over it is by doing what needs to be done. Once it is done, the guilt also disappears. As long as you harbour this guilt without taking steps, you will remain in misery. That is the simple logic of this guilt.

Another manifestation of this guilt happens when you can feel your ego surfacing in certain situations and you are unable to help it. When you can smell your ego but you are unable to control it, this guilt arises in you. This guilt is also good since it is a sign of your deep awareness of your own ego. It facilitates you to sincerely work towards eliminating that ego.

JUMPING BETWEEN THE PAST AND FUTURE

Guilt itself is a pull and push between the past and future. When you think of past incidents with updated intelligence you feel guilty. Similarly, with guilt, you anticipate the future, and destroy the future also. Either way, you miss the beauty of the present moment because of guilt.

The other day one of my close disciples was asking, 'Master, you are so casual, so innocent, so playful. But when it comes to teaching us, any word that you utter, simply becomes true! How can so much intelligence and intuition happen continuously?' He asked out of pure awe...!

I had a class that day. Before coming to the class, I was playing chess with one of our devotee's daughter. We had not finished the game, so I told her I would come back after the class and play. It was then that this disciple asked me, 'How you can be so playful, so joyful on one side, and on the other side, your words are so clearly coming to be reality!'

One thing you should understand: you are not able to experience this intuition because you are not able to fall into the present moment. You are always pulled by the past or future. Either you work and worry about the past, or you work and worry about the future. Something or the other is continuously going on in you.

Time is like a shaft. Visualize this one thing and understand: time is like a shaft. You are either pulled to this side of the shaft or that side of the shaft. But eternity penetrates time only in the present moment, at the center.

Because of your pull and push between past and future, you never feel relaxed. A deep craving exists all the time, either to achieve something in the outer world or inner world. Please understand that the craving to achieve something in the inner world is also craving for the future. Your craving for enlightenment is also a worry about the future. When you leave the past and future to be in the present, you will see that you relax from this craving.

ACCEPTANCE – THE BEAUTIFUL WAY OUT

Acceptance is a wonderful tool to fall into the present moment, to relieve yourself of the pull and push of the past and future. The first thing is to accept all the happenings of the outer world and accept all the happenings of the inner world. Whatever problems you have in the outer world and whatever problems you have in the inner world, just accept them in their entirety. Summarise all that you experience and label as problems and accept them.

Just try this small experiment:

Just relax for three days with complete acceptance. If you relax for three days without the pull and push in the inner and outer worlds are you going to lose all your wealth? Surely not! So there is no problem. In three days you are not going to lose anything. Why don't you give it a try? Just for three days, sincerely, utterly, accept everything in your life one hundred percent!

If you are not able to accept one hundred percent then accept that you are not able to accept one hundred percent. Even the acceptance of 'I am not able to accept myself in the inner world and outer world,' will make you drop from the pull and push between past and future. The moment you understand, 'I am unable to free myself form the pull and push. I am not able to accept my reality,' that very understanding will start doing its job.

The moment you accept something, you will simply fall into the present moment. The moment you fall into the present moment, the time shaft will become a servant for you. As long as you are below the time shaft, it will rule you. You will be pulled or pushed by the time shaft. The moment your consciousness is raised to the present moment, you will see that you are penetrating the time shaft.

When you penetrate the time shaft, the future is also clearly known to you. The past is also clearly known to you. The tremendous realization comes to you that the time shaft is only your projection! Try this experiment just for three days. If you can fall into the present moment, relaxing from the outer world and inner world things, in three days you will have a glimpse. 'What is life? What does it mean to live in the present moment? If this happens to you, you will experience such ecstasy, such a different space, such a different life that you have never experienced before.

Just for three days, don't try to alter anybody in the outer world. You have lived based on your philosophy for the last 30 years. Give me just one simple three day trial period. You will see that when you experiment with such great techniques, they work miracles in your being. They start a great alchemy process in your being. If you are not able to be sincere, accept that you are not able to be sincere. Even that sincerity is enough. You will start seeing a different space in you. That different space is what I call *nithya* (eternity).

Many women face the guilt of killing a life when they go through an abortion. Please understand that when they decided to abort the pregnancy, their intelligence was only at that level. If their intelligence gets updated soon, it is not their mistake.

Once a guy came to me complaining, 'I am suffering. I have 14 children.' I asked him why he chose to have so many children. He replied, 'Why? God gave me!' The problem is, we do all that we want to do in the name of God! We use Him as our 'dustbin'. We do all the possible nonsense and place the responsibility on Him.

So it is also with the guilt related to extramarital affairs. Be very clear that extramarital affairs show disrespect to another being. You have no right to disrespect. Will you let the other person do it too? What is the meaning of the relationship then? Man is centered on *muladhara chakra* – lust energy center, and woman is centered on the *swadhishtana chakra* – fear energy center. That is why man gives in to lust easily and woman gives in to fear easily. During the traditional marriage ceremony, in front of the sacred fire, the man promises to the woman, considered to be a representation of God, 'I shall give you security and release you from insecurity.' The woman promises to the man, 'I shall give you love and free you from lust.' Both of them decide to liberate the other from their weaknesses. But what happens once the ceremony is over? You start playing on the weakness of the other person. Knowing the other person's weakness should make you compassionate towards that person.

Instead, the man exploits the woman's fear and the woman exploits the man's lust in cunning ways.

A mature person cannot disrespect another person as if they are a commodity. If you see your wife as a commodity, you will continue to play your game with her. If you see your wife as a being, you will realize how much she has contributed in your life. You will never think of extramarital affairs. It is disrespect to your own body and inner space too. People who sell their bodies have no respect for themselves. When you do it, you reduce spirit to matter and that is disrespect because you are not just matter as you think. You are energy or spirit. Understand: when man faces insecurity, the woman should become a mother. When the woman becomes centered on fear, the man should adopt the role of father.

MANGALATVA - EVERYTHING THAT HAPPENS IS AUSPICIOUS

Understand that all guilt is foolishness. Why do we feel guilty? Because we feel we have done something wrong. But in truth there is nothing called 'right' and 'wrong.' In Existence, the basic law is *mangalatva*, such a beautiful word. *Mangalatva* means 'everything that happens is auspiciousness!'

Good or bad cannot be defined. It cannot be decided with your logic. Your logical ideas of good or bad are limited only to what you know as life and limited to the people directly around you. But life is not just limited to you and the people who are around you. If you look a little deeply, you will experience that life is beyond your logical comprehension and your logical understanding.

In Sanskrit we have a word *'Shivam'*. The word means 'auspiciousness.' You may think that the activity of Shiva is 'destruction' according to Hindu mythology. In the *Vedic* tradition the word Shiva means auspiciousness... causeless auspiciousness, or energy. That is the exact translation of the word *'Shiva'*.

Of course, the work of Shiva is destruction, but it is not destruction as we know it. In Sanskrit, there is a beautiful appreciation for the process of destruction. Actually, it is not destroying; it is creating space for new things to happen! That is the work Shiva does. Understand that you can see destruction as destruction or as creating space for new things to happen. If you see destruction from another dimension, it is actually creating space for new things to happen. The destruction energy from the other angle is nothing but the possibility for rejuvenation. It continuously keeps the whole thing alive! That is what Shiva does. His work is continuous rejuvenation.

You see, if you look at things with your logic, with a small vision, you can always complain, blame that whatever is happening cannot be called auspicious. If your vision expands, if you start looking at life as a bigger picture, from a bigger perspective, from a greater understanding, you will realize the truth that whatever is happening is auspicious.

The person who feels that the whole of life is auspicious or *mangala*, is enlightened! He is liberated. He doesn't have fear. He doesn't have difficulties. He doesn't have problems. He doesn't need any help. The very understanding that whatever happens is auspicious is enough for him. He has solved his life.

There are only two kinds of people on the planet Earth. One is the spiritual type that feels 'whatever is happening is auspicious and nothing needs to be added to it.' The other is the materialistic type that feels, 'whatever is happening, there is always something lacking or needing some adjustment.'

A small story:

A preacher gave a long and very inspiring talk about charity.

Then he sent his hat around for a collection.

The hat went around to the entire group and came back empty.

The preacher simply took his hat back and said, 'Thank You, God, at least my hat came back.'

Be very clear that you can make anything auspicious. When you are really in tune with the all-pervading auspiciousness, you will understand that whatever is happening is auspicious. The best thing possible is happening every moment. Whereas if you trust your logic, you will always be complaining. If you trust the cosmic Intelligence, the cosmic logic, you will always be relaxing and appreciating.

You can feel the cosmos as either order or chaos. It is your freedom, your choice. You can feel it as being a beautiful order. Just look around. Do you see any traffic light in the cosmos? No! All the planets are moving so beautifully. Digestion is happening in your body so beautifully. That is also part of the cosmic activity, is it not? Are you making an effort for the bread that you eat to get converted to blood? No! It happens in spite of you. Even if you sit and vegetate after every meal, digestion happens, does it not? That is what I mean. On the other hand, you can also say, 'There is so much chaos, so much fighting in every home, so much trouble in every house. The world is in chaos.' You can look at this angle or that angle. It is your freedom.

Whatever is happening is auspicious. In all our lives, at least once or twice we must have experienced this. Just look back at the moments when you took a major positive decision in your life. In those moments you would have had such confidence and courage. At some point in time you would have surrendered either out of joy or high energy or the decision that nothing better or nothing greater can happen in your life. You would have thought that whatever is happening is auspicious. On the contrary, when you are in the middle of some low mood it may be difficult to see that what is happening is auspicious. But when you come out of it successfully and review the entire situation, you are more likely to see that everything that happened was auspicious, was a good lesson and opened the door to new, beneficial experiences. If you remember this the next time a low mood strikes you, the depression is less and you recover sooner. You can open yourself to realize this truth of Shiva.

If your inner space is clear, you will be able to see everything as causeless auspiciousness and automatically, you will also work towards auspiciousness. All your fear, all your greed, all your guilt, all these things exist because your energy is taken away by the past memories that are occupying your inner space, just the way high resolution pictures occupy your computer's memory.

So how do we keep from getting caught in the trap of guilt? Respond with your intelligence to any situation. When a situation presents itself in life, instead of deciding based upon what you have learnt that you 'should do' or 'should not do', decide based on your intelligence, with a deep feeling of responsiblity. That is enough.

So, carry this understanding with you in your life. Guilt is baseless. Live out of your understanding of life, not rules. Everything happening in life will then be auspicious. Existence wants you to be your true self every moment - which is eternal, and pure bliss - *nithya ananda*.

MEDITATION

Re-living is relieving. The best way to relieve yourself of guilt is to relive it. Write it all down. Relive and relieve. Do not console yourself as your guilt surfaces one incident after the other. Sit in a meditative mood. Relive all the wounds that you are carrying. Close your eyes and enter into the guilt. Relive each guilt, one by one. Relieve by writing them out. Write it out in as detailed a way as you can. Husband and wife, or relatives, please sit separately. Start writing.

Has everyone finished writing? If not, there is no problem, take your time and write down everything. There is no need to hurry. Go deep inside and write slowly.

Now let me explain the meditation technique clearly. First, slowly, very slowly and consciously, feel that your head is being pressed inside your heart. Then clearly visualize that your head has gone into your heart region. Visualize that you are seeing through the heart. You are also breathing through the heart. You are relating with the entire world through the heart. The head is not there. There is just empty space above the neck. Just trust that this is true. Until all of you lose your head, you have to go on with the meditation.

First, you will be in the sitting posture where you will lose the head. Then, you will know how to breathe without the head, how to see without the head, how to smell without the head, etc. These are all very simple actions. Next, you should learn how to move your hands without the head, how to move your body without your head! Finally you will end up with a peak movement, maybe running or dancing. All your movements will be done without the idea or without the remembrance of the head.

Now, we will start with the meditation.

Sit down, close your eyes and tie your eye bands. You will need a little space for movement, so sit a little apart from each other.

Take slow and deep breaths, just for a few minutes. Along with it, feel that your head is being pressed into your heart, into the chest region. Become totally headless. You have no head now. You are headless.

Feel that you are breathing from the heart. Feel that you are seeing through the heart. Feel that you smell through the heart. Feel very clearly that you are breathing through the heart. Listen to everything around you through the heart. Listen to this music that is being played through the heart, not through the head. Listen through the heart, see through the heart, feel through the heart.

Stand up. Have the consciousness from the heart, and let your movements be as slow as possible. Remember that you are moving from the heart. Your centre is from the heart, not from the head. Again and again, forget the head. Move from the heart. Move as slowly as possible, but from the heart. Remember, you are a headless being. Move only from the heart... you are a headless being moving.

Stand in one place, there is no need to walk. Now, increase the speed slowly, very slowly. Remember to move from the heart, not from the head. Forget your head. You are a headless being moving. *(A few minutes pass)*. Stop! Sit down where you are. Just be, without the head. Sit only with your heart. Relax.

(A few minutes pass)

Slowly, very slowly, you may open your eyes.

You may take a break. Do not talk to each other. Maintain silence so that the process may be undisturbed.

Thank you.

CHAPTER 6

Etheric Body

The *etheric* body is associated with mental pain and suffering.

The *etheric* body is the space where the intense emotions are stored. Usually all of our intense emotions are those of pain only. You do not know any other intense emotion. If you know any other intense emotion, then you are a spiritual person.

Look into your life and see that pain gives you such an intense feeling. When you are depressed or in pain, you can see that you become very intense and your whole mind is centered. Your mind does not move to anything else. However, when you are in a blissful mood, have you experienced any bliss to that depth to which you have experienced pain? No! That is why I say, all we know is only pain.

The most frightening thing in the world for us is pain. All living beings are afraid of one thing, and that is pain. If you look deeply, you will find that people don't fear death even as much as they fear the pain that they will have to undergo at the time of death!

When it comes to fear, we have different types of fears: fear of poverty, fear of losing relationships, fear of contacting disease, fear of losing wealth, and so on. But the root cause of all these fears is pain! All the fears of man stem from the fear of pain.

And that is why people will endure even a major disease which doesn't cause pain, but they can rarely endure a simple headache!

Why do you have the fear of losing relationships? Because not being able to relate with that person anymore is painful! Why do you have fear of losing wealth? Because it is painful to hear others talk about your sudden poverty. Why do you have fear of falling ill? Because you may experience physical pain in some way.

WHAT IS PAIN?

Pain is that which is born out of resistance to the present moment. Pain is always born out of resistance to the present moment.

Pain can be physical, mental or emotional. Physical pain is the least of our worries. It is, in a way, a basic necessity for the body. Just imagine if we could feel no pain in our physical body. We might start styling our faces and limbs the way we style our hair today! Pain is the symbol of bodily wisdom. Pain is what makes us integrated human beings.

Contrary to what we believe, most of us are not 'living' with our entire body. We 'live' only in the upper parts, neglecting the lower parts of the body. Just try this: close your eyes and imagine yourself, your being. Call your name. Which part of your body comes to your visualization first? It would definitely be your face and upper limbs, certainly not the lower body parts. This clearly shows that we are not fully alive in every cell, in every limb of ours.

Even in our minds, we make this distinction. The upper limbs are the masters, the lower limbs the servants. When you create this separation, unknowingly, your energy or life force is channeled only to the body parts that you focus on with importance. Just touch your cheek. Doesn't it feel sensitive, alive? Now touch your foot. Does it feel the same? Notice that you are not as alive in your foot as in your cheek. Why is that? It is purely due to your lack of attention to your feet. You never feel your lower body parts in the same caring and responsible way in which you feel your upper body parts.

PAIN – NOTHING BUT RESISTANCE TO THE PRESENT MOMENT

On the emotional and mental level, pain is usually the result of some form of judgment that is constantly going on inside you.

Research reveals that emotional imbalance can deeply disturb the physical body. For example, sexual repression can result in back pain, or the sense of shouldering too much responsibility can cause pain in the shoulders.

A small story:

In Calcutta there were two small ashrams whose presidents were not on good terms with each other. One day a person of some authority arrived in one ashram and invited the president to join him in visiting the other ashram. The president was in distress. He could not refuse, but he didn't want to go either.

Suddenly the president developed a high fever which prevented him from leaving the place!

I saw this with my own eyes. As soon as the other person left, the temperature came back to normal again.

Haven't we all experienced 'Monday morning blues'? Whether we are children or we are adults, we experience this! When we are children, we display bodily symptoms of illness when Monday arrives after a long weekend. When we are adults, although we don't openly express our feelings, we do feel unease at having to go back to office on Monday mornings. When the mind and body pull you in opposite directions, there is every chance that dis-ease happens in you.

Every time you experience pain, it leaves behind a residue which becomes lodged in the body. By and by, this accumulated residue creates a negative energy field around you, which we call the 'pain body'. The 'pain body' is responsible for and controls most of our pain patterns.

THE POWER OF THE MIND OVER THE SENSES

The other day, a handsome young boy belonging to an orthodox family was brought to our healing center. His complaint was sudden blindness. His parents were weeping and told me that the boy was in excellent health, but had suddenly turned blind one week earlier. All medical tests revealed perfect vision, but he couldn't see!

After scanning his energy, I requested that I may spend a few moments alone with the boy. No sooner did he get the opportunity to talk to me in private, the boy poured out his troubles to me. He said that he was deeply in love with a girl, but had been forced by his parents to stop seeing her.

I immediately figured out the root cause of the problem. I asked the boy to get a photograph of the girl, and spend the next three days meditating upon it continuously.

His parents were taken aback at this unconventional solution, that too from a spiritual man!

But you will be amazed: the technique worked a wonder. In three days, the boy regained his vision perfectly. He was able to see like before.

How did this happen? See, when the boy was compelled not to see what he most wanted to see, his subconscious mind decided not to see anything at all. Just by the power of his intense thought, he became blind. His blindness was deeply psychological. Just imagine what tremendous power the mind has over the senses!

In the *Bhagavata Purana*, a grand epic of Hindu mythology, it is mentioned that Krishna and Radha took birth within a few moments of each other. Radha was a normal baby in every way, except that she wouldn't open her eyes.

A few days later, Radha's mother visited Krishna's house to see the baby Krishna. She took her newborn daughter with her. The moment Radha was brought in Krishna's Presence, she opened her eyes and beheld Krishna before her! Later in life, when questioned by a friend about this incident, Radha remarked, 'What else was there to see? It is for Krishna that I have taken birth. So I waited till I was taken to his Presence to open my eyes.'

This may only be a tale, but it illustrates the tremendous power of the mind over the body.

196

You Invite Pain Upon Yourself

Actually, pain is a requisition letter written by some part of the body to the mind saying, 'Please pay me some attention!' Understand: your attention is your energy. Wherever you direct your attention, there your energy is also directed, and in that direction you witness growth.

Actually, you invite pain upon yourself. Not many people will believe it if they are told that they invite pain upon themselves, like honored guests into their household.

A small story:

Once a man entered a restaurant and began ordering various food items. Platefuls of steaming food of various types made their way to his table. He ate with relish.

After a hearty meal, he finally signaled the waiter to stop bringing in the food.

The waiter duly returned with a long bill.

'What is this?' asked the man, looking at the bill innocently. 'Why have you brought me this? I haven't ordered anything like this!'

When you order food, you have to remember that you are ordering the bill also! In the same way, we invite pain and disease upon ourselves with our immoderate habits and stressful lifestyles, and then forget all about it and complain later when disease takes its toll.

One more thing: although we suffer because of our disease, we also enjoy it secretly in a way because it gets us attention from people. This is no wonder, because in the hectic pace of today's life, who has the time to pay attention to the other person unless they fall ill? Attention is a basic need for every individual. Psychology proves that normally a man can stay alive without food for up to 90 days, but without the attention of others he will lose his sanity in just 14 days! Attention is energy; it is a life-force. Though we are unaware of it, the craving for attention is so great, that to gain it, we create our own low-energy pools and gladly suffer the disease too.

> An engineer working in a large firm brought the same dish for lunch everyday.

> Every day he complained about how much he hated that particular dish. His sympathetic friends would share their lunch with him.

> One day, one of his friends finally asked him, 'Why don't you just ask your wife to cook something that you like for a change? How can she not be aware that you hate this dish?'

> 'What wife?' the man asked in surprise. 'I am a bachelor. I cook my own lunch!'

This may sound funny but most of us live our lives in very much the same way. Through our lack of awareness, we first invite pain upon ourselves, and then complain about it and resort to painkillers. We never identify ourselves as the root cause of the pain. We always throw the responsibility for the pain on others.

SELF-HEALING - JUST THE PRESENCE

If physical pain is perceived as the absence of your attention, then the remedy must be your presence. There is a simple and beautiful self-healing meditation technique that channels your 'presence' into the diseased limb. It is definitely a better option than painkillers, whose side-effects sometimes prove worse than the original complaint!

Let us say that you have limb pain. Lie down in a dark room. Focusing only on the part that is causing you pain, make a conscious effort to forget about the rest of your body. As you experience your painful limb, deliberately drop the word 'pain' from your mind.

Your mental chatter will continue to tell you that you feel pain. Switch it off. Feel deeply; experience with an open mind. Look into what is happening inside your mind in the context of the pain. You will soon see that your mind was just exaggerating the pain. Put all your awareness on the center of the pain, and it will soon shrink to become just a tiny pinpoint of pain. Concentrate completely on this point, and you will discover in a sudden moment that the pain has disappeared, and in its place is pleasure, or bliss.

PAIN AND PLEASURE - TWO SIDES OF THE SAME COIN

Pleasure is the opposite of pain - and like all opposites, one has no existence without the other. You cannot enjoy pleasure without suffering, without pain. It is significant that ancient Indian scriptures used the same word, pain, to imply both pleasure and pain - because pain is the ultimate result of both.

The root of pain and pleasure is the same. It is the same sensation with two names. If you have ever received a good massage from a friend or a professional, you will realize that the same massage would seem like sheer physical violence if you received it at the hands of a stranger!

On the other hand, bliss is that which arises when you drop the ideas of both pleasure and pain. And you have to drop them both together; there is no other way. Bliss is what floods you when both pain and pleasure have ceased to disturb you. Bliss is beyond pain and pleasure. It is perfect harmony, complete inner silence, and total peace.

If you try to understand the truth of your experience, it will be that 'pain' does not exist at all. Pain has only a negative existence. Like darkness, it is only an absence - the absence of awareness, that's all. As darkness disappears of its own accord when light is brought into a room, so also, pain dissolves automatically when the energy of your awareness is focused upon it.

You can use your pain as a tool to enter your being. You will find that pain itself can become a door to *ananda* - bliss.

A small story:

Two men were traveling through a forest on a dark, moonless night. Suddenly, a bolt of lightning flashed in the sky.

One of them began to tremble in fear. A storm! His mind was immediately caught in confusion. Should he continue to walk? Or should he find a safe place to stop until the storm was over? He began wishing that he had never decided to undertake the journey. He cursed himself as foolish and unlucky. In other words, he fell headlong into suffering with just a few strokes of lightning.

The other man simply used the moments of lightning flashes to take a better look at the road ahead, and kept moving. He made sure that he was traveling in the right direction, thanked the lightning for its help, and moved on.

Pain is just like this flash of lightning. It happens, but whether you suffer from it or learn from it is entirely up to you! Then you will realize that you are the cause of your own pain and only you can be the solution.

PAIN TEACHES YOU THAT YOU ARE BEYOND THE BODY

When you observe your pain deeply, innocence opens up in you. For the first time, you become aware that you are not the body. No pain can touch the real 'you'. Once you realize that you are beyond pain, you transcend pain to become a *dukkha ateeta* - one who has gone beyond suffering. You experience the rare freedom that arises with non-attachment to the body that you have carried all your life. You transcend your mundane life and enter into a spiritual plane. You then exist in the world as an *atman*, an enlightened master. The whole material world disappears and another world arises – of incomparable beauty, innocence, joy and compassion.

As the *Bhagavad Gita* says:

He who is ever established in the self, takes woe and joy alike, regards a clod of earth, a stone and a piece of gold equal in value, is possessed by wisdom, receives the pleasant and the unpleasant in the same spirit, and views censure and praise alike.

With awareness and practice, pain can become the magic portal to enter into *nithyananda* - eternal bliss.

Just to see with intense inner clarity, the nature and cause of pain will make pain evaporate because it no longer has a reason to exist in you. And this realization brings with it a state of absolute bliss, which is the state of enlightenment.

Enlightenment allows you to see for the first time that what you called happiness and contentment earlier were not true happiness and true contentment. Enlightenment showers real bliss upon you, real ecstasy. It gives you a taste of the real.

Pain - The Catalyst to Start the Quest for Truth

If you look a little deeply inside you, you actually need to be thankful for the pain and suffering that you experience. They are the catalysts that set you upon your quest for truth and transcendence.

Just look at your life. When you were happy about something, did you ever wonder about the meaning of life? Did you look inwards to see who you are, what life is all about? Did you feel the need to deeply know about the Ultimate Truth? No! When things are going smoothly we just blindly follow the same routine with barely any awareness or consciousness. There is nothing to disturb you from the routine so you continue without any awareness.

On the other hand, when pain happens in you, it makes you look at it objectively. It forces you to look deeper into life to learn what its mystery is all about. It is a blessing in disguise. It is the key that can open the door to the world of reality; the choice is yours to open the door or not. It can simply shake you out from both the dream state and the 'waking dream' state we are in. Understand, even if you are awake, you are not completely in touch with reality. You live in a world of your desires and fears and hence see things in the same light. Pain can be a great teacher which can simply jolt you out of the dream and put you in touch with reality as is.

With pain, your usual thought patterns are shattered and you begin to see things as they actually are. You begin to recognize a subtle distance between you and the pain and that it is not 'your' pain, not something that is a part of you by nature.

In fact, pain is simply the response you have chosen to a particular situation. Once you see that, how can you suffer anymore? You just let go of it.

The intelligent ones don't curse the pain or the person inflicting it upon them. They use it as a blessing to go in and see what the system response is, and try to cut the root of the pain. Pain can be a great teacher if you allow it to be. If in one instance, you properly research the cause and effect of pain within you, it can turn out to be the biggest turning point in your life. Such a powerful emotion, pain is.

ACCEPTING YOUR EMOTIONS OBJECTIVELY

Many people come and ask me, 'I get angry and hurt easily when someone insults me. How can I avoid this?'

I tell them, 'Why do you try to avoid it? To suppress pain, anger and humiliation will only cause it to stay in your system in a repressed form. Suppressed emotions can be dangerous - a little anger, a small feeling of hurt, can fester over time into a deep and lasting hatred. Try accepting your emotions without judging yourself.

Are you feeling hurt? Ok, now enter completely into the hurt feeling. Don't avoid it and don't reject it. Sit by yourself and enter into it.

Neither give yourself sympathy nor direct the hurt against the person who hurt you.

Simply watch the emotion as it plays in your system, that's all.

If you decide to do this sincerely, the process may take a while - maybe a few hours, even a few days. But at the end of it, you will see a transformation you never imagined! After all, emotion is energy, tremendous energy and pain is the strongest emotion in you. How long can so much raw energy circulate in your system? The moment you accept your pain with no rejection, welcoming its role in your life, the whole quality of pain changes. The same energy that was pain, anger or suffering is transformed into the blessed emotions of love and bliss. This is compassion, the silent force that moves in each of us, the force that transforms the ugly into the beautiful. And compassion brings its own reward. Just give yourself a chance and you can experience what I am saying! I don't speak philosophy. I speak out of experience.

LOVE AND PAIN

Why do love and pain always seem to go hand in hand?

In the first place, isn't your idea of 'giving freedom' to your beloved a very wrong one? Love itself implies giving the other total freedom, unconditional freedom. To say that you are giving a certain amount of freedom to the other itself shows that you are holding back a certain amount! No one understands that.

It is natural to want to possess your beloved; that is the play of the ego. It is difficult to imagine that your beloved may need space and time away from you. You try to do the right thing by 'giving freedom' to your lover. But when she actually uses that freedom, you end up feeling exploited. Actually, you never expected that she would ever use that freedom to do what she wants and be with whom she wants to be with. When you see her giving time and energy to something or somebody other than you, you start feeling possessive and cheated.

The reason that love usually brings so much pain with it is that lovers unknowingly force each other into the golden cage of their own expectations. But true love can never blossom in captivity. You try to imprison your lover and she does the same, time after time, until you end up feeling that love is so much misery that perhaps it is better not to love at all.

Love can be a door to joy and freedom, or it can become a living hell. To experience love as pain is to miss the whole point of love. There is a saying, 'If you love someone, set him free. If he is yours, he will come back to you. If he doesn't come back, he never was yours anyway.' This is the freedom any relationship deserves. When you understand this, you will start respecting the other person as an individual. You will not try to possess them as though they are an object.

PAIN AND SUFFERING – THEY ARE STEPPING STONES

To start with, we need to understand that suffering is not a state of life. It is a state of mind. It is not an event in your life. It is your response to an event. In a particular situation, whether you suffer or not depends entirely on your reaction to that situation.

When do you undergo suffering? Maybe when you fall ill or when your neighbor gets a new car or when your loved one leaves you or when your boss fires you or you lose some wealth.

Suppose you decided to accept these situations without anger or resentment, just as they are. Would you still suffer as much? After all, there is nothing inherently painful about your neighbor getting a new car. It is an event that happened in his life, that's all! The problem is that you carry so much history with the neighbour, so much jealousy because of that and therefore you feel suffering. The whole thing has been woven by your mind. If you take a look at it with a little intelligence, you can simply drop it. Similarly, when your boss yells at you, you feel pain. The pain would have been either because he reprimanded you in front of everyone or because you feel bad for having fallen short of his expectation at work, or because you feel you didn't deserve the firing.

Sit by yourself and think honestly about what the reason is. Once you find out the exact cause of the pain you can attend to it and get relieved from the root cause itself. If it is due to him scolding you in front of everybody, then the pain is actually a hurt to your ego. Ask yourself, 'What is there if everybody was watching? Why have I invested so much in what others think of me? Why am I so silly? Why can't I have my own meter to measure myself and not depend on others for it?' Ask yourself these questions. Try to take back your investment in other's opinions of you.

You will see that one instance of pain might liberate you from a huge block that you had in your life. Like this, sit and analyse the root cause of pain and see where you are stuck. For every pain, you are the problem. Your boss or your neighbour or your loved one or your wealth is not the reason. No one outside can be a reason for your pain because your pain itself is only your response to an external event based on your own investments. Depending on where you have invested your ego, you will suffer. If you work towards dissolving all those investment, you are intelligent.

Try to accept, to welcome, the inevitability of the moment without reaction. It is only your negative response to an experience that allows it to hurt you. Remember, no one or nothing can make you suffer without your silent permission.

Make a habit of witnessing experiences minus your personal judgment. Learn to recognize with clarity the causes of your suffering, both the obvious and the subtle.

An important thing you should know: one of the most deeply hidden reasons for suffering is that you could be enjoying it. For example, falling ill can become a source of pleasure if it fetches you the attention and care you have been craving. Look deeply at why it sometimes gives you pleasure to inflict pain on yourself or on others. Is there a better channel through which you can receive the same pleasure without the suffering?

Become aware - this is the first step.

Just as when a seed must first rupture before it can grow and blossom, pain and suffering can break down the defenses of your ego, leaving you open and vulnerable to Existence.

In the *Mahabharata*, there is a beautiful quote by Kunti, the mother of the Pandavas. She says, 'Oh Krishna! Let pain and suffering come from all sides in my life. They will constantly remind me about You, my Lord.' Kunti is asking the Lord to bless her with pain and suffering so that she may constantly remember Him for relief! In modern days, we need not go to this extent, but we can understand the potential of suffering in the context of our own liberation. Suffering has tremendous potential to integrate and transform us.

If you learn your lesson well, suffering can open your eyes to the unreality of suffering. It can teach you how unnecessary it is to suffer at all. This is what I call 'necessary suffering'! Once you learn your lesson through necessary suffering, you will handle suffering in a much more mature and beautiful way.

In our lives, we are continuously eaten by pain and suffering. If you have heard of the concept of *pralaya*, you can understand. *Pralaya* is the total destruction of the Earth as recorded in Hindu mythology. The real *pralaya* or destruction that happens in our life is pain.

Life itself starts with pain - the pain of the birth, the excruciating pain that you have to undergo at the time of taking birth. You have to come through a very small passage to be born. Imagine such a big body coming out of such a small passage. Because of this excruciating pain, you actually enter into a coma before you come out. According to energy science, according to the mystics, before entering into the world, you are pure consciousness and you know the reason that you are taking birth. But you enter into a coma and come out, which is why you forget the past lives, the past births. Life starts with excruciating pain and ends too at the time of death with excruciating pain.

Life is almost like a bridge between pain and pain. If you see the Golden Gate Bridge in the USA, just as the Golden Gate Bridge connects two places, life seems to connect pain to pain.

This body of yours can teach you a lot of things. If you can work on this body, it can teach you a lot of things. If you can establish a rapport with your body and observe it carefully, you will see that your body is the closest to God that you can get. It is such a natural thing given to you as a gift. It can teach you how not to fight Existence and how to flow with it. Every moment the body is trying to flow like Existence.

PAIN - THE TEACHER IN THE *KALI* AGE

There is one thing you need to understand: when the *Kali* age took birth (the fourth quarter of time as per mythology), it was deemed the age of darkness. All the sages and *rishis* were praying to the Lord, 'Oh Lord! Now the *Kali* age has entered, the enlightened Masters will not be available to the society. Living Masters will not be available to the society; only very few will be here. Then, how can society maintain the equilibrium? How can we save society? How can humanity be saved? Only with the living Master's grace, can people learn and live blissfully. Only with their guidance, can people learn spirituality and live a real life. Now that *Kali* has entered, how can the people be saved? Who will teach them? Who is the Master?'

Then the Lord said, 'Don't worry, I will teach the whole world continuously in the form of pain. Whenever pain happens to you, either physical, psychological or emotional pain, any pain... if you look at it, if you work on it, if you approach it with love and the mood to work on it, you will see that it is the greatest teacher. It will teach you and transform your life.' Have you ever wondered how we could look at pain with such a loving and learning mood? If you can internalize this one statement, then you have found the solution to all your problems. You can try it as an experiment to start with. The next time you experience pain, try to remember this statement and put it into action. You will see that it simply transforms your whole outlook.

A small story:

There was a big marriage ceremony between two lions. Suddenly in the centre of the stage, a rat came up and started dancing.

After a few minutes, somebody interfered and said, 'Hey, this is the marriage of lions. How dare you come up here and dance?'

The rat raised his head and said, 'Hey, before marriage I was also a lion!'

If you learn one lesson, if you can learn from one pain, you can learn all the lessons!

Anyhow, whenever pain happens you will see that the pain teaches you. If you don't learn the lesson, if you are insensitive, then you will continue to live in the same pain.

KIDS ARE THROUGH YOU, NOT OF YOU

Teach children also to look at their pain objectively and deeply. Don't teach them to suppress their pain. Teach them to handle it and look into it. One more thing, never beat your children. They are forms of God living with you! They chose you for their journey. They trusted you to be their guardians. I chose my parents. When I died in my last birth, I was totally in a meditative mood. So I had the conscious choice and chose my parents carefully, as people who would help me to reach my enlightenment in this lifetime. I chose people who would not disturb me in my growth or progress, who would let me walk in my path undisturbed.

In the same way, every child chooses you and trusts that you will be their guardian. So never beat them. Beating is not the way to teach. Keep them like flowers. Don't suppress them or disturb them. Teach them more through *your* life, instead of giving *them* regulations. You should live and show them how to live. They should just pick up the rules from your very body language. Your way of living should be an example for them to follow most naturally. That is the right way of parenting. By showing them compassion and love, a lot can be healed in them at a young age itself.

ETHERIC BODY MEDITATION

You are bliss by nature. Every time you breathe in, you are taking in *prana* from Existence. *Prana* is the life energy that air brings into our system when we breathe. It runs our very life and is the causative factor for us being alive. Air is only a medium that brings in the *prana*. We need *prana*, not air, for survival. Life energy is pure bliss. So in this meditation we will visualize that we are breathing in bliss every time we inhale.

You should understand a big difference between visualization and imagination. Visualization is not the same as imagination.

211

Imagination is day-dreaming; your mind creates situations that can have no existence in reality. For example, you are sitting in the office physically but your mind is in Hawaii imagining that you are enjoying yourself on the beach. Body is in the office but mind is somewhere else, just fantasizing. Imagination clearly means that you are not completely in the present; you are out of touch with reality.

Visualization, on the other hand, is seeing that which exists in reality but you find difficult to realize practically through your physical body. Visualizing yourself actualizing your potential is an example. Your potential is reality. Because of your own conditioning, you find it difficult to actualise your entire potential. But as a step towards actualizing it, you can very well visualise that you are actualizing it. That is visualization.

As of now, you have not experienced bliss as your very nature. But bliss is your nature. There are people, enlightened Masters, who over the ages have declared that you are bliss. To experience this truth, this reality of Existence, you can take the help of visualization, which is a very powerful tool that we underestimate.

As of now, because we don't realize the truth of our very nature, we are unconsciously contributing to the collective negativity by breathing out our negative emotions and suffering into the world. Now we are going to break this negative cycle and reverse it.

Get ready for the meditation. Close your eyes. Tie your eye bands.

Etheric Body

In this meditation, we are going to do just two things with full awareness.

When you breathe in, visualize clearly that you are inhaling the suffering from the world. Because your very nature is bliss, visualize that the fountain of bliss spontaneously happening inside you is transforming the entire suffering into bliss. Visualize the bliss energy spreading to every part of your body, penetrating every pore, and every cell of your body.

When you breathe out, visualize the bliss energy from inside you just radiating out to the world.

Very deeply visualize that you are breathing in darkness, and breathing out gold light; you are taking darkness in, breathing gold out.

Visualize not only *your* pain but the whole world's pain and suffering in the color black, and take it in.

Now, continue to immediately start breathing out. When you breathe out, feel that you are breathing out golden light - the bliss, joy, or ecstasy.

Put your whole consciousness and awareness into this and visualize.

(At the end of the meditation)

Om Nithyanandam.

Relax. Slowly, very slowly, open your eyes.

We will meet for the next session. Thank you.

CHAPTER 7

Causal Body

The causal body is associated with the deep pain that happens at the time of death that results in coma. The causal body is experienced in deep sleep, in deep darkness. Darkness is a beautiful energy we have been associated with right from our birth, right from when we were in our mother's womb.

DARKNESS - THE REJUVENATING ENERGY

We originate from the darkness of our mother's womb, and we also get rejuvenated every day in darkness when we fall into deep sleep, and ultimately, we disappear also into darkness at the time of death! Darkness is energy. In the *Vedic* tradition, Mother Kali is represented as dark energy. *Kali* in Sanskrit means darkness.

Each and every one of us by our own nature has a layer of darkness around us. This body is called the causal body.

We should understand what happens exactly when we fall into deep sleep.

Whenever your body needs rest, automatically the mind is pulled down and inserted into the causal body. It is like a battery; when it is discharged, that battery is taken out and inserted into the re-charger. There is also a particular time for recharging. In the same way, after your excitement for the day, the mind will be automatically pulled, because it needs some rest. It will be inserted into the causal body.

In the causal body, you are in darkness, but you don't want to rest in darkness. So what do you do? You continuously jump around in your mind. When you fight with darkness, when you don't want to rest in darkness until you get recharged for that recharging period of half an hour or one hour, you create side effects which are called depression and worry.

Actually, depression is a natural phenomenon which is supposed to happen, which gives you the rest that you need. Nature gives you rest for you to get back your energy. If you can go deeply into depression, you can go deeply into excitement also.

Please understand: A person who can't get depressed can never get excited. If you know how to travel with the low mood, with the low current, then you will know how to fly with the high mood also! If you don't know how to travel with the low current, you will never be able to go to the peak of the high mood also.

Darkness is the causal body. It is the place where you actually get rejuvenated. It is the layer from which you actually receive energy. When you sleep, you feel so totally refreshed because you are actually inserted into the causal body, into the darkness.

Two things happen when you cooperate with the darkness: one is, you don't resist depression if it happens. Also, you will not create depression at all.

Be very clear: depression can never depress you if you simply depress the depression! As long as you resist it, it is depression.

When you allow it, it is rest, it is deep rest. It is actually the time when you are with yourself. The problem is that you don't want to be with yourself but you are being pulled into it. Then you fight with it. Then you name it depression, worry, suffering, everything.

You must have seen in your life times when you are in the office and suddenly you get a call to go home immediately. You simply obey the order, right? You don't have any problem in doing that. In the same way, you just need to know how to travel with the depression, with the darkness.

You see, sometimes during a weekend, you go around and have a good time. When everything is over, you come back to your house. But when you get up the next day, your body and mind will have a hangover, is it not? You will feel like giving it rest. You won't want to move anywhere. You just feel like lying down. Your mind doesn't want to work. But what do you do? You forcibly start moving around and creating further activity for yourself.

STOP HATING LAZINESS AND IT WILL DISAPPEAR

You have a very deep hatred towards laziness. If you actually stop hating laziness, it will actually disappear from your system.

A small story:

Once a man went to his friend's house. His friend was a very cunning and diplomatic person. Diplomacy and cunningness go hand in hand. You can always see that the people who are innocent, will never be diplomatic. They will not know what diplomacy is. But the cunning persons will know diplomacy very well.

The friend somehow wanted to drive away this man. He suddenly called his wife and said, 'Bring some coffee for him'.

The wife shouted, 'There is no sugar, no milk. There is nothing in the house!'

The man got up and gave his wife a kick saying, 'Fool! You do not know how to treat a guest. You don't have anything to offer my friend. Is this the way to take care of him? Is this the way to treat a guest?' He started shouting and screaming.

She started weeping and wailing.

The guest saw this and said, 'Oh sorry! Because of me, all this is happening. Don't worry. It is time for me to go to another function. Let me go.' He got up and walked out.

When the man left, the host smiled and said proudly, 'See how I played the right drama and sent him out!'

The wife retorted, 'No! It was me who played it up and sent him out.'

Then the host replied, 'I acted as if I beat you, and he ran away.'

She said, 'I acted so well as if I was crying and he ran away.'

At that point, the man walked in saying, 'I acted as if I have gone but I have come back!'

Whenever you don't take care of the guest properly, he might just suddenly simply disappear from your house. In the same way, when laziness comes as a guest, don't pamper it too much and don't even resist it. Just don't bother about it. Don't hold on to the idea that you are lazy.

DEPRESSION, DEEP SLEEP AND DEATH

As I said earlier, your body is like a re-chargeable battery. It is like a battery getting discharged. It will be simply removed and put inside the charger for recharging. But the battery is not ready to wait until it gets fully recharged. It wants to again jump and play inside the toy. Understand that when you don't allow the recharging to happen, when you resist the recharging process, you create depression.

If you don't resist and allow the process to happen for a few moments, then depression will drop you. You will see that once the batteries are recharged, they will be simply bubbling. You will have the total energy to experience the ultimate excitement.

The time for recharging differs for every person. But once you know the knack of how to cooperate with the charging process, then the time will reduce and the quality will also improve. So it is the knack of cooperating, the method to cooperate with the darkness that you need to learn.

You see, this is the darkness, the ultimate darkness.

If you allow yourself to be recharged for a few minutes, you will come out of the depression. If you allow yourself to be recharged, if you cooperate with this darkness, you will come out of sleep also. If you work totally on darkness, you can come out of death itself because all these three are the expressions of the same thing: that is darkness.

Understand that depression, deep sleep and death are all the outcome of the same darkness layer. If you know how to work with the darkness in the ordinary life, the depression will disappear. Also, the third thing, that is the fear of death, will completely disappear from your system. When this happens, you will not fall into coma before you die. You will die consciously. As of now, 99 % of us die only by falling into a coma. This is the worst kind of death you can have... falling into coma and dying.

Don't think that coma means 'no pain'. The whole death process will start with pain. You *will have* pain. From the outside you won't feel the pain, but inside, it will be excruciating. When the pain becomes too much, you will have a built-in mechanism of a pain killer. To make you forget the pain, the coma is the built-in painkiller system.

Whenever your body needs rest but your mind is continuing in an excited and restless mood, your body cannot rest. Unless the mind itself is pulled inside the causal layer, the darkness layer, your body cannot rest. Unless your mind is black, your body will not become black. You will not allow your body to be black. So your whole body and mind will be pulled and inserted into the black hole. If you resist that moment, and think, 'Oh I have depression.,' you create depression by thinking you have depression. If you don't resist that moment, you will simply go inside and come out with a fully regenerated feeling. So it will be more like a complete rest rather than depression.

Integration Vs Schizophrenia

The causal layer is also called the *kaarana shareera* in Sanskrit. It is the layer which we are stuck in when we want to do something but we end up saying, 'I know it is right, but I am struggling. I know but...'

If you are caught in this, you are dead... over! You will neither achieve this nor that. Nothing can be done by you. You will be stuck with this one idea for many births. This is what we call '*kaarana shareera*' - giving reasons.

If you feel, 'I know what you are talking is right but I am not able to do it,' it means that you are caught in the *kaarana shareera*. You will never be able to get out of this layer unless you take a strong step and put your foot down to the whole nonsense. If you are caught in this layer, be very clear – nobody can save you. Nobody can save you. Do not be caught in the causal layer. That is what I call evil. When you are caught in the causal layer, you are like different fragments living inside one body. You are fragmented.

Anything fragmented is hell. Only something that is integrated is effective. You are either integrated or just schizophrenic. In my own life, I can say how integration, integrated devotion, was responsible for everything that happened. Integrated devotion is the real devotion. Schizophrenic devotion is not devotion at all. If you say, 'I know it is right but I am not able to get there...' the whole thing is over!

Integrated Devotion – From My Own Life

The reason for my first deep spiritual experience is that I never had that schizophrenic attitude in my inner space. One of my great inspirations was Annamalai Swamigal. I was so inspired and impressed by all the masters and mystics I was associated with in my young age. Also, the inner space was so pure at that young age, and there were no other heroes in my space except these masters. The masters were my heroes and in every step, I used to think, 'How will they behave? Let me behave like that. What and how will they do? Let me do like that.'

I used to go for a circumambulation of the sacred Arunachala hill very often. The circumambulation is totally 16 kilometers. I used to go late at night. When I had a little fear, I used to ask myself, 'How will Annamalai Swamigal behave? He won't bother about fear. Then let me also be like that!' and I would continue the circumambulation without fear!

Let me tell you about one incident:

> One day, maybe around the time when I had my first experience, it was raining heavily. I was doing the circumambulation. There was heavy rain, thunder and lightning. Immediately I thought, 'How will Annamalai Swamigal behave? He won't bother about it. He would just continue to walk. Let me also do in the same way.' I continued to walk.
>
> As I walked on, I was passing through the common crematorium where people were cremated in that place. In India, both cremation and burial are done in the same place. I was walking in that place because when you go round the hill the path goes through that crematorium also. It is the town's cremation ground.
>
> Suddenly I saw a dog biting something and eating. When I went near, the dog started barking at me. At first, when

fear arose, I thought, 'How will Annamalai Swami behave? He won't bother. Let me just move on then.' I started moving. Anyhow, when I started moving, the dog got scared and ran away.

When I went nearer, I saw that what the dog was biting was a dead body which was not completely buried and had come out in the rain and lying on the road. Just imagine a twelve or thirteen old boy at midnight, seeing a dead body without its head, because the head is in the dog's mouth!

The moment the fear started, it did not even reach my being completely; even before that, even before the fear stroke could happen completely, the awareness was so intense and I thought, 'How will Annamalai Swami respond now? He would just walk around and go. So let me just walk around and go.' I went... that's all.

I just took a detour and walked on. I did not even turn back and see. I just walked. The fear stroke did not even touch my whole body. The fear stroke, which was like a pebble, which was about to start, did not even open up.It did not even reach my body. The heat or the shivering, or the shaking was not even there in the body. It had just died.

Just the decision, 'If Annamalai Swamigal does, I will do,' did the whole thing... over!' When any thought came up from inside, I would think, 'How will Annamalai Swami respond to this thought? How would he respond?' If I get the response, 'He will not have this thought,' I would just say to myself, 'Then forget about it. It's not mine.' Over!

See, the person who inspires you or impresses you, becomes the hero of your inner space, especially if you are still young. These great masters impressed me so much. In every situation, internally I would calculate, 'How would these great masters have behaved?' and whatever came to my mind, I would do the same.

For example, if there were some sweets, my brothers would jump, 'Hey, I want this much as my share!' I would simply think, 'How would Annamalai Swami react in such a situation? He won't bother. He would just give away such things.' I would also then just keep away from the whole thing.

Clearly, the entire inner space was so deeply conscious and ready for the spiritual experience. That is why, just a small push, just a small inspiration from Annamalai Swamigal was able to put me into the first spiritual experience. This is what I call 'Living Enlightenment!'

LIVING ENLIGHTENMENT

When you live the Master's body language, you live enlightenment. Whenever any thought comes into my body or into my inner space, the first thing I would think would be, 'How would he behave?'

It could be anything... related to clothes or food or anything... If I feel a little lazy to meditate or to walk, I would think, 'How would Annamalai Swamigal be in this situation? How would he handle this situation?' Naturally, he would not bother about the laziness. He would just get up and meditate, that's all. So I used to do just that. He became the scale for everything. All the great Masters became the scale for me for everything that I did from morning till night. They became my life center.

One day, I asked Annamalai Swamigal about a dream that I had, and I also asked him what he saw in his dreams. He replied, 'I don't have dreams!' I was shocked. I asked him, 'You don't have dreams at all?

Discourse 'Living Enlightenment', Los Angeles, Nithyananda Poornima 2007

Then how can I have dreams?' That night I clearly remember that when I was having a dream, I said to myself in my dream, 'I cannot have dreams because Annamalai Swamigal does not have dreams.' You will be surprised... The dream just disappeared!

The inner space was so thorough, so innocent, and so direct, that it just happened. Even if I felt cold or very warm, I would ask myself, 'How would Annamalai Swamigal feel in such a situation? He won't bother. Then I too won't bother. There were no further questions or arguments inside.

In your life also, to get out of the *kaarana shareera*, this is the most direct and powerful technique. In any situation, think 'How will the Master respond? How will the Master face this situation?' You will see that a new door opens out of nowhere! This is what I call 'Living Enlightenment'.

You don't need anything else. This one thing is enough. Even if you are sitting, if thoughts come up, think to yourself, 'If Master was sitting here, what would be coming up? Naturally silence. Then why am I thinking? Silence!' Over! Nothing else is needed. If your mind steps in and says, 'No, no! I know it's true. I know it, but it is too much.' Then think, 'If Master's mind says this, how would He respond to it?' He would have just finished the mind off at that moment! That's all, nothing else.

Take this one message with you and let this message become the very life in you - the message of Living Enlightenment. Actually, this is what I call 'relationship with Master' as well. Relationship with the Master is not just doing some *puja* or offering some flowers to Him or worshipping Him once in a while.

Feeling connected to Master means just living **Him**. When you *live* the Master, you feel connected to Him. Only then you are expanding also. Only then something is happening to you. Otherwise, you are just a schizophrenic person. You will have ten different faces. Sometimes you will behave nicely. Sometimes you will behave rudely. Sometimes you will be with lust. Sometimes you will be in a worshipping mood.

Just integrate yourself. No *kaarana* or reason should be told. Just allow the whole body and mind to imbibe the energy, spirit and inspiration of the Master. It should go so deep into your inner space that while dreams start coming in, you should say, 'Would Master have dreams? No. Then relax.' It should go that deep into your inner space! And it is perfectly possible also. When this starts happening, many times you will see that you are aware within your dream itself!

One person came to me and told me, 'Master, I had a dream that a ghost was trying to catch me. Within the dream, I remembered you, and suddenly the ghost left.' This means that even inside the dream, the faith that the Master will save you has gone inside. When that can go inside, this can also go inside! It is not that in the dream a ghost will catch you. The dream itself is a ghost which will catch you!

Carry this one message: 'How will the Master behave in this particular situation?' Any problem can be solved with this one thought. Anything in the internal world can be solved, because Paramahamsa is a person who knows all the possible experiences one can undergo on planet Earth. Only such a person can be called Paramahamsa. If he is not aware of a particular experience, Existence makes him go through that experience so that he becomes a Paramahamsa. So whatever you go through, or went through, or are yet to go through, I have gone through already. Understand that. So there is no space that you can say I have not gone through!

MEDITATION

Now let us enter into the layer of darkness.

Sit straight. Throw out all the colors that are there in your mind. Keep only darkness in your mind. You have to chant

227

the *ooooo kara* – the *ooooo* sound. Understand, it is not *Om* or *Hoooom*. It is just *ooooo*.... You will continually push the air out as much as possible. Don't bother about breathing in. Just keep pushing air out continuously by chanting this as deeply as possible. By pushing the air out, the body will breathe by itself. Take a small breath in, and then chant *ooooooooo*. In the small gap that is there between the final exhalation and the next short inhalation, the body will take in air by itself. So, put all the effort to just throw out the air with the *oooo* sound. Throw everything out totally.

I will guide you through the meditation. You will be made to visualize a dark cave, a dark cave inside which you are sitting and meditating. Then you will be able to enter into the layer of darkness.

So, please sit with your eyes closed and tie your eye bands.

Start chanting the *ooooo kara*

Put your whole effort on only exhaling; just exhale. Throw out all your *prana* (Life giving energy), life, everything... just throw them out.

(After 20 minutes)

Stop.

With all your effort, keep exhaling through the nose. Do not intone any sound. Just exhale.

(After 5 minutes)

Stop.

Visualize a deep and big forest wherein there is a deep and dark cave. You are sitting inside the cave. Visualize all the walls of the cave. It is a cave within a single rock. The ceiling of the cave is also rock surface. There is just a deep darkness - soothing, relaxing and joyful darkness; comfortable darkness.

Totally comfortable and secure with the darkness, you are alone, sitting and meditating. Feel the darkness. It is covered by layers of darkness over darkness. Darkness is totally drowned in darkness.

You are just in your mother's womb, the same comfortable darkness of your mother's womb. Feel the utter relaxation, the utter rest, with no responsibilities, only total, comfortable, peaceful darkness. You are sitting inside the dark cave and meditating on the darkness. Feel the cave. Visualize yourself inside the cave. Visualize that you are comfortably sitting and meditating on the deep darkness. You only know one word: darkness... darkness... darkness.

Inside the cave you are connected to the darkness of the universe, the darkness from which the universe was born - the darkness of your mother's womb from which you were born. You are just filled with that live darkness. There is no other thought except darkness. Become the darkness. Feel that the whole thing is just darkness. Your body has disappeared in the darkness. Penetrate into the deeper and deeper layers of darkness. Just become pitch black darkness, nothing else.

The whole space is filled with thick darkness. The darkness is much more intense and dense than the Earth itself. Just taste the experience of the deep and peaceful darkness.

(After a few minutes)

Om Nithyanandam.

Relax. You can open your eyes.

Please carry this darkness with you for the next half hour - the darkness of your mother's womb, the darkness that is the deep comfort. Rest and relax in the darkness of no responsibility, only freedom. Carry this darkness of rest and relaxation with you until the next session. Avoid speaking to anyone. Do not look more than four feet in front of you. Try to look down at the ground. Carry this peaceful darkness with you.

SHARING FROM AN NSP PARTICIPANT...

After the NSP, I really understood how to face fear. It was such an exhilarating feeling. As I was driving back one day, a vehicle suddenly veered in my direction. Normally I would have had my heart in my mouth, but to my very pleasant surprise, I remained very calm and negotiated the vehicle. There was no panic; it was such a huge relief. I must admit, this has remained with me to this day. Even if some child or vehicle comes across my path while I am at the wheel, I don't panic unconsciously.

After the NSP, the feeling was just like as if you have been unchained, unfettered and are flying. Looking back, I think it was not so much the content as being in His presence that transformed me. One experience of the NSP is the consciousness of sleep. During the darkness meditation, I was clearly able to be aware that I am floating on thoughts and the next morning, Swami asked, 'Do you now know that what you thought of as sleep is actually floating on thoughts?'

The overall experience of the NSP is that it took me deeper into another dimension; one that I did not even suspect existed.

Sri Nithyananda Sajeeva
Businessman, Mysore

CHAPTER 8

Cosmic Body

The cosmic layer is the sixth energy layer. This is the body of pleasure. This is what is perceived as heaven. The very energy from this layer expresses itself as pleasure. Whenever the energy emanates from this body, it expresses itself and you feel pleasure, you feel joy. It is a very deep layer; that is why you feel it very subtly.

But this energy, when it comes out, has to cross the pain layer to come out, so you will always find that your pleasure will have a coating of pain! That is why, when you are enjoying something, you will always feel, 'When will this enjoyment disappear?' And because of this, you will not enjoy it fully also.

This is why our joy and pleasure always seems contaminated. Our pleasure has to travel through the pain and the guilt layers. That is why it is contaminated.

IN THE GAP LIES THE REAL JOY!

Actually if you see, the moments of happiness or joy happen when the mind stops. This may happen for just a few moments, but the impressions and the relaxation from dropping of the mind will be tremendous. When I say the mind stops, I mean, the mind gives a gap sometimes. For example, when you see nature you will be capturing thousands of scenes continuously. But at one point in time, the mind will give a gap. It is this gap that becomes an unforgettable memory!

Let me tell you an incident from my life.

> This was during my wandering days before enlightenment. I was walking from one city to another in India. On the way to a place called Omkareshwar, there is a thick jungle and a river flowing between the two hillocks that are completely made of marble stone. Between the two hillocks, the sacred river Narmada flows.
>
> On a full moon night, I was just walking with a stick in my hand, rotating the stick and singing to myself. I was walking alongside the river. I was going down a small valley, and when I reached its end, I looked up and saw a big cliff in front of me. I saw on both sides, the two big hillocks shining in the full moon. Because it is white marble, it was simply shining in the moonlight!
>
> The river was so beautifully flowing with a mild murmur. Suddenly I saw that both the hillocks were bridged! There was a physical connection between them in mid air. I went a bit near and saw that the whole thing was a honeycomb! The honeycomb was at least 400 feet long!
>
> When I saw that, in just one moment, my mind gave a gap. Even now, I can see that moment. It was so ecstatic! I can remember that moment as such indescribable joy. Both the hillocks were simply connected! And the moment I perceived that, the mind gave a gap. Whenever you disappear into the nature, this often happens.

Touch The Deep Core of Pain - Go Through to Something New

Let me tell you another incident from my life.

I was on the banks of the Narmada river in Omkareshwar again – the place where Shankara became enlightened.

I had done many, many types of *tapas* (penance) and tried different types of meditation techniques. Actually, I literally killed myself with these meditation techniques. Finally, a very sudden and deep depression landed on me. I had a deep feeling of being cheated and thought to myself: for the sake of enlightenment I have left my family. Whatever has to be done according to the *Vedic* scriptures, almost everything has been done. But still, it is not happening. Only days are passing.

One day suddenly, maybe in the evening at around four, I felt excruciating pain along with the deep depression. I felt that nothing more could be done, that there is no need to live anymore, because whatever has to be done is done. I thought that either I had to become enlightened or I had to die. I never spent any time in my life earning money or learning how to live. I don't even know how to live! Even now I can't count. I can't count numbers too far. I never learned anything towards life, so I thought either I had to become enlightened or I had to die.

I was convinced that the whole idea of enlightenment was just a concept. I thought it was never going to happen in my life. I felt that at least there is no possibility for it in my life. So I decided, 'Let me commit suicide.' It was such an excruciating pain that made me decide to commit suicide.

I entered the Narmada river - a very powerful and aggressive river. Between the two hillocks, it runs - very deep and powerful. It has big falls as well. I thought, 'Let me commit suicide. It is not going to be any more than two or three minutes. I will be flooded away.'

I started walking. When the water started coming up to my hip, in the terrible fear, I just shut my eyes tightly and continued walking. I continued walking and walking. I could feel the water continuously rising. At one point, I felt my breath to be very painful. I was breathing the pain inside, the suffering inside.

I was breathing the pain inside. So much of pain had gone inside and at one moment, something hit me. Suddenly something broke. When the breath came out, it came out as complete bliss!

But I found that I was continuing to go inside the river. I was just moving. Since I had my eyes tightly closed, I don't know how much distance I would have walked. When the breath came out with bliss, I felt completely rejuvenated. It was as if the whole of life had entered me. I fell down and saw that I was on the other shore! I do not know what had happened. What I am telling you is the simple truth.

I do not know what had happened in between… Whether I walked through the water, or I walked on the pebbles and rocks, I don't know. I thought that maybe the river is shallow in the part that I walked, but I heard from at least fifty people that it is not less than 200 feet. I don't even know swimming till date. When I fell on the ground, I saw that I was on the other shore, that's all.

Suddenly, I could very clearly feel that Narmada was laughing at me. The river Narmada is considered a virgin girl. She has always been considered to be a virgin girl. I very clearly felt she was laughing at me!

I wanted to share this experience just to tell you that when you touch the deep core of pain, you will see that bliss opens in you!

FAITH IS YOUR ANTIDEPRESSANT

Deepak Chopra says 90% of the people who live with the faith in God live in a more joyful and happy way. They have much less depression than those who had no faith in God. Even if the concept of God cannot be proved by spiritual people, even if the faith in God is only a hypothesis, it helps you to live with tremendous joy and happiness. He says that even if it is a hypothesis, it is perfectly alright because it supports life and joyful living. It makes living on the planet Earth much satisfying.

You drink because you wish to escape from yourself. Man pours to fill; women eat and fill. Men drink, women eat. Addiction to food is because you feel empty inside. Once you understand the purposelessness of what you do, you will lose these addictions.

When you wake up in the morning, just laugh! If you cannot feel free to laugh in your own home, where else can you laugh! Laugh at how purposeless everything is. Release yourself from the nagging restlessness. There is no need to sell your inner space to have outer space. You can retain joy inside and still have the outer space to enjoy.

MEDITATION

What can be the best meditation to work on the layer of happiness? Just laughing... that's all.

If you laugh continuously for 42 minutes, you will get enlightened.

-Zen Buddhism

The laughter we are talking about is not just the plastic smile we wear on our faces most of the time. It is not social laughter. It is uninhibited, complete laughter with your whole being. Every cell, every nerve fiber, should vibrate with the laughter.

You must have heard of the Laughing Buddha. It is common to see the Laughing Buddha statue in many houses as a good luck show piece. This Laughing Buddha used to go from village to village and all he used to do was stand up on the village square and start laughing. His laughter was so total that not only his belly, but his whole body used to shake with laughter. Just seeing him laugh, all the villagers who were gathered watching would start laughing! Within minutes the entire village would be roaring with laughter. In the gaps in the laughter, when the mind was choicelessly still, the consciousness of the village would be simply uplifted! Without a single word uttered, the entire village would be in meditation. Such is the simple but extremely powerful meditation of laughter.

Laughing is what works directly on the bliss within you. It is laughing that brings out the bliss energy. It breaks the solidified layers, melts them and spreads the energy throughout the body.

So in this meditation, you have to laugh till I say 'Stop!'

Sit down and close your eyes. Start breathing. Breathe as deeply as possible. Start laughing.

(A few minutes pass)

Relax.

This is such an energy giving meditation! You can experience the real heartfelt laughter, the full belly laughter. Laughing is the forgotten language. The Master's laughter is of an entirely different quality. It is the laughter of a child. It is innocent laughter. Actually, in laughter, you and the Master, both of you meet. Laughter puts you in touch with the very core of your being - eternal bliss, *nithya ananda*.

CHAPTER 9

The Initiation: Be Un-Clutched

This session's subject is about how to be un-clutched, the science of inner bliss. What do I mean by the words, 'Be un-clutched'?

THE IDENTITY GAME

We have two identities: one which we show to the outer world and the other, which we believe as the inner world. The identity which we project to the outer world, is how we want society to recognize us, how we want society to respect us. In Sanskrit, we use the word *ahankar* for this. The identity which we project to the outer world is *ahankar*. Usually it will always be a little more than what we are. The identity which we believe in the inner world, as we are, is *mamakar*, which will always be lesser than what we are. *Ahankar* will always be a little more than what we are, and *mamakar* will always be a little less than what we are.

On the outside we will always be projecting a little more than what we are. Inside, we will always be concluding a little less than what we are. This is what we call the superiority complex and the inferiority complex.

Our life is nothing but the fight between these two worlds. If you are spending your whole energy expanding your *ahankar*,

241

the identity which you project to the outer world, your life will become materialistic. If you are spending your whole life chiseling and developing the *mamakar*, the identity which you think is *you*, your whole life becomes moralistic, suppressing.

Working in the outer world with *ahankar*, and working in the inner world with *mamakar*, both lead to only more and more suffering, more and more depression.

The person who works on *ahankar*, on trying to prove to others, on trying to develop the identity which he shows to the outer world, ends up in depression of success around the age of 40 or 45. What I mean is, you will have achieved all that you wanted to achieve, but you will feel depressed not knowing what for you wanted to achieve it.

The basic truth is that you are much more than these two identities of *ahankar* and *mamakar* that you carry. You are beyond the identity which you project to the outer world, and the identity which you believe as you in the inner world. You are beyond these two.

Figure 14: Water Bubbles

This is the truth. When you un-clutch from these two identities, suddenly you realize, you are beyond these two; these two can never bind you.

PAIN SHAFT OR PLEASURE SHAFT

Let me expand on the word 'un-clutching'. What do I mean by the word 'un-clutching'? As of now, constantly you are connecting all your thoughts and creating shafts in your mind. For example, the headache which happened in you ten years ago, the headache which happened nine years ago, the headache which happened eight years ago and the headache which happened yesterday, are all independent experiences which happened in your life. For the sake of nurturing memory, or for the sake of easy reference, you put all these headache experiences together in your mind. You store all these memories in one area in your mind. You archive it this way just for utility, just for reference. But by and by you start believing that they are really connected!

In the initial level, you archive them for the sake of easy reference. Just like how you file your office work, you archive these incidents also. You put them all in one file. After some time you start believing that all those experiences are connected.

The suffering which happened ten years ago happened for a different reason, for a different purpose, and it was a different place and totally different experience as well. The suffering which happened nine years ago was for a totally different reason. It was also a different experience. The suffering which happened eight years ago was for a different reason, for a different purpose, and in a different place. When you start believing they are connected, you create a shaft. If you connect all the painful memories, you create a pain shaft. You think, 'My life is suffering. My life is pain.' You start believing that your whole life is a chain of suffering, a long chain of suffering.

When you start believing that your whole life is suffering, you have created a pain shaft, and you will wait in your life only for painful incidents so that you can elongate this shaft. You start looking to develop that shaft.

One more thing you should understand is that whatever you believe in or not, that you expand. If you believe something, you will again and again see that same thing happening in your life. That is why again and again, *Vedic rishis* say you create and see what you want to see, not what *is*. You create what you want. Whatever you believe, you will create it and expand it.

Once you start believing that your life is painful, you are waiting unconsciously for painful incidents to happen, in order to strengthen that belief, to strengthen your judgment. We don't usually collect arguments to pass judgments; we collect arguments to *support* our judgments. The judgment is ready; we only collect arguments to support it.

When you are clear that your life is a pain shaft, a big chain of essentially unrelated pains, you are waiting for some more incidents to support your faith, more judgments to support your belief. A person who believes that life is a pain shaft will unconsciously create and elongate the pain shaft.

Second thing: whenever you are adding painful incidents unconsciously, consciously you will be trying to break the shaft also.

Sometimes you believe that your whole life is a chain of joyful experiences. Of course, usually we don't believe life to be this way, but just assume this for now. It is very rare to believe that your life is a shaft of joyful experiences. If you do, then constantly you are in fear, thinking, 'will it continue?' You think, 'will it continue in the same way?'

Understand clearly that if you believe life is a shaft of pain, you do two things: unconsciously you gather more and more incidents and strengthen your faith, and consciously you try to break it, fighting to stop it. On the contrary, if you believe that it is a joyful chain, unconsciously you will be in fear that it will end, and consciously you will try to prolong it.

Understand these two big dramas that happen in us. When you believe it is a pain shaft, you try to break it consciously. When you believe it is a joy shaft, you try to elongate it consciously. But the big difficulty, the important thing that we forget, is that you can neither break the shaft nor elongate it because the shaft itself does not exist!

The shaft does not exist. When you started archiving all the incidents from your life for the sake of easy reference, by and by you started believing that they are existentially connected. You connected all the incidents of your life for the sake of utility. But after some time, you start believing that they are existentially connected to each other and believe your life to be either a pain shaft or a joy shaft. When you start believing it as a pain shaft, you try to break it. When you believe it to be a joy shaft, you try to elongate it. But one important thing you forget is, you can neither break nor elongate the shaft, because the shaft itself does not exist!

It's only your faith, or your belief which makes these things happen.

YOUR MIND IS NOTHING BUT ILLOGICAL, INDEPENDENT, UNCONNECTED, AND UN-CLUTCHED THOUGHTS

So many thoughts are flowing in your mind constantly.

Try this: sit for ten minutes and write down all your thoughts without editing them, without judging them, just as if a transcribing software is connected to your mind. Then read what you have written. You will understand that all your thoughts, whatever is moving in you, are illogical, independent, completely unconnected and un-clutched thoughts! Try to do this in your house when you are relaxed. Just sit and pen down whatever is going on in your mind.

If you start judging your mind while writing, you will interrupt the natural flow of thoughts. If you start judging your thoughts, you are actually teaching your mind to play a hypocritical game with you. Whenever you judge your kids and express your judgment to them, you are actually teaching them to hide things from you, that's all.

Do not judge. Just plainly see what is going on, and pen the whole thing down. Then, read what you have written. You will understand that your thoughts are illogical, independent, unconnected and un-clutched. You would be sitting here and thinking, 'I think I should go to the office tomorrow.' The very next moment you would think, 'I need to go to Australia to settle that deal this week.' Then the next moment, you would think, 'I wish I could attend my kid's annual day celebrations.' Is there any correlation between your office, Australia and your kid's annual day celebrations? No!

Your thoughts are just like water bubbles in the fish tank. They just appear and disappear.

If you look a little deeply, suddenly you will understand, that by your very nature you are un-clutched. There is a gap between one thought and another thought, just like how there are gaps between the water bubbles in the fish tank. But the gaps are too small; you are not able to perceive them and so it looks like a continuous stream to you. Although they are independent bubbles coming out of the same source, they look like a stream to you.

In the same way, if you look a little deeply into your thoughts, you will realize that your thoughts by their very nature are independent. For example, if you see a dog on the street, suddenly you will remember the pet you used to play with when you were a child. Then you will remember your teacher you taught you when you were a child. Next, you will remember the house where your teacher used to live. If you look at it logically, you will see that the dog in street and the teacher are not connected. There is no logical connection between the two, but your mind simply flows with thoughts like these. If you look a little deeply, you will understand that your thoughts are illogical, independent, unconnected and un-clutched. But the problem is, you can't live in this wilderness. You can't live with this natural flow because you need a clear-cut idea about everything. So you pick up your thoughts and connect them in the way in which you wish to. If you believe that life is joy, you pick up all the joyful thoughts and connect them. If you believe that your life is pain, you pick up all the painful thoughts and connect them to create a shaft of pain.

Whatever you believe about life, thoughts related to that, you pick up and create a shaft. If you see what is going on in your mind, it will be an illogical mixture of pain, joy and every other emotion possible. Not only that but the depths of the thoughts will be so different that you will not be able to make any logical statements about them! You will not be able to come to any logical conclusion about them. As such, what is happening is, that completely illogical, independent, unconnected and un-clutched thoughts are just emanating from your mind, that's all. What you do is, you collect all your painful memories and create a pain shaft, or collect all joyful experiences and create a joy shaft.

Not only that, you start firmly believing in the shaft as well. Then, the trouble starts, because you will try to elongate or break the shaft, but you will not be able to it. You can neither elongate it nor break it because the shaft does not exist; because by your very nature, you are un-clutched! By your very nature, you are an un-clutched being. But societal conditioning causes you to create these shafts. There starts the conflict between your genuine nature and that which is created by your mind.

By Nature, You Renounce Your Thoughts Every Moment

You need to understand an important thing about renouncing: you don't need to renounce any thing. People come and ask me, 'Should I renounce everything to achieve enlightenment?'

I tell them, 'Don't renounce what you have. Just renounce what you don't have. That's enough!'

You carry so many things that you don't actually have, like your fantasies and your fears. Greed gives rise to fantasy, and fear itself is nothing but negative fantasy. We are living with so many things that we don't really have. Our fantasies, our fears, our worries - all of these things that we are living with, we don't really have. They are creations of our mind.

So just renounce what you don't have. That is enough. Then automatically, whatever you have, you will live with. Understand, the shaft which you have created for yourself is the original sin that you have committed. By connecting thoughts, by clutching into your thoughts, you commit the first sin.

Understand that by your very nature, you are an un-clutched being. By your very nature, you are an unconnected, independent, causeless being! You don't need to renounce anything because by nature you cannot hold on to anything. It is only when your mind plays up, you start thinking that you need to renounce many things. Actually you can't hold on to things even if you wish to. People come and tell me, 'I am so depressed. I don't know how to come out of it.' I tell them, 'Just try to hold on to it!' You will not be able to!

For half an hour, sit and try to hold on to the depression. You will see that you can't. Try your best to sit and meditate on your depression. Suddenly you will come back and tell me that you are not able to meditate on it any more because it is not there!

249

By your very nature you are un-clutched. What do I mean by this? You see, any thought will come up only if the previous thought has died. No two thoughts can co-exist. Until the earlier thought is renounced, you can't have a new thought. The fact that a new thought is happening in you proves that the earlier thought has been renounced. Fortunately you can't have two thoughts at the same time. Even if you suspect you are schizophrenic, meaning you have contradictory thoughts within you all the time, you can't have two thoughts at the same time.

All these ideas such as 'unconscious', 'split personality', 'schizophrenia', etc are modern day sins. In those days, the priests gave life to the concept of sin to create guilt in you and rule you. In the same way, the psychologists and psychiatrists created these words such as unconscious, split personality, schizophrenia, etc to aid in their profession. Understand: these are all the modern day terms to exploit you, nothing else.

This might be shocking to you because you always believed that there is something called the unconscious, that there is something called split personality, there is something called schizophrenia, etc. But just look a little deep inside, and you will understand, the very fact that you are having new thoughts means that the earlier thoughts have been renounced. It is similar to trashing your emails. But the problem is, you also decide to pick up your emails back from the trash!

Every moment thoughts are being renounced by you, by your very nature. Whenever a new thought appears in you, it means that the old thought has been renounced. But even after renouncing, you try to pick up the thoughts from the trash can and create a new shaft. It's like you feel that some valuable thoughts have been dropped in the trash can and so you pick up some thoughts from it. You pick them up and put them near your bed. You also spray a little perfume on it to keep it a little nice. You try to decorate it.

Just do a few basic things to get liberated from this life and death cycle.

First, have a clear understanding that you are creating a shaft, a shaft of pain, or shaft of joy, and trying to fight with it, by either trying to elongate it or break it.

Second: don't even think that you have to un-clutch yourself. By your very nature, you are an un-clutched being. So stop creating a shaft, and you are un-clutched.

You don't need to un-clutch. People come and ask me how long it takes to teach meditation. It takes only two words: be un-clutched. To teach what is *not* meditation takes one or two years for me. To teach what is meditation takes only one minute. You don't need to learn meditation. All you need to do is stop creating the shaft.

Constantly you are creating the shaft: the pain shaft or the joy shaft. And you think your mind is flowing with a certain logic. When you stop creating the shaft, suddenly you will realize you are un-clutched by your very nature.

The moment people hear this truth, they feel shaken. They think, 'What will happen to my ego if I un-clutch? What will happen to my property, my wealth, my name and fame, and all that I created based on my outer world and my ego?

What will happen to my 'feeling of mine', my holy personality which I created by my penance, discipline, mediation and all those things? What will happen to 'I' and 'mine' if I remain un-clutched? When you have a great amount of vested interest in your 'I' and 'mine', when you are holding on to too many things based on 'I'and 'mine', then it is very difficult to understand you are un-clutched by your very nature.

INTELLECT VS WEALTH

Try your best to create something based on *ahankar* - 'I', and feel fulfilled; you will never be able to. In the same way, try your best to create something on your *mamakar* – 'mine', and feel fulfilled; you will never be able to. There is a story of Brahma and Vishnu searching for the head and foot of Lord Shiva respectively. This incident is part of a mythological recording. It happened in my native place, Tiruvannamalai where the sacred Arunachala hill is. It is a spiritual nerve centre. I call that place a spiritual incubator. Just like how premature babies need an incubator to supply air and all the basic things, so also for enlightened beings   to land on the planet Earth, you need a spiritual incubator to protect and help them, and allow the whole expansion to happen before they settle down in their body. Tiruvannamalai is such a spiritual incubator.

> The story says Brahma had to find Shiva's head and Vishnu was asked to find His feet. If you know the background of Brahma and Vishnu, you will be able to see how beautiful the story is. Who is Brahma? He is the husband of Saraswati. Saraswati is the Goddess of learning or knowledge, symbolically signifying intellect or the head or the 'I' - *ahankar*.

Who is Vishnu? Vishnu is the husband of Lakshmi, Goddess of wealth, symbolically signifying possession or the 'mine' - *mamakar*. The story says Brahma started searching for the head, the *sahasrara* of Shiva. Vishnu started searching for the feet.

Vishnu came back after some time and said, 'I am not able to find Your feet. Please forgive me. I realize no one will be able to find it either.' He understood the truth and surrendered.

But Brahma who was going upwards to find Shiva's head, continued. Suddenly, he came across a flower (called *Tazhampoo* in Tamil) which was falling downwards from Shiva's ear. He learnt from it that it had been traveling for four ages of Brahma in order to reach this point of travel. Brahma realized the futility of his own mission but did not want to accept the situation. He requested the flower to come as a false witness to Shiva to say that Brahma had seen the head of Shiva. The flower agreed. Brahma went to Shiva with the flower and the story. Shiva at once knew the truth and got angry. He cursed Brahma and the flower for lying. Later, when Brahma understood his mistake and surrendered, Shiva graced the two of them.

You need to understand the story well. Vishnu is the embodiment of wealth, Brahma of intellect - *ahankar* and *mamakar*, that is, I and mine. **Neither by wealth nor by intellect you can achieve enlightenment...** that's the truth of the story.

One important thing, if you dig in the line of wealth, *mamakar*, you will get frustrated like Vishnu. You will face the depression of success and you will become so humble. You will fall only to understand the truth. You will surrender easily if you dig in the line of *mamakar*. Very soon you will realize that wealth cannot take you to God. That is why Vishnu surrendered so quickly to Shiva in the story. That is the real significance of choosing Vishnu, beholder of wealth for this role.

On the other hand, the intellect is so strong like Brahma, that you will not only be unable to find Shiva, you will not be willing to surrender either! But once you complete your ego trip, and discover the futility of the intellect, you receive the Divine grace.

If you travel in the line of *mamakar*, in the outer world, at least at one point in time, you will understand, and you will experience the depression of success and turn towards spirituality. You will say, 'Enough. Let me rest. I understand that enlightenment can never be achieved in this line.'

But the person who travels in the line of *ahankar*, the line of intellect, not only does he not achieve, he will not even be able to understand that he *cannot* achieve. The intellect or the ego becomes so sharp, and so subtle, that he will cling on to false claims and false techniques to declare that he has achieved it. Those false claims are the *Tazhampoo* flowers, the false witnesses!

The person who travels in *ahankar* in the outer world, who projects his identity in the outer world as well as the person who travels in *mamakar*, who projects his identity in the inner world, both will not be able to understand the truth.

'SELF-DEVELOPMENT' IS NOT POSSIBLE

Almost all these self development techniques are done to give you the feel-good feeling; nothing but the feel-good feeling.

First thing: understand that your self can't be developed because it doesn't exist the way you think it does. Try your best. I have conducted hundreds of self development programs. With that authority I am telling you this. With that clarity I am speaking.

I can give you some simple tips and techniques to develop your own self-development program. All you need to do is make sure that the person who is attending the program should feel good for two to three days, that's all. You are successful, nothing else is necessary.

There are best sellers on how to maintain relationships, how to influence others, how to stop worrying and start living etc. These books talk about how to live happily with your wife, how to stop suicidal tendencies. But you will be shocked to hear, that the authors of these books themselves would have committed suicide in their lives, or would have had the most unhappy of marriages!

In order to write best sellers or to deliver a self-development program, it is very easy. Just three tips are enough. Write what you can't practice! Second: write it in such a way that you will only talk about the problem. Third: never give a solution! Just with these three tips, you can become a self-development guru. Nothing else is necessary. Write what you can't practice; try to complicate it as much as possible; never give a solution. These three are more than enough.

You see, your self can't be developed because it does not exist. If you have done enough of spiritual practices you will understand what I am saying. Second, if you have done enough of techniques to keep you in one shaft, be it verbalizing or visualizing, then you will understand what I am trying to say. Verbalization means chanting *mantras*. Visualization means meditating on various forms. If you have tried any of these intensely, you will understand the truth of what I am expressing. If you have not tried, then please try.

If you have tried enough, understand the truth that by your very nature, you can't connect things and create a shaft. I have seen people who chant *mantras* for 30 or 40 years and they come and ask me how to concentrate on the *mantra*; how long it will take to make their mind settle down and focus on the *mantra*. I tell them, I am not sure how long it will take, but I am sure that it is surely not going to happen in this life! Understand, it is very difficult to connect and keep to one line. You are fortunate that you can't be clutched! You should feel fortunate that you are by nature un-clutched. It is like this: while by your very nature you are un-clutched, you try to clutch and cause misery to yourself! One more thing is that since by your very nature you are un-clutched, you can't be in bondage also. You come under the clutches of bondage only because you forcibly clutch onto people and relationships. Each person and each interaction is independent. That's all. You form a shaft and make the relationship also one of pain or joy and fall into bondage because of that.

If you worked too much in the outer world creating more and more wealth, the idea that you are un-clutched by your very nature comes as a big shock to you! You start thinking that you can no longer attend to your outer world duties. If you had been pursuing the inner world, you may start thinking, 'If I am un-clutched, then what will happen to all the spiritual practices I did? If I am un-clutched, then why did I do so many meditation techniques; why did I do so much of penance? Why did I control myself to keep such discipline? What have I done? What am I doing? Is everything useless?'

So now we have a big problem. If we understand and accept the truth that we are un-clutched, all the work that you did based on your *ahankar* and *mamakar*, becomes useless! Understand: whether you believe it or not, it is useless. Nothing can be done about it. You can strongly believe again and again that it is not true. You can try and cover yourself up with all sorts of lies to dodge the truth, but whether you believe it or not, understand it or not, by your very nature you are un-clutched. You *are* un-clutched.

BEYOND IDENTITIES

You need to understand only these two things: the identity which you are showing to the outer world and inner world - both are not what you actually are. You are much more than these two. Second thing: you don't even need to renounce these two identities because by your very nature you are un-clutched from these two identities!

When you constantly believe you are connected to these two identities, you start working to identify with them. When you want to disconnect from these two, you start working to un-clutch from them. Both are not necessary because you neither need to strengthen them them nor un-clutch from them, because by your very nature you are un-clutched!

What do I mean by again and again saying you are un-clutched? Let me explain. Let us say that you are sitting. The moment you decide to stand up, it means that you have renounced the thought of sitting. The moment you decide to walk out, it means that you have renounced the thought of sitting and listening. The very fact that a new thought has appeared, itself means that the old thought has been renounced. This is what I mean when I say that by your very nature you are un-clutched. You cannot have two thoughts at the same time! That is why I say that by nature you renounce the first thought when the second comes and so on. By nature you are a renouncer! You don't need to make any effort to renounce. Fortunately that is the way you have been designed by Existence! If you understand this, it is enough. Just the mere understanding will cause you to stop picking up thoughts back from the trash can. You will also understand that you don't even need to renounce both your identities because the identities which you are carrying are anyway not you!

When you understand this, suddenly there will be so much space available in you to yourself! The moment you understand that you are beyond these two identities, the tremendous inner healing will start happening in you. You start accepting yourself. The moment you understand you can't develop yourself anymore in the way you were thinking, and that you are much beyond the self you are thinking, you begin the ultimate self development process.

Someone goes to *Bhagavan* Ramana Maharishi and says, '*Bhagavan*, prescribe some spiritual practice for me.'

Bhagavan says, 'Meditate.'

The man goes away and after two years, he comes back and says, '*Bhagavan*, I am not able to meditate.'

The Initiation - Be Un-clutched!

Bhagavan says, 'You have achieved the results of meditation.'

The man says, 'I don't understand. I tell you that I am not able to meditate and you tell me that I have achieved the result of meditation.'

Bhagavan says, 'Understanding that you are not able to meditate is the result of meditation.'

Let me tell you an important business secret: techniques are given to people to make them understand that they are not able to practice them. It is very shocking, but it is the truth. Techniques are given to people to make them understand that they are not able to practice.

Of course, I myself give techniques and meditations to over one million people. More than one million people have been initiated. Let me be very clear: techniques are given to people so that they understand that they can't practice. What do I mean by this? As you practice, suddenly you will start realizing, there is something deeper. Ramana Maharishi says beautifully, 'You are asked to meditate to make you understand you can't!' You will realize that the more you struggle with the understanding that you can't, the deeper you will travel. All you need to do is understand this truth.

For spiritual practice or whatever words you may use, understanding that you are much more than two identities is the aim. Understand that you are not clutched; that is enough.

You may start asking 'How will I do my job if I am un-clutched? How will I take care of my things? Will I not just lie down in my bed?' Understand that the moment you ask these questions, it means that you have a little hatred or vengeance against your routine like your job, or taking care of your family. That is why, the moment you get an excuse, you want to escape from it!

By asking this question, you are merely expressing your anger or violence against your routine, nothing else. Everyone invariably harbours vengeance against their routine and responsibility. They will continue to play their role no doubt, but with a deep and subtle vengeance. That is the truth.

When people ask me if they can just leave everything and be un-clutched, I tell them, 'Alright, don't do anything. Just be un-clutched. Let us see for how many days you can lie in your bed!' How many days do you think you can lie in your bed? For ten days maybe? Maybe until your *tamas* (laziness) gets exhausted, you can lie down. Understand: you have a certain amount of *tamas* in you. Until your *tamas* gets exhausted you will lie there. But after that what will you do? Naturally you will start working. You will start moving!

So you don't have to be afraid that if you are un-clutched you will not do your daily routine. I tell you, what you think as *you* is not at all necessary to run your day to day life. This is the basic truth. What you think as *you* is not at all necessary to run your day to day life. This might hurt. But truth always hurts us.

See, our mind is such that if someone is happily independent of us, we can't tolerate it. It is too much to take. Constantly we should feel that we are needed. Understand, what you think as you is not at all necessary to run anyone's life or even your day to day life.

So let me summarise the truths that we have just discussed.

First thing: you are much more than these two identities of outer world and inner world that you are carrying in your life; the identity which you show to the outer world and the identity which you show to yourself.

The second thing is that you don't need to un-clutch, you are already un-clutched.

The third thing is that all you need to do is stop creating the shaft that you are constantly trying to create. Constantly you are referring to your past experiences of the same kind and connecting them and creating some idea. Constantly you are creating an idea about everything with the help of the shaft. You have around ten to twelve shafts of pain, joy, painful joy, joyful pain, etc., with which you simply play one after another. You just see the scence around you and pick up any one shaft and start to connect, that's all. All you need to do is stop connecting and creating shafts.

LIFE IS NOT A UTILITY

The problem is, you always think that life has to have utility. Two kinds of societies have been created. One believes that man will work and he can be controlled only if he is constantly taught that he is not enough. He can be made to work only if he is controlled through fear and greed.

The other group believes that man will express his energy if he is fulfilled. The focus is on making man feel fulfilled and then the expression of the energy does all the work! The Eastern *rishis* believe that man will express his energy to the maximum if he believes he is fullfilled. That is the first truth you are taught in Eastern mysticism, by the Eastern mystics: you are full and fulfilled.

When the Whole is removed from the Whole, the Whole remains as the Whole. This is the essence of man. It tells you to express yourself just out of your fullness and that if you do so, only your fullness will still remain! This is the truth of your existence. When the whole system operates from this truth, you don't run based on fear and greed. But the Western society, the Western social system, is made to believe that man will work only through fear and greed. That is why you are taught in your colleges and universities that life has got some utility and that you have to go behind that for fulfillment.

Please understand that life has got no utility. It has got a *purpose*, but not utility. Utility is when you live life and get some product out of it. Purpose is when you enjoy life and express the purpose of life, which is fulfillement! Purpose is entirely different from utility. In utility, you are constantly hypnotized into thinking that you are not enough unto yourself and that you need to achieve a product to attain fulfillment. But with the Eastern *rishis*, you are constantly taught that you are enough.

Understand, the Indian lifestyle, the *Vedic* lifestyle, is based on 10,000 years of research and development with more than ten million inner scientists. When I say inner scientists, I mean the *rishis* who were full time scientists, working in the inner world. 10,000 years of inner research and development, and at least ten million inner scientists are behind the technology and strength of the *Vedic* culture, and there is only 0.6 % registered psychiatric patients and 0.6% patients of depression.

We are talking about 10,000 years of research and development, 10 million inner scientists and inner science laboratories! Not only that, there are at least ten million ashrams and places where congregation – *satsang* – happens everyday! Everyday gatherings happen at temples and *satsang* centers in the name of spirituality. It is not a holiday religion, or weekend religion, or weekend congregation. It is an *everyday congregation*!

Even if you see the crime rate of people from the *Vedic* tradition, it is negligible. If you understand that you are full and express your fullness, your whole attitude will be one of pure compassion. You will attract more and more joyful experiences in your life. On the other hand, if you believe strongly you are not enough unto yourself and start running based on fear and greed, you will attract only more fear and greed experiences.

One more thing: by your very nature you will reproduce what you believe. Anything, if it has to survive, should reproduce itself. If you believe your life is running based on only fear and greed, you will reproduce fear and greed in yourself and in everyone else also. You will reproduce that same fear and greed in everybody you see.

When you think you can run only on fear and greed, you forget you can run gracefully, that you can live gracefully. If you are handling a child, and you say, 'Hey! Do this and I will give you candy,' or, 'If you don't do this, I will discipline you,' it is alright to a certain extent. Until the child stabilizes, it might be needed to once in a while wield the consequence. But after growing physically also, if you should be handled through fear and greed, it means you are mentally retarded. You have not grown.

A child can be handled with fear and greed, but *you* don't need fear and greed. When you ask the question, *what is the utility value in this?*, be very clear that what you are asking is based on fear and greed.

The more I travel outside India, the more love and respect I feel for the *Vedic* culture. I am not able to help myself in this regard. People ask me why I wear this *rudraksh* string, why I wear this *kumkum*, why I wear all these things. I tell you it is because simple things like these beads, and this *kumkum*, the great, enlightened Masters of the *Vedic* tradition have developed after 10,000 years of research and development! Nothing was ever done without proper research and development. They spent their whole lives and used their whole bodies as inner science laboratories, and did vast research and development.

Currency is beautiful and needed for life. But it is too poor a substitute for the explosion of your consciousness. You cannot run behind currency at the cost of your consciousness! It is beautiful to maintain your body and your mind. It is good to maintain your lifestyle, food, clothing, basic things etc. But I tell you, there is something much more than all this. There is something called your consciousness.

You are constantly taught to live a consumerist lifestyle so that you will be pulled to buy all the consumer products that are sold. It is a pure and effective marketing strategy. Your life is too precious to be wasted through somebody's marketing strategy. Your body cannot be used as someone else's income source. You are drilled with all sorts of ideas. Your entire software is programmed by them. Because of this, your hardware is spent in fulfilling their vested interest, that's all.

Let me clarify one thing: kids should not be handled through fear and greed. Only when you don't have the patience to explain, you use fear and greed. Not only that, only when *you* have fear and greed, you will create fear and greed in them. Understand: the person who is a leader for you, has he gone beyond fear and greed? No! Then what does it mean? It only means that he is expressing his fear and greed through his command.

Whatever frequency you live in, you will attract people of that frequency. You do this unconsciously so that you feel always comfortable and strong. So naturally, if you are in the fear and greed frequency, you will create the same type of fear and greed based people around you.

PAINFUL MEMORIES - HOW THEY GET REGISTERED

Painful memories get registered because you need to learn lessons. You need to update yourself, you need to develop yourself. Maybe for that reason you start recording the painful memories. When you refer to them again and again, it becomes a painful memory itself! Memories that you record in your system are not wholly true. You record only what you need.

Also, you don't need to renounce them. Whenever you try to renounce them, you actually strengthen the memory having to do with them. You don't need to create a law for yourself that you should not refer to your memory either, because by your sheer un-clutched nature, you will forget it the next moment. It will simply disappear! For example, the moment you decide to stand up, you renounce the decision to sit. Am I right? You are constantly renouncing. So if you allow the process to happen, your painful memories will simply disappear.

But by consciously trying to renounce them, you only strengthen further. They are strengthened when you try to renounce them. People come and tell me that they constantly repeat positive affirmations such as, 'I should stop smoking, I should stop smoking,' but it is not working. Why?' All these creative visualizations create only more and more trouble. Because in the very words, 'I should stop smoking,' the word 'smoking' is there as a contradicting word. You are not only empowering 'I shoud not', you are also empowering 'smoking'. That is why by repeating this so called affirmation you are unable to quit smoking!

When you decide 'I should get rid of this headache,' you are constantly remembering the word headache also. So what you need to do is this, whenever these memories rise, have a glass of water! The moment you decide to have a glass of water, your greed has disappeared; your fear has disappeared! But you say it comes back. How? Your faith in it is what brings it back; that is the basic problem.

You feel frustrated about it coming back. But if it comes back, it also means that it leaves you right? Why don't you then celebrate those moments when it left you? Why do you constantly remember only the moments it comes back? A young man came and asked me, 'I am suffering a lot because of my lustful thoughts and fantasies. What to do?' I told him, 'Just have a cup of coffee.' He was surprised. Unless the lustful thought has left you, you can't have a cup of coffee. You can't have the thought while having a cup of coffee. Only if it has left you, you can move to the coffee, but what do you do? You bring it back while you are having coffee. That is the problem.

It is so easy to renounce a thought. You ask me how it can be so simple! It *is* simple. The problem is that you are constantly taught that it is not so simple. If you really understand the whole process, it is so simple. Constantly people are telling you that it is not so easy. But I am telling you that it is so easy. Nothing needs to be done. Just a simple understanding is enough.

People come and tell me, 'I have a constant fear of death, what should I do?' I tell them to come and sit, and have a cup of tea. When they are having tea I ask them, 'What happened to the death fear?' For *that* moment, it is not there! So all you need to do is have tea. Understand what I am trying to convey through the tea. Your fear of death can be replaced with just the thought of having a cup of tea! That is all it is worth. But you empower it so much and allow it to wreck your life.

One elderly person - a well read scholar came to me and said, 'I am constantly searching for enlightenment. For the last 35 years, I have been searching. Please teach me meditation for enlightenment.' I sat down and started talking to him. I asked him about his family, where he is from and those types of things. He was with me for four hours. He did not even remember his first question again! He did not remember because his question had only that much depth. It did not come from his being. So just remember that your thoughts rarely have depth.

You see, all your negativity has only one power, and that is the faith you place on it, that's all. Understand that it is a simple game, that's all. You do not need to work for un-clutching. People ask me again and again why they fail when they try to un-clutch. I ask them why they are connecting their past failures with their present failures. When you connect your past failures, you create one more shaft: failure shaft.

The failure which happened nine years ago, the failure that happened eight years ago, and the failure that happened yesterday, are independent incidents. Why do you connect all of them and influence the experience that is yet to happen? Just relax and stop connecting, and suddenly you will see such deep inner healing happening in you, such deep peace happening in you. Suddenly you will see that you have dropped out of the war that was going on within you.

I tell you, when you become a drop out, when you drop out of this war, when you drop out from this whole game, suddenly you will realize that the whole thing is just a psycho drama that is happening. Because you are constantly supporting it, you are constantly creating these shafts.

Let us spend a few minutes un-clutching now. I will give you a few tips on this un-clutching, and you can just experience how this un-clutching works on you. If you have done some techniques earlier, you will see that this technique will straight away bring you to your inner space.

Now we will spend a few minutes un-clutching. Close your eyes. Just do not connect any words. Whatever words are rising in you just let them rise. Don't connect them with any other thought. Just don't create the shaft. Just un-clutch. If you feel bored, or if your mind asks what to do, just un-clutch from that thought also. Don't even connect with that thought. Just sit and be un-clutched. If your mind connects with a thought just un-clutch. Unclutch from both the identities. Do not create, maintain, or destroy any thought.

(After the meditation)

Om Nithyanandam.

You may open your eyes slowly.

CHAPTER 10

Nirvanic Body

The next layer is the *nirvanic* body. The Master lives in the *nirvanic* body. From the *atman* to the *nirvanic* body is where he lives. Only the *nirvanic* body and cosmic body can meet. No other layers can meet. You meet the Master in laughter. Laughter is like a bridge between you and the Master. It can transmit energy directly from the Master to you. When you sit in front of the Master and laugh, you can immediately feel the energy transfer happening.

The *nirvanic* layer is associated with bliss. It is so subtle that it almost doesn't exist. It is almost the *atman*, just the step before. What is the way to explore this last step? What is the way to bring out the energy of this last step? By totally cutting yourself from the past.

THE QUANTUM JUMP BEYOND

No evolution will help; only revolution will help. This moment of touching the *nirvanic* body is the moment when the seed takes the decision to sprout. When the seed is sprouting, the seed will experience agony. In Christianity, this is called as 'The dark night of the soul'. The moment when you take the decision to make the jump, you take the decision to go beyond. You take the decision with all your consciousness, with all your energy, to go beyond the body and mind.

When you realize that everything you are experiencing is just your own conditioning, you suddenly wonder, 'Is this life really worth living? So many desires, so many sufferings, so much of guilt, so much of pain... Only one layer of joy, and that also is through the layers of pain!'

Look at your whole past. Read what you have actually written. Almost for everybody, the past is more like a wound which needs to be operated upon, or thrown out from the being.

When you consciously decide to drop the past, you can actually drop it. Understand a few things: your past is simply your conditioning. When you understand it is the only conditioning, can't you drop it? As long as you think it is *you*, you can't drop it. But if you understand that it is your conditioning, you can simply drop it. When you psychologically drop it, even physically the whole thing will change! That is the beauty of it.

RELATING WITH THE MASTER - JUST LOVE

The *nirvanic* layer is the layer that the Master is always in. So how do we relate with the Master? When you come in front of the Master, just feel a deep love, that is all. Feel a deep love in front of him, that is enough. Nothing else is needed. Nothing else needs to be done. There is no other code of conduct to be followed.

Many people come in front of me and do all sorts of things like either showing off too much or displaying too much humility. The ones who show too much humility are the cunning ones. The really innocent ones will just come and sit on the seat on which I am sitting or just next to me! And I always find that

these innocent people are not only good to me, they are good to everybody. People who put up all sorts of show know only how to act, not how to be. So there is no need to know how to act, just be, that's enough.

A small story from Ramana Maharishi's life:

One farmer went to Ramana Maharishi's ashram and tried to sit with him. Because he had knee pain, he sat on a small stool. Some of the ashramites shouted, 'Oh, you cannot sit in front of *Bhagavan* on a stool. You are to sit only on the ground.' *Bhagavan* gestured to them and laughed. On the roof, a monkey was sitting right above Ramana's head. He asked, 'What will you do about this monkey? He is sitting right above my head!'

So understand that all these codes and protocols are just foolishness. I don't see any juice in it. When you can have tears of love, tears of gratitude in your eyes, that is the real thing. That is the real way to conduct yourself in the presence of the Master, nothing else is needed.

A Second Birth

If you really understand whatever is taught and whatever is spoken, will you be the same person when you go back? No! You will never be the same person. You can never be the same person. So naturally when you meet the Master, you will be reborn. You will have a second birth.

There are three types of *garbha* (womb). One is the *garbha* which is carried by the mother - which gives birth to a child. The next is the *hridgarbha*. If you carry a great ideology in your heart, if you give birth to a book, or a painting or a great scripture, these are all from your *hridgarbha*. If you carry the Master's presence or the deep gratitude in you, you give birth to yourself through *gnanagarbha* – the womb of wisdom. So the Master totally destroys your past. He makes you drop from your past, and gives you a new life.

Realize Your True Nature - The True Revolution

Only a total disconnection from the past can help you grow. There is no question of evolution, it is always only revolution. Evolution can never happen; only revolution can happen. So just drop from your past, just decide totally, consciously, and drop from your past. Don't think, 'Oh, I do not know how to put this whole thing into practice.' No! Simply throw the old personality out. Don't respect your old habits that threaten to come back. Don't respect the old body; don't respect the old mind; don't respect the old conditioning. Simply decide, 'This is how I am going to live from now onwards. This is the way I will live... over!'

Nirvanic Body

A small story, which is a very powerful story:

Once there was a rat in a king's palace. The king wanted to kill the rat.

One day he called his soldier and ordered him to kill it.

When the soldier entered the room, suddenly from somewhere the rat jumped on to his face. He lost his balance, got frightened and ran out of the room, shouting, 'No, no, no! Oh king, the rat is too big. I do not think the rat can be killed by anybody.'

Seeing the frightened, and shivering soldier, the king got frightened and thought, 'Oh, this rat is something totally different, I do not know what to do.'

He called the palace cat and ordered it to go and kill the rat.

The soldier told the cat, 'Don't think it is an ordinary rat. I went and was totally shaken, so be careful.'

Anyway the palace cat got ready with all his paraphernalia. He exercised for two to three days at the gym and took a special diet of food. On the day of the fight, he entered the room. Again the rat jumped on the cat's face. The cat got totally frightened, lost its balance and ran out.

Now, the rat became a challenge for the whole country. Even the palace cat could not do anything about it! So the king announced, 'Anybody who kills the rat will be given a special prize. So, many cats were brought. They tried to catch the rat but just couldn't.

In a remote village, an old man had a cat. He thought, 'Why not try my cat?' He asked the cat, 'Will you kill the rat in the king's palace?' The cat said, 'Why not? Let us go.'

The man brought the cat. It was a very lean cat. He let the cat inside the room. The cat simply killed the rat, and came out!

The king asked in utter disbelief, 'How did you do it? Even the palace cat could not do it! How did you have the courage? How did you do it?'

The cat replied, 'What? I am a cat. It is my nature to kill a rat. I just caught the rat, that's all!'

Understand that while your nature is so clean and straightforward, simply being influenced by past experiences and undue conditioning only makes you spoil your real nature. You always think, 'No, the last time I tried and things were a failure. Nothing worked. I think this time too, the same thing is going to happen.' Don't have all those past things in your memory. Even the idea 'the last time I failed' is past. Cut it from the very root. Drop from the very root of the past.

Someone came and told me, 'Swamiji, last year alone, I stopped smoking 27 times!' Just imagine. Understand: it is you who gives energy to the past. The past can never control you on its own because there is no entity called 'past'! The past is actually dead. It is you who gives it life.

BLISS IS CHOICELESSNESS

By the time you reach the *nirvanic* layer, you will be without *samskaras* and at the doorstep of enlightenment. You have to let go now to reach enlightenment. It happens on its own. It cannot be *made* to happen. It is like river water. It stays in your hands as long as your hands are open; once you close your hands to possess the water, there is no water.

Bliss is like a flowing river. It is choicelessness. If you try to make bliss a choice, it will be absent. If you can understand the purposelessness of life as a part of the grand plan of Existence, you will reach this layer. The river flows without a purpose right? Does the river have any purpose? No! Yet it flows so blissfully.

The ego believes that there is purpose to life - material, relational and spiritual. The more purposes there are, the stronger your ego feels. If you drop all purposes and still hold on to the purpose of enlightenment also, it is futile. Only when you realize that life is totally purposeless and you drop your ego, will enlightenment happen to you.

BLISS IS THE PATH AND THE GOAL

Even if you apply your strong logic you cannot find the purpose of Existence! The purpose of Existence is bliss, that's all.

How can we enjoy without possessing, without making something our own? We are like water bubbles on a wave in the ocean. Each bubble catches hold of a few more bubbles and calls them wife, husband, father, son, and collects shells thinking they are jewels. The bubble does not understand that it can burst any moment and once it bursts, none of this will hold good.

When you are ready to digest that everything is purposeless, whether material, relational or spiritual, only then life acquires meaning. The moment you have a goal, you miss the path.

The mind always waits for something to happen. It waits for salary - weekly, monthly, yearly, five yearly. If someone offers you 100 years' salary and asks you to die tomorrow, will you die? When you measure your life by paycheck, you reduce your spirit to matter. Your ego is stuck on what you see as a purpose in life.

> An elderly lady came to me with her son. She wanted me to take him into the ashram as a *brahmachari*. I was surprised since usually no parent would like the child to be a *sannyasi*. Vivekananda is great, but no one wants his son to be a Vivekananda. I asked her why she wanted him to be at the ashram. She said that he is mentally not sound. I told her I run an ashram not an asylum!

We have many reasons why we cannot do things. By the time you finish one responsibility, you will have ten more waiting for you. Running becomes your conditioning, not relaxing.

When you are young, you tell yourself that you will relax after you graduate from university; then you shift the goal post to marriage; then to children; then to educating children; then to their marriage. Can you relax after you are 60? By then you have missed the path itself.

The primal sin you can commit is to miss the path of life by following goals. When you live, allow your being to be blissful. When you start hurrying, think about what you are hurrying for; do not allow restlessness in you, thinking that it will settle down. That will never happen. If you are not able to relax into the present moment, even after fulfilling your responsibilities you will not be able to relax. Whenever you run, just think why and what for.

You may have a big house, drive a big car, and people around you might always be praising you. But can you carry anything of this with you? Can you carry with you even one single cheque book? No! It is all purposeless. When you understand the purposelessness, healing happens. If you allow this understanding to happen, even if you are abused, you will heal. The understanding itself will guide you.

You may be thinking, 'All my life I have had a purpose, and my life has been fine. But now you say everything is purposeless.' Whether you like it or not, that is the truth.

Your seeing me is a dream. Scriptures say that the moment you see an enlightened Master, you become enlightened! Understand, seeing me is not the same as looking at me, which is what you do. Looking is with eyes; seeing is with the being. The closer you come to the Master, the more your understanding of him changes. Your maturity allows you to see me differently as you grow.

People get a shock when I tell them about the purposelessness of life. Restlessness hides the purposelessness from you; it hides the path with the goal. Please understand this and be healed. All your dreams of the future, and all your guilt of the past will disappear; all ephemeral joys and suffering will vanish.

In Tiruvannamalai, my hometown, there was a saint by name Yogi Ramsuratkumar. He was as innocent as a child. Whenever people came to him, whatever their problem was, he would say 'Alright'. When someone died, he would say, 'Alright'. If someone's son was getting married, he would say, 'Alright'. I asked him, 'Swami, why do you say alright to everything?' He said: everything is just purposeless. Whatever you think has a purpose has no meaning.

Whenever you remember the truth of purposelessness, healing will happen, and suffering will disappear.

You need courage to pursue the truth. Life will then take on a different path. You will live as a liberated soul. You will never drop your job, relationship or wealth. You will drop only what you do not have. You will drop the mental associations. You will drop the fantasy of a throne and start enjoying the seat on which you are sitting. When purpose is dropped, meaning will happen.

RESTLESSNESS - WHY YOU BECOME TIRED

You actually become tired not by doing things, but by thinking of how much you have done. The play of the mind makes you tired and dull. You constantly struggle; you are restless. Once you understand why you feel tired and dull, you will switch track. When you switch track, you will never think that you are doing anything great. You think you are doing something great only because the mind makes it out to be so. The moment you understand this and your mind loses its power to do this, you start working without ego and you will work ten times more! Then, your inner space will be so pure. Even if you have achieved great things, you will not bother about it.

We just finished installing the largest Venkateshwara deity in the USA. In fact it is one of the largest stone statues here. All it took was a phone call. I do not think I did anything big for it. By the time you finish the word building game, you will become tired. Instead, you can finish the work itself.

If you work towards a purpose, you calculate at every 10% step of finishing the job. By the time you reach 50%, you are tired. You start thinking that you are doing something big.

THE COURAGE TO BREAK FREE FROM THE PAST

Now it is time to enter into the *nirvanic* layer – the seventh body. Actually if you travel up to the seventh layer, there will be no suffering that can hold you back from enlightenment or from relaxing into Existence.

Only one thing will be there: the remaining seeds of *karma* - just the old memories or a little bit of emotional attachment to the old memory; that's all, nothing else. If you have the courage to move on from your emotional memory or your emotional attachment, this *nirvanic* layer also will be cleansed. There is nothing in this *nirvanic* layer which can hold you back.

Actually if you do this whole program intensely, it is a straight route to enlightenment. Do it as much as possible, and it will enrich your life. It will cause tremendous physical and mental healing in you. But the aim of this program is not just physical or mental healing, but the healing of your entire being.

I have designed this program to get you out of the *bhavaroga* – worldly life. If you are intense, this single technique that you are going to do now, can completely liberate you from the entire past. In the *nirvanic* body, all you need is the courage to take the jump.

All you need to do in this *nirvanic* layer is to break free from the past. One important thing: just take a few minutes and think back...Now practically you have your complete biography in your hand, am I right? You have your biography in the papers that you are holding in your hand. If you have written properly from as much of your life as you remember, you will have your entire biography in your hand. Now ask yourself: the way in which you lived in the past, is it perfectly alright or do you feel there is a need for some improvement? Naturally you will feel that you should improve or develop it, am I right? If at all you think, if at all you feel there is a need for development, that there is a need for transformation, please understand that you have to drop the *whole* past mental set-up. You can't say, 'No, there are some good things that I will take, and all the bad things I will drop.' No! Either you erase the whole program or you live with the whole program, that's all! There is no such thing as taking a little bit and leaving the rest.

Be very clear: if you think it is garbage, you have to dump the whole thing; or you have to carry the whole thing in your head. You can't say that you will pick up pieces of the garbage, arrange it nicely and put a little perfume over it and live with it. No! Either you throw the whole thing out or keep the whole thing with you. If you consciously decide that you need transformation, then throw the whole thing out.

Drop the Emotional Attachment to Your Memories

Immediately the next question will be, 'If I throw away everything, will I forget where my house is? Will I forget who my wife is?' Will I forget who my relatives are?' Be very clear, you will not forget where your house is or who your wife is, but you will forget the loaded memories or the loaded emotions associated with the house or wife.

When you forget, when you drop the emotional attachment to your memories, you are free from the 'burden' of the past. All these words appear to be too big, but I tell you your visualization has enough power, enough capacity, enough energy, to achieve this state.

The big problem is that we don't believe we have something called inner space. Just as you have an outer space, you have something called as inner space. Consciously you can clean this space.

All that we are going to do in the seventh layer is, consciously keep the inner space clean. To tell you honestly, it is not that you can throw away all the negative engrams. Whether it is desire or guilt or suffering or joy or anything else, it is not that you have worked on all the engrams completely. There will be a little bit remaining in some corner. Now it is time to dig deep in all the layers at once and throw them out. Re-live completely all the six layers, and relieve them! Reliving is relieving.

Breaking Free from Your Mental Setup

In the *nirvanic* layer, all you are going to do is only this one thing – breaking free from the past.

Always, the seed is afraid to break. It says, 'No, let the tree happen, only then I will break.' The tree in turn says, 'No, let the seed break, only then I will happen.' The seed has to break to allow the tree to grow! Only when you break free from the past mental set up can you create a new mental set up. You will be able to create a new mental set up only if you create the space for it.

Now, consciously, and a little violently, we are going to throw away our negative engrams. Not only consciously, a little violently also. You are just going to push your unconscious away from you. Or you are just going to bring your unconscious to your consciousness. The moment you bring it to your consciousness, it will be burnt away. You don't need to do anything special. Just bring it to your conscious zone, and it will be just burnt away.

If Shiva opens his third eye, it is just enough... *Manmata* (lust/ cupid) will be just burnt away. *Manmata* is a character from Hindu mythology used as a symbol of lust or unconscious. Now all of you are going to do the same thing. Actually it is a metaphysical story: Shiva opening the third eye and *Manmata* being burnt.

There is no real person called *Manmata* standing with a big sugarcane bow and flowers as arrows. And neither did Shiva actually open his third eye and direct fire on *Manmata* to burn him away.

If this really happened, then Shiva is a criminal; he has committed murder! It is a metaphysical story. When you open up the Supreme Knowledge, when you open the *gnaanaagni* - fire of intelligence in you, it just burns away all your negative engrams; all your negative engrams are burnt away. That is the meaning of the story. Now it is time for you to open your *gnaanaagni* or throw all your engrams into the fire of consciousness.

Breaking free from the past is the ultimate liberation. Now you are going to open your conscious being to your engrams. You are going to open your engrams to conscious energy. You are literally going to burn all your engrams. The book in which you have written about all your *samskaras*, is going to be put in the fire, so that you are rid of the *samskaras* once and for all.

WHAT YOU THINK AS JOY IS ALSO NOT JOY

You may think, 'Why should I put all my joyful moments also in the fire?' Whatever you know as joyful moments are not the completely liberating joy, please understand that. They are just superficial joys. Drop them, and you will see a new dimension of intense joy rising in you. Just have the courage and drop all your joys, whatever you understood as joy into the fire. You will see that you will enter into a new dimension, and a different kind of joy will rise in you.

It is like this, when you were a small child, playing with toys was a joy. But now, the very dimension of your joy is different, is it not? Do you enjoy playing with toys now? No! The whole dimension has changed. Do you feel that you are missing all your toys? No! But if I had told you when you were a child, that there is a different dimension in which you can enjoy, would you have been willing to listen to me? No! In the same way I am telling you now that there is yet another deeper dimension waiting for you. So, just place your trust and take the jump.

The very depth of the joy will change. Right now, like how the children play with all the human dolls as mother, father etc, you play with real human dolls calling one your mother, one as father, one as sister, one as brother, one as aunt, etc. You are just playing with all these dolls. Now just relax and drop these dolls. You will understand that your life is something far more valuable and higher than these dolls.

BLISS IS THE VERY MEANING OF HUMAN CONSCIOUSNESS

You are not here as a citizen of some country or belonging to some caste or creed or related to some religion or belonging to some community. You are just a liberated individual being, pure consciousness, who is supposed to relax into the bliss within you.

Somebody has given me a letter. It reads, 'Master, please show me the way to intense and eternal peace.' This is the way. It is time to drop layer after layer of conditioning. You are continuously made to believe you are male, you are female; you belong to this religion or that; you belong to this state, or you belong to that country; you have this much of wealth or you are poor. Now it is time to relax from these ideas.

LIFE IS A PSYCHODRAMA

Actually if you drop your conditioning, you will have something called your inner space where you can rest when you wish to. When you are haunted or tortured by conditioning, you can go inside and rest. If you have a resort or an inner space to rest in, you will be able to work much more beautifully. You will be able to play the psychodrama of life much more beautifully.

I always tell people, 'You thinking that you are a disciple and you thinking that I am a Guru is also a psychodrama!' Don't think that only *your* life is a psychodrama; you thinking of me as a Guru is also psychodrama. Because you want to think that way, you think of me as a Guru and I look like your Guru, that's all. As you want, so I appear. I am just a mirror. The Master is just a mirror. The whole thing is just a psychodrama. You are living in a psychodrama. Understanding that the whole thing is a psychodrama and the ability to relax from it only can help you in the *nirvanic* layer.

In the *nirvanic* layer, all you need to understand is this: whether it is your profession, or your relationships or your spirituality, the whole thing is just a psychodrama! You have an idea about yourself. You have strongly positioned yourself in some spot. You have decided about yourself and set yourself a few clear rules. From that point, you are continuously working and measuring and doing things. But you forget that the base itself is not there. The base which you have created itself is just an illusion. *Nirbana* in *Paali* language means *Nirvana*. The very meaning of that word *Nirbana* means 'nothing'.

There is nothing in all this! Please be very clear: all your activities are centered on you, what you think as *you*. For example, you think you are a person by name Raman. That is the starting point. From that you start: Raman, Raman's wife, Raman's daughter, Raman's family, Raman's property, Raman's spiritual growth, Raman's physical body, Raman's mental health, Raman's economic status... the whole thing is centered on you, but you don't realize that Raman itself is not there! You are trying to continuously protect yourself, physically, mentally, emotionally, economically, spiritually or socially. But the very being whom you are trying to protect is not there.

THE STORY OF THE PARAMAHAMSA

This story actually happened to me as a *darshan*, as a vision, as an experience. It is from this that I created our institution's emblem. If you see our emblem you will see the *Paramahamsa* bird in it. The *Paramahamsa* is our emblem. I had a beautiful vision or experience, from which I created the emblem.

Ramakrishna speaks about the great Swans – the *Paramahamsas*. These great Swans are actually enlightened Masters who take a bird body just to go around and see their territory! They are metaphysical birds, seen only through enlightened eyes or by people who are living in the higher consciousness zone. Of course, only if you are enlightened, you will be able to stay in the higher consciousness; that is different!

The *Paramahamsa* never comes down to planet Earth. It just flies high in the sky, enjoying and expressing its freedom; expressing its own bliss. Sometimes it descends in height and flies closer to Earth.

The *Paramahamsa* lays its egg while it is in the air. Within forty percent distance of touching the ground, the egg will hatch. Within sixty percent distance, the small one will emerge and grow wings. Before touching the ground, within ninety percent distance, the small one will just take off and fly back into the air. It will never touch the ground! It will never touch planet Earth. These are called the *Paramahamsas* – the supreme Swans that are untouched by worldly matters, who represent enlightened consciousness since birth.

There is a small story about these great Swans:

Figure 15: Paramahamsa flying over the lake

The Swan is flying high in the sky. When the reflection of the Swan falls on lakes or the ocean or a river, when the reflection falls on the water, all the fish in the lake start jumping, 'Oh, some new fish has come, some big fish has come!' They all start jumping on the reflection and play with it. The very sight of the reflection fills them with joy.

Some fish will jump this way, and some fish will jump that way. Some fish will think, 'What a beautiful fish, what a wonderful fish this is,' and they will be jumping this way and that. Some fish will start calling the other fish, 'Hey come quickly, come and see this beautiful fish, this pretty fish!'

Figure 16: Fish jumping over the Swan's reflection thinking it is a new type of fish

Some fish will even put a fence around the reflection and declare, 'Only *we* can go near this fish!' Some fish who jump towards the reflection will feel that the fish is hugging them. They will go back and write reminiscences, 'Oh... this fish is so great, so loving, radiating compassion; what amazing love and compassion!'

Some other fish start purchasing neighboring land - real estate, thinking the Swan may come there. Some other fish claim, 'I am the brother of the Swan, I am the son of the

Swan, I am the beloved of the Swan.' The whole drama happens!

Some fish who jump a little away from the reflection will feel as if the Swan is kicking them out; as if the reflection is kicking them out. They will go out and say, 'No, no. This fish is arrogant. He is not as loving as what these other fish have told me. In books I read that it was very loving and compassionate. I went there and the swan kicked me out. It is not as compassionate as what these fish say.'

If the water is calm, the fish see one kind of reflection of the Swan. If the water is turbulent, they see another form of the Swan. When they move with the water, they see yet another form of the Swan. They argue with each other, claiming that what each one sees is the real Swan; all by looking at the reflection! Each different perception of the reflection is held on to by either individual fish or groups of fish. The Swan just keeps flying, and the fish just keep arguing. When they do not see the swan's reflection, the fish have no recollection of the reflection that had filled them with joy just a while ago. Their memories are short and they are back to their eating, mating, fighting and dying!

Suddenly the Swan starts flying over land. The reflection which was appearing on the water suddenly disappears! Immediately all the fish start crying, 'What happened? Our Swan has disappeared! What happened to our Swan?' But they never understand that the Swan never landed on planet Earth in the first place to disappear now!

Different types of fish come around the reflection. There are some fish that are very busy - just jumping this way and that way. And when these fish jump this way and that way, the reflection starts moving because of the ripples created by the fish. And these fish will think that the Swan is moving. The fish cannot distinguish between the reflection and the source. They are too excited about the 'big fish' in the water. Some fish feel they are even getting enlightened. They feel that the closer they are to the reflection, the faster they will get enlightened!

Of course, wherever the reflection falls, automatically, ashrams and communities and temples just stand up! You don't even have to do anything; they will just stand up! If the reflection falls on Malaysia, all the Malaysian fish will gather and the temple will be built! If it falls on Los Angeles, all the Los Angeles fish will gather and the temple will be built! If the reflection falls on Bengaluru, all the Bengaluru fish will gather and the temple will be built! If the reflection falls on some other country or city, all the fish will gather and naturally, the ashram will be built!

Figure 17: Fish try to capture the Swan in various frames

Suddenly the Swan starts flying over land. The reflection which was appearing on the water suddenly disappears!

Immediately all the fish start crying, 'What happened? Our Swan has disappeared! What happened to our Swan?' Some of the fish start cursing the Swan, 'What is this? Believing this Swan, we built such a beautiful house and raised all the real estate around this building. Now each building will go for five lakhs.' Yet, the Swan flies on blissfully untouched by the drama that is going on with the fish. But they never understand that the Swan never landed on planet Earth in the first place to disappear now!

The whole thing is just a drama! In the same way, in your life too, you have started thinking that you have a soul. Of course, you have a soul, but that soul is entirely different from whatever you understand as your soul. It is just like your misunderstanding of the Swan's reflection. But based on your own understanding, you start protecting yourself and creating a fence around you. You create a house, family, relations, social security and wealth, then decide, 'Oh! I need spiritual growth also.' Then you go to some Guru and start searching for spirituality also.

But you forget that the very Swan has not happened! There is no Swan in what you are seeing. You are just playing with the reflection.

The problem is, the reflection itself is so graceful, so beautiful, that most of the fish have no motivation to look up! The fish are quite happy building walls and fences in the water, with the belief that they possess the Swan.

But there are some intelligent fish... who think... 'No! **This does not seem to be a fish. This seems to be something else.**' Some intelligent fish will suddenly think this way. These fish are what we call devotees!

There are some other very few but more intelligent fish. They will see the reflection and say, '**No, it is not even something else, it is just a *reflection* of something!**' And they will look up...and see the Swan flying! These are the disciples!

Figure 18: Some fish look up!

Understand? There are many levels of fish. There are fish that will jump *this* way, towards the reflection and feel that the reflection is hugging them. They will feel that He is very loving, caring and compassionate. They will go back and write reminiscences. This is one level. Or they will make a website for Him, or they will write a book for Him.

There are some fish that will jump *that* way, away from the reflection and say, 'No, no, that fish kicked me out. It is not loving or compassionate.' This is one group of fish.

Some rare, intelligent fish will look and say, 'No! This is not even a fish like us. It is something else...'

Figure 19: You are also a Paramahamsa!

You see, there is a beautiful *sloka* – verse - in the *Bhagavad Gita* which says: whoever thinks that the Guru is a better human being, has abused the Divine Presence. The Guru is not a better human being; he is completely disconnected from this very idea of human being! He is a different species altogether!

So only a few intelligent fish get an idea: No! He is not a better fish or a big fish or anything. He is not even the same species which we think we are. The very quality, the very idea is totally different. Those people who feel this, who are fortunate enough to have this *click* start becoming devotees! Only they start living around or start practicing very sincerely whatever they caught in the expression of the Swan.

Understand: the people who come and go...that is the fish that claim He is loving and compassionate as well as the fish that jump out and say, 'No, not like that, everything is business...' both the fish are only 'consumers'. The fish that start looking, that start feeling, 'No, this is not a fish, it cannot be just a fish like us...'- that fish is an investor!

Only when you have this doubt: *No, this is not just a fish, it is something else,* you are ready to *look up* and see the source. When you *look up* and see the original fish...the original Swan...you understand the truth! Not only that... Suddenly you will see...**you were also never a fish, you were thinking that you were a fish!** Suddenly you will see...*'Arrey*! **I am also a Swan!'**

Then, you will just fly and play with the Swan!

Until you see the Swan flying, you do not realize that you too are a Swan. You are a Swan, who for some reason, fell into the water, and forgot you can fly. You are just tumbling this way and that way, struggling to survive, thinking that you are a fish.

This is the truth.

Understand one important thing: whether the fish are jumping and moving the reflection, or they are feeling that the reflection is loving and compassionate and hugging them, or they feel that everything is just business and hating it, or if they look a little deep and find out the reality of the Swan, throughout all of these stages, the Swan does not even *bother*.... He is not even *touched*. He is neither touched nor bothered! That is the beauty! His reflection falls on the lake for only one purpose: expecting and seeing if maybe a few fish will look up; that's all! Maybe a few fish will look up...

Nirvanic Body

Understand:

In the first level, when you jump and say that he is compassionate, *you are a fish, and the reflection is also a fish.*

If you jump out and say, 'No, no, it is not as we think; it is all just foolishness,…' again, *you are a fish and he is also just one more fish.*

In the third level, when you look at the reflection and say, 'No, no, this is not a fish,' then, *you are not a fish and He is also not a fish.* He is a reflection and you are also a reflection of the reflection. That is why you are able to feel that it is something else.

Then, in the fourth level, when you *look up, He is a Swan and you are also a Swan!*

Along with *your* transformation, you will feel the higher experiences of Him. And by seeing the higher experiences of Him, your further transformation will happen; both are inter-connected.

When you see the divinity in an idol, it is the first level. When you see the divinity in a living human being, in the Guru or Master, it is the next level, and it is called *Guru Bhakti* – devotion to the Guru. You will see that *Guru Bhakti* suddenly leads to *Atma Bhakti* – devotion to the Soul! The Guru just turns the devotion that you have on him towards yourself and says, 'What is inside *this* system, is inside *that* system as well. *Tat Tvam Asi* – You are That!'

The reflection of the Swan happens everywhere for the one reason that maybe a few fish will look up. But understand one thing: especially the ones who are the organizers… I always tell them, these rituals, rites, temples, ashrams, everything is for service, for the public. You should remember only one thing: **do not forget to see the Swan**. Some fish are so busy collecting pebbles to add to the height of the temple, they forget to look up and see the Swan. Early morning, the Swan may no longer be there; only empty water will remain. They will be stuck with the memorial they built. The Swan would have disappeared.

All you need to do is **look up**! Look up at the real Swan instead of being caught in its reflection! Just look up and you can simply see that you are also not a fish; you also have wings and you also can fly just like the Supreme Swan or *Paramahamsa*. You are Him.

Before the Swan disappears, do not forget to *look up* and see the Swan. Sometimes, people just play around and miss. They forget to *look up* and see the Swan, thinking that it is going to be there forever.

So, do not miss...

If you can meditate on this one story, I tell you, you will be liberated this moment! If you can, keep your focus only on this one understanding, just like a Zen koan. Remember: you have never happened as you think you have; whatever you think as you is not you.

The root of you is non-existence – *nirbana. Nirbana* means *nirvana* which is 'non-existence'. Just imagine: to protect something which is non-existent, you are torturing yourself so much. The stream is flowing; if the fish is trying to push the stream, or if the fish tries to stop the stream, will the stream even know about it? Whether you try to become enlightened or you take on a stand against enlightenment, God doesn't even know anything about it.

All the fish on seeing the Swan think, 'Let us stop this stream. Let us have a barricade and stop this stream.' If all the fish line up in the stream and try to stop the stream, do you think they will be successful? The stream will not even know that the fish are trying to stop it!

In the same way, you not becoming enlightened, or you not realizing what reality is, your *atman* doesn't even know. You are not connected to your being even that much. So whatever you think as you is just non-existent.

A small story:

One born blind man went to the doctor. The doctor said, 'I will do an operation on your eye. You will have your eye sight back, and then you can walk without your stick.' The blind man said, 'Doctor, I understand that you will do an operation and I will have my eye sight back. But how are you saying that I can walk without my stick?'

Unless the man has his eye sight back, he will not be able understand how he can walk without a stick. Just intellectually, you cannot convince the man that he will be able to walk without his stick!

THE GREAT ENLIGHTENED BEINGS - *PARAMAHAMSAS*

The great enlightened Masters are the *Paramahamsas* who touch planet Earth taking a human form, with a mission, from time to time. A *Paramahamsa* is one whose spiritual awakening leads to enlightenment even before adolescence. Such a being never touches ground; his spirit soars high well before it is enmeshed in the web of worldly reality. *Paramahamsas* are rare beings whose innocent wisdom pierces even the most hardened heart and mind.

In such beings, the divine *kundalini* energy, which is the universal energy that flows through every individual, that is stored in the *muladhara chakra* (the energy center at the base of the spine) never moves downwards as it does with normal beings at adolescence.

In all humans, this energy moves upwards to downwards leading to sexual awakening and the desire to fulfill the need for procreation. In the case of the *Paramahamsa*, the *kundalini* energy is awakened before puberty, and it moves upwards instead of downwards at the time of spiritual awakening, without causing any desire for sexual pleasure.

The energy within the Paramahamsa stays pure, uncorrupted, and exceptional. Their purpose in life is to communicate to the rest of humanity this truth that has been gifted to them, in the hope that at least some others would glimpse this truth for themselves. Each *Paramahamsa* communicates this message in his own inimitable style. Ramakrishna, forever in divine ecstasy, inspired others through devotion or *bhakti*. Bhagavan Ramana Maharishi, another great *Paramahamsa*, communicated his message mainly in silence, through a process of discrimination. There are others who by their touch and at times by a mere glance imparted their wisdom to disciples who were ready to receive the truth. In whichever way they may impart the truth, it is not to be forgotten that they happen on planet Earth for only one reason: with the hope that at least a few of us will **look up** and see the Truth, and become That.

LOOK INSIDE, WHATEVER YOU THINK AS YOU IS NOT THERE

Understand this one thing: if you really look inside yourself, whatever you thought of as being you will not be there. It will disappear the moment you look inside. Whatever issues are the base for your suffering, where those issues are rooted, that very root is non-existent. That is why I tell you, your name itself is non-existent!

That is why in Zen they say, meditate on how your face might have been before your birth. Just visualize how your face might have been before your birth. Will you be able visualize? No! If you are 50 years old now, just 50 years ago you were non-existent. Whatever you think as you now, was non-existent 50 years ago, am I right? And 50 years later, you will be again non-existent. Why are you then suffering so much? Why are you torturing yourself just for these few years of drama? The whole thing is just *nirbana*!

Meditate on this one *sutra*. Don't bother about what others are thinking about you, because they are bothering about what *you are thinking about them*! It is just a drama that is happening continuously; you don't have time to stop and look, that's all.

You don't have time to open your eyes and see. You don't have time to relax for a few minutes and watch reality because your inner television is never switched off even for two seconds. You don't even know that the television can be switched off or there can be a few moments when the scenes will not appear, when the screen will be blank.

Here I am trying to tell you, that just because the screen is continuously filled with scenes, don't think what you are seeing is the truth. It *can* be switched off. You can switch it off, you can relax. It is time, at least for the next half an hour, relax and meditate on the face which you had before your birth.

YOU ARE A HAPPENING, NOT A BEING

One more thing: to understand the whole thing as 'Nothing', you don't need much spiritual practice. All you need is simple knowledge of English - to understand my words.

Listen carefully:

You are not a noun, you are a verb.
You are not a being, you are a happening.

Understanding that you are not a being is what I call *Nirvana*. The moment you understand that you are not a being but a happening, tremendous freedom and liberation happens to you. You don't have to protect yourself anymore. You can be so open and free. You don't have to have any guarding mechanism against everyone and everything.

Immediately your mind will say, 'No, I may have physical pain, or somebody may hurt me. If I don't protect myself, I may fall sick.' Please be very clear: I am not asking you to go and jump in the river. No! I am not asking you to allow yourself to be hurt. When I say don't protect yourself, I don't mean: enter into the river Ganga and watch what happens! Your mind is always playing these games. That is the problem. When I say don't protect yourself, immediately your mind will say, 'Oh! He says I have to jump into the Ganga.' No. The second statement is not made by me. It is made by your mind.

You have to understand your mind first. For example, if I tell you, 'There are two doors, and one door is open,' what do you conclude? The second door is closed! But this statement is not made by me. Then, who is it made by? Your mind!

When I say now, 'You are a happening, and you don't have to protect yourself,' there is no need for the second statement from the mind. Just internalize the first statement. Then, as and when situations arise, you will have enough intelligence and you will see that things happen automatically.

You Have Innate Intelligence to Face Your Life

Understand that you have enough innate intelligence to handle your life. You take the body with inbuilt intelligence. Not only that, the more years you live on planet Earth, the more experienced you become and therefore you should feel that much more confident to conduct the remaining years of your life on planet Earth. You should not bother about protecting your being, about protecting your ego. Just trust your innate intelligence - *swa-buddhi* – and live an open life. Then automatically only auspicious things will happen in your life.

Spontaneity - The True Intelligence

You have innate wisdom - *swa-gnaana*, to take the right decision in every passing moment; to handle your personality every moment, and to decide spontaneously every moment.

Because you don't trust that you have spontaneity, you try to keep all these records in your head, so that you can decide based on these records. But you miss one important thing –

situations continuously keep changing! Whenever you decide based on the decisions of your predecessors, be very clear: you are taking outdated decisions. Likewise, in life also, if you decide based on your past decisions, you are outdated. Then you can't be considered as a living being. You are live-dead!

YOU ARE NOT THE REFLECTION OF THE *PARAMAHAMSA*, YOU ARE THE *PARAMAHAMSA*!

Be very clear: whatever you think of as you doesn't exist. The moment you relax, a big load is taken away from you. That is what I call liberation. There is nothing to protect because you are just *nirvana* – Nothingness!

Just as an experiment today, drop whatever you think of as you and relax for a few minutes. I am not asking you to relax forever. When you go back tomorrow morning, you can carry it with you. Just today, as an experiment, relax. If you do this, you will understand that what is happening with your whole being; how you are continuously creating new struggles for yourself by trying to protect the reflection of the Swan.

First understand that you are just a reflection of the Swan. The moment you understand, you *become* a Swan! You are just the reflection of a *Paramahamsa*. The moment you understand that, you become a *Paramahamsa*!

Whether you want to be a reflection of the *Paramahamsa* or a *Paramahamsa* itself, it is up to you. Even if you think that you are a reflection of the *Paramahamsa* as of now, you are a *Paramahamsa*! Even if you think you are a reflection, be very clear: you are not the reflection, you are the real Swan!

You may try hard to think that you are only a reflection; you may try to protect as much as possible; to struggle as deeply as possible, but the whole thing is just like the futile efforts of the fish.

You may say, 'All these things are good to listen to, but let me think of my next routine. Tomorrow what I am supposed to do. Let me think of my life's pending decisions, and what I am supposed to do next.' If that is the case, it is perfectly up to you. Try to protect yourself, nothing wrong, but suddenly one day you will realize that someone inside you wakes up and understands or experiences that what you were protecting all these days was just a shadow.

We worked these four days continuously on your mind so that you can understand this single truth; this one single truth. If your mind is too crowded with your own thoughts, you will not be able to understand. If too many fish are jumping on the reflection of the Swan, you can't understand that it is a reflection. All I did in these four days was ask the fish to move a little away, to give a little space so that you can just see and realize that it is not the Swan, but just the reflection of the Swan. The moment you understand it, you will play the game of reflection so beautifully! The moment you understand this, the moment you realize this, if you are a doctor, you will become a much better doctor because you know that it is a game you are playing; so you will not suffer with it.

Let me explain to you why this understanding will liberate you. It is like this: you are sitting here with me now in this room. As long as you know that the exit door can be opened any time, and that you are free to move any time, you will be comfortably sitting here. The moment you feel it might be locked and the key might not be available any time you will not be able to sit here comfortabiy. You will first try opening the door! You will first try to escape! In the same way, if you don't understand that life is a game, you will hurt yourself and you will hurt others, taking the whole game too seriously. Taking the whole game too seriously is the only mistake that you make. The moment you understand you are just *Nirbana*, you will see that physical well-being and mental well-being simply happens!

There is a beautiful verse written by Ramana Maharishi addressed to the sacred hill Arunachala as his very beloved. The verse says: I thought you are my God and you will protect me. I came to you, but suddenly now I see, you have simply destroyed me completely! Whatever I thought as 'me' is not there now. *I* am missing!'

That is what I am telling you now. Many of you have come to me for healing, thinking that I will protect your body, your mind, and your life. Understand: the moment that you understand there is nothing to be protected, everything is simply protected.

YOU ARE DIFFERENT EVERY MOMENT

Your body is not the same body that was there yesterday. Your mind is not the same mind which was there yesterday. If your mind and body are both not the same, then who are you? How can you say that you are the same person who was here yesterday? How can you say that?

If your body is not the same thing which was there yesterday, and if your mind is not the same thing which was there yesterday, how can you say that you are the same person who was here yesterday? What you think of as you now is not the same you that you thought you were yesterday. Then how can what you think of as you be true even at this moment?

Yesterday is different from today. Then how can you think that there is some continuity in you? When you think that there is some continuity in you, you start protecting yourself; you want to protect the continuity. You want it to be saved, preserved... and the problem starts. Just understand that you are fresh and different every passing moment.

You Are Not As Solid As You Think You Are

The moment you understand that there is no need for any protection of your identity, there will not be any suffering, and you will understand that the whole thing is happening just like small bubbles in the ocean! Any minute, the bubbles will disappear!

There is nothing to protect. There is nothing to care for. There is nothing to grow. Understand that you are just liquid. The very understanding that you are liquid is enough to liberate you. Just a simple understanding that you are not as solid as you think is more than enough.

Contemplate on this one thing and relax from whatever you think of as you for the next half an hour; you will emerge as a new being. At least you will have a glimpse, one glimpse of who you are. When I say 'you' I mean capital letter Y-O-U, not small letter 'y-o-u'. Please sit as as you are and close your eyes. Allow these words to merge in you. Whatever understanding happens let it happen.

The Master is there to awaken this understanding in you. Ramana says: The Master is a *simha swapna* - a nightmare where a lion is chasing you! You *will* wake up even if you are in your deepest dreams in the waking state. However thick the veil of illusion may be, you will wake up.

MEDITATION

Sit down on the floor. Whatever you understand by these words let that sink into you.

See clearly that you are just liquid. See very clearly what prevents you from realizing this. See where you are stuck: whether it is your social position, or it is your fear of health, or it is the fear of losing your relationship, or the fear of losing your wealth. Just see where it is getting stuck and stopping you from experiencing that you are liquid, that you are fluid. At least understand that which stops you from realizing it. If nothing stops you, then relax into you.

You are not the same person as you think you are. There is no need to protect you, because you don't exist. You are just the greatest illusion created by you, and supported by worldly illusions.

Forget about tomorrow. There is no need to bother about it. Realize this truth now; that is enough. Don't bother about the consequences of this realization. Don't analyse whether it is positive or negative. Relax bothering about the consequences; just see the truth. Don't worry about how many times you missed in the past. Even if you have missed ten thousand times in the past, it is alright. *Now* there is a possibility, you can capture it! Just catch it.

(After the meditation...)

So, we have gone through the meditation to drop the entire past. Now you know where you are stuck. Whatever thought came into your mind repeatedly during this meditation, is where you are stuck. That is what you need to drop.

When you are finished with all these seven layers, the final touch will happen by the Master's grace. Actually that is what happens when you put your entire effort. If your effort has been intense, the Master's grace happens automatically. When you open up and throw out everything, the Master will be there to heal everything. This is what happens in the meditation during all the seven layers. You throw everything out and the final touch is given by the Master's grace.

Now, we are going to have only these two sessions: the session of expelling everything from the past and receiving the Master's grace. The meditation which we are going to do now is called *vraja* homa. It is the meditation done by the people before taking *sannyas*. Don't worry; I am not going to give you *sannyas* now! This is normally the meditation done by people who are taking *sannyas*.

Of course when I introduced this meditation to the public, some traditional swamis criticized me. They asked, 'How can you give this to everyone? It is specially for us.' I said, 'Only because of this secrecy, we lost the real science of *Ayurveda* medicine; we lost the real science of *Siddha* medicine; we lost all the ancient surgery methods; we lost so much of our knowledge. So I believe that when something can give results, it should be shared with the whole world. This is such a highly powerful meditation technique that can transform beings; why not give it to the whole world?' Therefore, I brought it out!

Now I am giving it in all our NSPs. After all whose property are these meditation techniques? They are all our ancient *rishis'* (sages) property. Why were they created? They were created for the sake of the whole world. It is not meant to be monopolised by some small group of people. It belongs to the whole world. Knowledge belongs to the whole world. No one can say that it is only for them. That is the reason why I brought it out.

I want all of you to understand the importance of this meditation so that you will enter into it with intensity.

The first part of the meditation is the Nithya Dhyaan meditation. It cleanses and energises the vital energy centers in your body which are responsible for the swaying emotions and stored negative memories. It brings intense awareness into your system to awaken the inner intelligence. It can create an explosion in your consciousness that can steer you towards a life of totality.

Nithya Dhyaan is a technique that gives you what you need to balance yourself and experience complete harmony between your body, mind and spirit; to harness the inner intelligence as a propelling force to excel in the inner and outer worlds.

It is a guided meditation technique for 35 minutes comprising five steps. Please listen to the instructions carefully.

Step 1: Sit in *Vajrasana* (if not possible, sit cross legged or on a chair) with hands on your hips. Close your eyes and breathe chaotically for seven minutes.

Figure 20: Chaotic Breathing

Step 2: Continue to sit in *vajrasana* (if not possible sit cross legged or on a chair). Form *'chin mudra'* with your fingers (form a circle with thumb and forefinger of both hands, palm upwards), and placing your hands on your knees, hum intensely for seven minutes. When you hum, keeps your lips together and produce the *'mmm'* sound.

Step 3: You may now sit cross-legged on the floor if you wish to or continue to sit in *vajrasana*. For the next seven minutes, you will take your awareness from the *muladhara chakra* to the *sahasrara chakra*. Dwell on each *chakra* for one minute with total awareness on that *chakra*.

Figure 21: Chakra awareness

   a. Take your awareness to the *muladhara chakra*.
     Your *muladhara* is pure
     Your *muladhara* is filled with energy
     Your *muladhara* is overflowing with bliss
     Your *muladhara* is radiating *nithyananda*
     (After 1 minute)

b. Take your awareness to the *swadhistana chakra* which is two inches above the *muladhara*.
    Your *swadhistana* is pure
    Your *swadhishtana* is filled with energy
    Your *swadhistana* is overflowing with bliss
    Your *swadhistana* is radiating *nithyananda*
    (After 1 minute)

c. Take your awareness to the *manipuraka chakra* which is located at the navel center.
    Your *manipuraka* is pure
    Your *manipuraka* is filled with energy
    Your *manipuraka* is overflowing with bliss
    Your *manipuraka* is radiating *nithyananda*
    (After 1 minute)

d. Take your awareness to the *anahata chakra* which is located at the heart center.
    Your *anahata* is pure
    Your *anahata* is filled with energy
    Your *anahata* is overflowing with bliss
    Your *anahata* is radiating *nithyananda*
    (After 1 minute)

e. Take your awareness to the *vishuddhi chakra* which is located at the throat center.
    Your *vishuddhi* is pure
    Your *vishuddhi* is filled with energy
    Your *vishuddhi* is overflowing with bliss
    Your *vishuddhi* is radiating *nithyananda*
    (After 1 minute)

f. Take your awareness to the *ajna chakra* which is located
    in the region between your eyebrows.
    Your *ajna* is pure
    Your *ajna* is filled with energy
    Your *ajna* is overflowing with bliss
    Your *ajna* is radiating *nithyananda*
    (After 1 minute)

g. Take your awareness to the *sahasrara chakra* which is
    located in the crown center.
    Your *sahasrara* is pure
    Your *sahasrara* is filled with energy
    Your *sahasrara* is overflowing with bliss
    Your *sahasrara* is radiating *nithyananda*
    (After 1 minute)

Figure 22:
Gratitude

Step 4: For seven minutes, just be un-
clutched in silence.

Step 5: Take your awareness to the
sahasrara chakra. With your awareness
only on your crown center, just relax. Smile
and relax.

With your whole being, offer your
gratitude to your beloved mother for
giving you this body. Remember and give
your gratitude to her with all your being.

Offer your gratitude to your beloved father
for giving you this life and providing for all your needs.

Offer your gratitude to all the doctors and nurses who received
you when you came to planet Earth.

Offer your gratitude to all the people who built the hospital or
home where you were born.

313

Offer your gratitude to all the people who took care of you when you were an infant.

Offer your gratitude to all those who worked for your food, clothes and living when you were young.

Offer your gratitude to all the teachers who gave you primary education.

Offer your gratitude to all your young age friends who made your life happy and blissful, who shared their innocence and joy with you.

Offer your gratitude to your brothers and sisters and other relatives for nurturing you and caring for you.

Offer your gratitude to all the people who gave you professional education, who helped you stand in your profession; who gave you the courage to stand on your own feet.

Offer your gratitude to all the people who helped you financially, whenever you needed it.

Offer your gratitude to all the doctors and nurses who took care of your health, who gave you medical assistance whenever you needed it.

Offer your gratitude to your spouse for giving you love and security in your life.

Offer your gratitude and love to your children for coming into your life.

Offer your gratitude to all the people who encouraged you and gave you inspiration in your spiritual life.

Offer your gratitude to all those who have served you in one way or the other all through your life: the milk man who delivers milk, the grocer, the laundry man, the garbage collector, your servants, your driver, all these people whom you take for granted.

Offer your gratitude to your enemies and those who have hurt you, for making you strong and forgiving by virtue of their behaviour towards you.

Offer your gratitude to all those who helped you physically, mentally, socially, economically and spiritually.

Remember each one of them and offer gratitude, taking your own time.

Offer your gratitude to your body and all its parts one by one.

Offer your gratitude to your mind for its miraculous functioning.

Offer your gratitude to all the spiritual Masters.

Offer your gratitude to the Master who has given you this *Nithya Ananda Spurana* experience.

Offer your gratitude to the Divine, to the Whole, to God, for making all these things possible in your life.

Now you will read whatever you have written in your book about all your *samskaras* and re-live them completely once more in all the four layers of desire, guilt, pain and joy. You have 15 to 20 minutes to relive the whole thing. Relive them and be relieved from them. You will realize when you do this that you don't even feel connected with those memories now! This happens because of the deep meditation that you did for each layer. You will feel that the memories are moving away. Relive everything and bring them out. You can visualize as if bulldozers are moving the earth and bringing out the whole thing. Visualise that the whole thing is just moving away from you. Finally, offer everything into the fire. Here, we will have a fire which is energized with the *mantras* - chants from the *Upanishad mantras*.

The Master's love is the greatest medicine which can heal the past. The Master's grace can simply heal the entire past and totally cut you off from the past, giving you a new birth. You are then reborn; you become *dwija* - twice-born. At the time of *sannyas*, this same fire ritual is done. To cut your self completely from the past is the ultimate initiation.

Let me explain the whole initiation process. First, the *mantras* are chanted. The meaning of the *mantras* is: I am burning all my past, all my ideas of any relationship, my ideas about desires, my ideas about worries, my ideas about depression, my ideas about aggressiveness. These *mantras* touch each aspect of our past one by one and just burn the whole thing in the fire.

Once you put everything into the fire you will feel so refreshed. When you do the cleaning consciously, it happens this way; you are totally cleansed, and you are out of it. Consciously offer everything to the fire. You will see that the entire past is cut off from you. This is the way to come out of all the seven layers. In the end, the final touch, the Master's grace, or the Master's blessings completes the whole process.

In the *vraja homa*, the intention is to purify the whole world, the whole universe. Of course when you are purified the whole world is purified. Understand: you are going to disconnect yourself from the past consciously, totally. Don't think: how will my imagination work for me? Imagination can do miracles. Sit for a few minutes and imagine that all your wounds, all your suffering, all your guilt, all your pain, all your tears, all your joy, all your desires, all your *karmas* are getting burnt.

If you wish to, you can sit and read the whole thing you have written once, so that it will be easy for you to remember. Just relive the pain, relive the desire, relive the guilt, relive the past. From first line to last line of what you written, read all of it. Relive your entire past; the gist of your entire life and relieve yourself from desire, guilt, pain and pleasure.

First, undergo all the desires; then undergo all the pain; then undergo all the pleasures. Relive all the moments deeply, and as vividly as possible. Only when you live the *karmas*, the *karmas* will leave you. Otherwise it will be just a hangover in you.

When you really live it, the very reliving becomes relieving. So take your own time, and put all your emotion and imagination in every step, doing it as slowly as possible, as deeply as possible with no urgency. Relive it; only then you can relieve it.

(The group finishes the meditation)

SHARING OF EXPERIENCES OF NSP PARTICIPANTS...

I wanted to express to you the deep impact the NSP program with Swamiji Nithyananda had on me. The experience was profound even though I still haven't fully comprehended its scope, as the process continues to unfold. Swamiji touched my heart and every part of my life, and left me in a state of bliss.

Dr. Tom Glew BSc. ND.

During the Shiva Sutra meditation, upon my first meeting with him, I was in the back of the room and Swamiji said, 'Now feel my energy'. I was suddenly consumed by light and bliss. I felt as if I was floating in space with the biggest smile across my face - like the Cheshire cat in Alice in Wonderland!

During the NSP program, we covered the 7 energy bodies. Part of our exercise was to write down all our desires, our past guilts, emotional sufferings, and our joys. I feel like Swamiji took a squeegy and wiped the slate clean. If I had to re-write all of these things again, it would take me a 10th of the time. I know that I have a choice now to be concerned with these small details which only create more stress, more suffering. I seriously came away with the belief that these things really don't matter. I now know I can be in a space where I am full of divine bliss all the time.

It took me a week to come back to earth after being with Swami for the weekend. Suddenly all the small stuff no longer mattered. What matters now is the truth, that it is our birthright to be blissful beings, free from suffering.

I am so honored to have had this experience. Without a doubt, this was the most powerful time of my life.

Kristin Campbell
Neoalpine Yoga, Whistler BC

APPENDIX A

Significance of The Spiritual Name

Many people tell me after the NSP that they feel they have emerged as new beings; they feel they have been born again as a new person. Of course, you will realize at the end of the program that it truly *is* a new birth. That is why you have a choice to take a new name, a spiritual name, given by a Master.

At the end of the NSP, you have a choice to get a spiritual name from me. The new name which I give, the spiritual name, is like constantly reminding you to nurture the psychological revolution which has happened in you through this program; to nurture the new life, the new understanding which happened in you. When a psychological revolution has happened inside you, and you enter into a plane of higher consciousness, again and again if you remember your old name, you will be allowing it to pull you back to the older familiar plane with your old mental habits.

Your name is a very powerful thing for you. Let us say your name is John, and you are sleeping with a few people in a room. If somebody walks in to the room and calls out, 'John', immediately and unconsciously, only you will wake up and respond! This is how deeply your name has been embedded in your unconscious. Your name can be a powerful technique for realizing your Self.

Another important thing is that whenever somebody calls out your name, you are suddenly jolted into a split moment of deep consciousness and awareness of yourself. You must have experienced a situation where you are sitting in a big classroom and suddenly the teacher calls out your name for something. You might have even been dozing off, but the moment you hear your name being called, you will break from the sleep or whatever thought pattern, and you will be jolted to the present place and time!

Our name has tremendous influence over our state of mind. I meditate *upon your being and give you a name which will put you on your path to enlightenment. This spiritual name indicates the spiritual path which will suit the innate nature of the person and lead him to the ultimate flowering of the individual and actualization of its potential.*

Every time we call a person by his spiritual name, we remind him about his path to enlightenment. By and by, the name will enter the very core of his being.

If you have the right spiritual name given by an enlightened being, the very name will take you to the depth of your consciousness. It will connect your mind and consciousness. It will be like a bridge for you to enter into enlightenment. It will tell you how your way of life should be, how you can achieve enlightenment, how you should take care in your life.

Significance of the Spiritual Name

There are thousands of ways to live a life on planet Earth. To give you the proper guidance meant for only you, the Master chooses the name. Your name is like a *mantra*.

Let me give the definition of the words engram or *samskara* and *mantra*.

Any word which is inscribed in your inner space, which binds you, which suffocates you, which brings you down in your consciousness, is *samskara*, engram.

Any word inscribed in your inner space which liberates you, which takes you to higher consciousness, which takes you to a more joyful and blissful state is a *mantra*.

Mantra and *samskara* are almost the same, but *samskara* binds you, while *mantra* liberates you. *Mantra* is the antidote for *samskara*. If you are given your name by a person who is yet to get enlightened, who still lives in unconsciousess, then your name become a bondage for you. If you are named by an enlightened being, by a person who lives in superconsciousness, your name is a method or technique to liberate you. Your very name can be used as a technique for enlightenment.

If at all your spiritual name can be used in the social setup in which you are living, that is the best thing, because the whole day from morning until night, either you will be using the name or someone else will be using the name to address you. When this happens, understand that every moment becomes a spiritual practice for you! Your name is the right word from an enlightened Master, given to you as a technique. Every time it is repeated, you are entering into the zones of higher consciousness. Every time you remember the meaning of it, you move to a different plane.

People come and tell me, 'The spiritual name you gave is so beautiful. Whenever I remember the name, I feel fulfilled. Whenever I remember the name along with with its meaning, whenever I meditate on the name and its meaning, I feel like I am overflowing!' The spiritual name can take you to the deepest level of your being.

One more thing: any other word is only addition to your already existing collection of words, but your name is your very center. Your name is the center, and everything else is only an addition. That is why in the *Vedic* tradition, we use only Gods' names as names of new borns. That is why we have chants for every God that desribe the God through 1008 names. Such chants are called *sahasranama*. *Sahasranama* is used for two different purposes. One: to address the Gods; second: to pick up names for your children. The elders in the family will first refer these *sahasranamas*. They will see which your family deity is, what your astrological birth data is, then refer the *sahasranamas* to find a suitable name for you.

Here, an enlightened Master straightaway gives you your spiritual name which can take you to your enlightenment. Many people ask me if it is compulsory to change the name legally. Understand two things: unless you change your name legally, you will not completely changeover to the new name in your everyday life. You will entertain a mix of your old name and spiritual name all the time, thereby defeating the very purpose of giving the name. Secondly, unless I make it mandatory to change your name legally, people don't take this seriously. Just out of curiosity to know what name I might give them, they sign up for a new name. So just to make people more aware and conscious of the whole process of giving a spiritual name, I tell them it is better to change their names legally.

About Nithyananda

It was under the glow of the spiritual magnet Arunachala in the energy center of Tiruvannamalai in South India, that Nithyananda was born - as Rajasekharan, to Arunachalam and Lokanayaki on 1 January, 1978. The family astrologer predicted that he would be a king amongst holy men.

At the age of 3, Nithyananda was associated with Yogiraj Raghupati Maharaj, a yoga guru who took him through rigorous training and prepared his body, with apparent foresight into the energy explosion that was going to happen in the young body. From the age of 5, Nithyananda took to deity worship with great passion. He showed profound commitment to the rituals he practiced with the deities. Just a few years later, he came in touch with Mataji Kuppammal, a deeply pious lady who initiated him into *Vedanta* and *Tantra* and started his scriptural learning at that young age. Encountering many mystics from the town of Tiruvannamalai, he received esoteric teachings from them.

At the age of 12, he had his first deep spiritual experience: while sitting on a rock on the Arunachala hillock, he suddenly had a 360 degree panoramic vision, and experienced becoming one with everything around

The earliest picture of Nithyananda in meditation taken when he was 10 years old

him. This experience further inspired him to forge ahead in his journey inwards.

Academics at school and polytechnic came naturally for Nithyananda. With only the attention he gave in classes, he passed all his grades with distinction. He obtained a diploma degree in Mechanical Engineering from a leading private Polytechnic in Tamilnadu.

Nithyananda meditating in Arunachala

At the age of 17, he left home driven by the irresistible urge to jump into the real life that he was seeking. He wandered through the length and breadth of India studying Eastern metaphysical sciences and meeting many masters and mystics. He visited many great shrines, ranging from the Himalayas in the North, to Kanyakumari in the South, from Dwaraka in the West to Ganga Sagar in the East. After enduring

intense meditation and other austerities, he attained eternal inner bliss...the state of *nithyananda*. At the age of 22, Rajasekharan became Paramahamsa Nithyananda.

Guided by Divine Vision, on Jan. 2003, Parahamamsa set up his

Flagging off construction at the mission site, Bangalore

mission headquarters in Bangalore, India, in the land of mystical and sacred banyan tree.

Today, Nithyananda is an inspiring personality for millions of people worldwide. From his experience of the Truth he has formulated and makes available the Technology of Bliss to every individual. His methods empower us to be physically and mentally fit, with sound spiritual strength in both the inner and outer worlds. Millions of people around the world have experienced radical transformation through his techniques in short periods of time.

Nithyananda gives the tools to live a creative and productive life, guided by intuition and intelligence, rather than by intellect or instinct. He shows the way to excellence in the outer world and radiance in the inner world at the same time. His programs guide one to fall into the natural space known as meditation.

He says, 'Meditation is the master key that can bring success in the material world, and deep fulfillment in your space within.' His powerful techniques and processes that comprise the meditative programs help the flowering and expansive explosion of the individual consciousness.

Nithyananda cooperates with scientists and researchers the world over, to record mystic phenomena through scientific data. He intrigues the world of medical science with results from his own neurological system. From the astounding observations, scientists feel that the potential for altering the rates and progression of diseases like heart ailments, cancer, arthritis, alcoholism, etc. are beginning to look achievable.

About Nithyananda Mission

Nithyananda Mission is Nithyananda's worldwide movement for meditation and transformation. Established in the year 2003, the Mission continues to transform humanity through transformation of the individual.

Sacred banyan tree, Bidadi ashram, India

Nithyananda Mission ashrams and centers worldwide serve as spiritual laboratories where inner growth is profound and outer growth is a natural consequence. These academies are envisioned to be a place and space to explore and explode, through a host of activities, from meditation to

Hyderabad ashram, India

science. They offer Quantum Spirituality, where material and spiritual worlds merge and create blissful living; where creative

intelligence stems from deep consciousness. **Nithyananda Dhyanapeetam** is the spiritual wing that takes care of the spiritual activities of the mission.

Los Angeles Temple, USA

Seattle Temple, USA

Many projects are in development at the various academies worldwide; and new academies are being established to provide services in varied fields to humanity at large.

A diverse range of meditation programs and social services are offered worldwide through the Foundation. Free energy healing through the Nithya Spiritual Healing system, free education to youth, encouragement to art and culture, satsangs (spiritual circles), personality development programs, corporate

Salem ashram, India

programs, free medical camps and eye surgeries, free meals at all ashrams worldwide, a one-year free residential spiritual training program in India called the Life Bliss Technology, an in-house *Gurukul* system of learning for children, and many more services are offered around the world.

Columbus ashram, Ohio, USA

Ananda Sevaks of the Nithya Dheera Seva Sena (NDSS) volunteer force comprising growing numbers of dedicated volunteers around the world, support the mission with great enthusiasm.

Offerings from Life Bliss Foundation (LBF)

Life Bliss Foundation is the teachings wing of Nithyananda Mission that offers specialized meditation programs worldwide, to benefit millions of people at the levels of body, mind and spirit. A few of them are listed below:

Life Bliss Program Level 1 - Ananda Spurana Program (LBP Level 1 - ASP)

- Energize yourself

A *chakra* workout program that relaxes and energizes the seven major *chakras* in your system. It gives clear intellectual and experiential understanding of your various emotions - greed, fear, worry, attention need, stress, jealousy, ego, discontentment etc. It is designed to create a spiritual effect at the physical level. It is a guaranteed life solution to experience the reality of your own bliss. It is a highly effective workshop, testified by millions of people around the globe.

Life Bliss Program Level 2 - Nithyananda Spurana Program (LBP Level 2 - NSP)

- Death demystified!

A program that unleashes the art of living by demystifying the concept of death. If you know the process and purpose of death, you will live your life in an entirely different way! It creates the space to detach from ingrained and unconscious emotions like guilt, pleasure and pain, all of which stem from the ultimate fear of death. It is a gateway to a new life driven by natural intelligence and spontaneous enthusiasm.

Life Bliss Program Level 3 - Atma Spurana Program (LBP Level 3 - ATSP)

- Connect with your Self!

This is a breakthrough program that analyzes clearly the workings of the mind and shows you experientially how to be the master of the mind rather than let it rule over you. It involves the whole tremendous intellectual understanding coupled with novel meditations to produce instant experiential understanding.

Life Bliss Technology (LBT)

Life Bliss Technology (LBT) is a one-year residential program for youth aged between 18 and 30 years of age, on practical life skills. With its roots in the Eastern system of Vedic education, this program is designed to empower modern youth with good physical, mental and emotional health. By nurturing creative intelligence and spontaneity, and imparting vocational skills, it creates economically and spiritually self-sufficient youth.

Above all, it offers a lifetime opportunity to live and learn under the tutelage of an enlightened Master!

Nithya Spiritual Healing

- Healing through Cosmic energy

A unique and powerful means of healing through the Cosmic energy, this is a meditation for the healer and a means to get healed for the recipient of the healing. Nithyananda continues to initiate thousands of Nithya Spiritual Healers worldwide into this scientific and time-tested healing technique which has healed millions of people of ailments ranging from migraine to cancer.

Nithya Dhyaan
- *Life Bliss Meditation*

 Become one among the millions who walk on planet Earth – Un-clutched! Register online and get initiated.

Nithya Dhyaan is a powerful everyday meditation prescribed by Nithyananda to humanity at large. It is a formula or a technique, which is holistic and complete. It works on the entire being to transform it and make it ready for the ultimate experience of enlightenment to dawn. Each segment of this technique complements the remaining segments to help raise the individual consciousness. It trains you to un-clutch from your mind and live a blissful life. It is the meditation for Eternal Bliss.

If you wish to be initiated into Nithya Dhyaan, you may visit http://www.dhyanapeetam.org and register online. You will receive through mail, a *mala*, bracelet, a spiritual name given by Nithyananda for your own spiritual growth (optional), Nithya Dhyaan Meditation CD and Nithya Dhyaan booklet in a language of your choice, personally signed by Nithyananda (mention your choice in the comment column).

Nithyananda says, 'My advent on planet Earth is to create a new cycle of individual consciousness causing Collective Consciousness to enter the Superconscious zone.'

To achieve this,

Hundred thousand people will be initiated to live as *Jeevan Muktas* – liberated beings experiencing 'living enlightenment', and 1 billion people will be initiated into Nithya Dhyaan – Life Bliss Meditation – designed to cause a shift in the individual consciousness on planet Earth.

Contact us

USA:

Los Angeles
Los Angeles Vedic Temple
9720 Central Avenue, Montclair,
CA 91763
USA
Ph.: 1-909-625-1400
Email: programs@lifebliss.org
URL: www.lifebliss.org

Florida
International Vedic Hindu University
113 N. Econlockhatchee Trail, Orlando
Florida, 32825
Ph.: 626-272-4043

New York
Queens Vedic Temple
129-10 Liberty Avenue, Richmond Hill,
Queens NY 11420
Ph.: 718-296-1995

Ohio
Ohio Ashram
820 Pollock Rd,
Delaware, Ohio
Ph: 740-362-2046

Oklahoma

Oklahoma City Vedic Temple
3048 N. Grand Blvd.
Oklahoma city
OK 73107
Ph.: 405-833-6107

Missouri

St Louis Vedic Temple
8201 Nithyananda Ave,
House Springs, MO 63051
Ph.: 314-849-6760

Washington

Seattle Vedic Temple
2877 152nd Ave Ne building 13
Redmond Washington 98052
Ph.: 425-591-1010

Phoenix

Phoenix Temple
6605 South 39th Ave,
Phoenix, AZ 85041
Ph.: 480 388 2490
Email: vedictemplephx@yahoo.com

MALAYSIA

Malaysia Ashram
No. 14, Jalan Desa,
Gombak, S Taman,
Desa Gombak, Kuala Lumpur, Malaysia
Email: nirantaraananda@gmail.com
Phone: + 603 337 10980/+ 601 223 50657/ + 601 788 61644

Klang Ashram
No 62, Jalan Serempang Dua,
Off Jalan Sungai Betek,
Taman Betek Indah,
41400 Klang, Malaysia

INDIA

Bangalore, Karnataka
(Spiritual headquarters. Vedic Temple located here)
Nithyananda Dhyanapeetam
Nithyanandapuri
Kallugopahalli, Mysore Road, Bidadi
Bangalore - 562 109
Karnataka
Ph.: +91+80 27202801 / 92430 48957
Telefax:: 27202084
Email: mail@nithyananda.org
URL:www.nithyananda.org

Varanasi, Uttar Pradesh
NithyanandaDhyanapeetam
Leelaghar Bldg,
Manikarnika Ghat,
Varanasi
Ph.: 99184 01718

Hosur, Tamil Nadu
Nithyananda Dhyanapeetam
Nithyanandapuri,
Kanuka Estate, Nallur post,
Hosur - 635 109
Krishnagiri District,
Tamilnadu
Ph.: 99947 77898 / 99443 21809

Hyderabad, Andhra Pradesh
Sri Anandeshwari Temple,
Nithyananda Giri,
Pashambanda Sathamrai Village
Shamshabad Mandal
Rangareddy District - 501 218
Andhra Pradesh
Ph.: 91 +84132 60311 / 60044
Mob.: 98665 00350 / 93964 82358

Salem, Tamil Nadu
Nithyananda Dhyanapeetam
Nithyanandapuri
102, Azhagapurampudur
Salem – 636 016
Tamilnadu
Ph.: +91 94433 64644 / 94432 35262
(Behind Sharada College)

Namakkal, Tamil Nadu
Nithyananda Dhyanapeetam
Nithyanandapuri,
2/200, Tirumangkuruchi Post,
Namakkal – 637003
Tamilnadu, INDIA
Ph.: +91 +94433 88437

Tiruvannamalai, Tamil Nadu
Nithyananda Dhyanapeetam
Nithyanandapuri,
Opposite Rajarajeswari Temple
Girivalam path
Tiruvannamalai
Ph.: 94449 91089 / 94432 33789

Pattanam, Tamil Nadu
Nithyananda Dhyanapeetam
Nithyanandapuri, Puthupatti road,
Pattanam
Rasipuram (Taluk) - 605602
Namakkal disrict
Ph.: 04287 222842

Rajapalayam, Tamilnadu
Nithyananda Dhyanapeetam
Nithyanandapuri,
Kothainachiarpuram,
Rajapalayam,
Virudhunagar District
Ph.: 04563 260002 / 94426 23768

Pondicherry, Tamilnadu
Nithyananda Dhyanapeetam
Nithyanandapuri,
Embalam to Villianoor main road,
Embalam post,
Pondicherry - 605 106
Ph.: 94420 36037 / 97876 67604

Poompuhar Aadeenam, Tamilnadu
Shivarajayoga Mutt
Opposite Poompuhar College
Melayur Post
Seerkaali Taluk
Nagai District - 609 107

For a list of centres worldwide, visit www.nithyananda.org

Suggested for further reading

- Guaranteed Solutions for lust, fear, worry ....
- Nithyananda Vol. 1 (The first volume of a biographical account of Nithyananda)
- Life Bliss Program Level 2 - Nithyananda Spurana Program
- Follow me IN! (Life Bliss Program Level 3 - Atma Spurana Program)
- You can Heal (Nithya Spiritual Healing)
- Meditation is for you
- Bliss is the path and the goal
- The only way out is IN
- Rising in love with the Master
- Bhagavad Gita series
- Uncommon answers to common questions
- Open the door...Let the breeze in!
- Nithya Yoga - The Ultimate Practice for Body, Mind & Being

To purchase books and other items, visit www.lifeblissgalleria.com or contact us.

Visit http://www.youtube.com/lifeblissfoundation to view over 400 FREE video discourses of Nithyananda.